C000057399

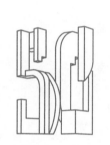

CHIMAMANDA NGOZI
ADICHIE

SHERMAN
ALEXIE

BIANCA
BAGNARELLI

JESSE
BALL

EDUARDO
BERTI

CARRIE
BROWNSTEIN

LILLI
CARRÉ

LUCY
CORIN

REBECCA
CURTIS

LYDIA
DAVIS

HARIS A.
DURRANI

BRIAN
EVENSON

JAMES
FOLTA

SOPHIA
FOSTER-DIMINO

SHEILA
HETI

JOHN
HODGMAN

ELI
HOROWITZ

KRISTEN
ISKANDRIAN

JESSE
JACOBS

HEIDI
JULAVITS

DAN
KENNEDY

ETGAR
KERET

ZAIN
KHALID

ANDREW
LELAND

JONATHAN
LETHEM

VALERIA
LUISELLI

SARAH
MANGUSO

THOMAS
McGUANE

CARSON
MELL

STEVEN
MILLHAUSER

JOHN
MOE

KEVIN
MOFFETT

WENDY
MOLYNEUX

DAN
MOREY

APARNA
NANCHERLA

TUCKER
NICHOLS

PATTON
OSWALT

JEFF
PARKER

KEATON
PATTI

BENJAMIN
PERCY

JASON
POLAN

ISMET
PRCIC

MATTHEW
SHARPE

CORINNA
VALLIANATOS

VAUHINI
VARA

SARAH
VOWELL

SARAH
WALKER

DIANE
WILLIAMS

SEAN
WILSEY

KEVIN
YOUNG

© 2017 McSweeney's Quarterly Concern and the contributors, San Francisco, California. All rights reserved by us and those who created the contents of this issue, our fiftieth, good god.
Back in 1998, we had thoughts of four issues. Just to prove that we could do it. Now, almost twenty years later, this endeavor endures, kept alive through the hard work and belief of far younger people who come through our doors as interns, stay as staff, and keep all this alive and improve it daily. This issue is testament to how it can work. We welcome Ruby Perez, Sunra Thompson, and Claire Boyle as interns. They stay on as staffers, in customer service and other entry-level positions. They stay a bit longer, and because the office currently contains only four humans, and everyone has to do everything, they grow into the roles of publicity director, art director, and managing editor. And they suggest a special fiftieth issue. We had no idea such a milestone was approaching—though the existence of Issue 49 should have been a clue. We say yes, Issue 50, good, fine. They say, Let us do something special for such a milestone. We say yes, of course, sure. They suggest publishing fifty authors we have long known and loved, and we say sure, fine, good luck. They—these very young people!—send out queries to all of these people, some of whom we have known twenty-five years but from whom we would never deign to ask such a favor ourselves. And what happens? A cascade. A gorgeous cascade of new work from many beautiful people. Fifty people. We hear from Lethem, who sends his new work, which rips off our skull in the way he is accustomed to doing. We hear from Lydia and Vowell and Hodgman, all of whom were there back in the day, whose faith in this operation made us weep then and does so now. How did we all find our way through these last twenty years? Wars were started, became fiascos, were wound down. We elected two imbeciles and one philosopher-king. We talked about sending humans to Mars. Then we forgot it. Now we are remembering again. We became a nation never more divided and we citizens struggle daily to maintain our hope and humanity and vigilance against crimes against our own. Today we read about Chaldean Christians from Iraq being deported back to that broken country. Christians who came here decades ago, and who are now being sent to a country that we broke, to a country riven by interfaith violence—also our doing. They will not stand a chance, but here, on our shores, the outcry is muted. Muted because these men and women committed crimes. Some were caught with drugs. Some wrote bad checks. And now they are being deported, sent to the desert to die, and few care, none but their families and the ACLU, which alone seems to be capable of providing hope against the ever crueler and more maniacal policies of the Madman-Child and his many enablers. We live in a nation of ever-heightening meanness and we are exhausted, so tired of cruelty carried out in our name. But we are energized, or temporarily distracted, by the contents of this, this Issue 50, compiled by Ruby and Sunra and Claire—all of them led by Kristina Kearns, peerless captain and fearless forager of funds. We thank them and we thank you. We thank you for purchasing or borrowing this issue. We thank you for subscribing, if that's what you have done. We thank you for supporting new writing in America—especially the short story, increasingly a form under threat of extinction or at least diminished relevance. Remember when the short story thrived and was in some ways the medium of the day in this nation? One would think, in this era of ever-shorter attention spans, that the short story would enjoy an ever-upward trajectory. But this is not so. Fewer and fewer writers publish short story collections, because publishers publish fewer and fewer of them, because readers buy them less and less yearly. Why? This is difficult to parse. This is worth discussion. But in the meantime we thank you. We hope you enjoy these pages. We love these pages and we love you. Not in a romantic way. Maybe in a romantic way. Would you like it that way? It is up to you. Be loved in the way you find most right. That's the best we can do, now or ever, as humans, this temporary species flourishing—for we are, in many ways we are—on this blue space-rock hurtling toward oblivion. Be loved in the way you find most right.

In this fiftieth issue, we thank all staff members past and present; all the helpers and passers-through and hangers-on; board members; and also our landlord, a very noble man.

BARB BERSCHE · SARAH MIN · TODD PRUZAN · SEAN WILSEY

ERIKA KAWALEK · DIANE VADINO · KEVIN SHAY · CHRIS GAGE

ELI HOROWITZ · SCOTT SEELEY · ELIZABETH KAIRYS

LAWRENCE WESCHLER, EARLY BEACON AND LOVER OF ALL THAT FASCINATES

JORDAN BASS · ANDI WINNETTE · CHRIS YING · D. ARRICK

MEAGAN DAY · RUSSELL QUINN · ELIANA STEIN · CHRISTOPHER BENZ (D-AK)

JULIET LITMAN · ANGELA PETRELLA · MR. ANDREW LELAND

DARREN FRANICH · MICHAEL GENRICH · MIEKA STRAWHORN · (& ALL AT 826)

JESSE NATHAN · DOMINIC LUXFORD · SAM RILEY · (& ALL AT VOW)

EVANY THOMAS · YOSH HANE · KATRINA ORTIZ · JENNIFER BROUGHTON

DAVE KNEEBONE · BRENT HOFF · MICHELLE QUINT

JULIE WRIGHT · LEE EPSTEIN · LAURA FOXGROVER · ALVARO VILLANUEVA

ADAM KREFMAN · BRIAN McMULLEN · CAITLIN VAN DUSEN

GIDEON LEWIS-KRAUS · GREG LARSON · GABE HUDSON · CALVIN CROSBY

CHRIS MONKS · JOHN WARNER · BRIAN CHRISTIAN

IAN DELANEY · JORDAN KARNES · ANNIE WYMAN · ORIANA LECKERT

LAURA HOWARD · DAN McKINLEY · DANIEL GUMBINER

SHANNON DAVID · DANIEL LEVIN BECKER · TED GIOIA · LAUREN STRUCK

VENDELA VIDA · EM-J STAPLES · CLARA SANKEY

CASEY JARMAN · WALTER GREEN · CHELSEA HOGUE · RACHEL KHONG

ETHAN NOSOWSKY · ALISON SINCLAIR · ISAAC FITZGERALD

BRIAN DICE · GINA PELL · ISABEL DUFFY-PINNER · JEREMY RADCLIFFE

NATASHA BOAS · KYLE BRUCK · CAROL DAVIS · JULIA SLAVIN
CATERINA FAKE · NION McEVOY · JED REPKO · ROBERT COULY

ASSISTED BY: Angela Hui, Matthew Keast, Molly McGhee, Anna Sanford, Clara Sankey, Laura Van Slyke, Mara Veitch, Miranda Wiebe. FURTHER SUPPORT: Vendela Vida, Andi Winnette. WEBSITE AND HUMOR EDITOR: Chris Monks. WEB DEVELOPMENT: Brian Christian. PUBLICITY AND EDITORIAL ASSISTANCE: Ruby Perez. DEVELOPMENT: Shannon David, Theodore Gioia. ART DIRECTION: Sunra Thompson. COPY EDITOR: Daniel Levin Becker. EDITORS-AT-LARGE: Jordan Bass, Daniel Gumbiner. FOUNDING EDITOR: Dave Eggers. EXECUTIVE DIRECTOR: Kristina Kearns. MANAGING EDITOR: Claire Boyle.

JACKET & ENDPAPER ILLUSTRATION: Bianca Bagnarelli

MCSWEENEY'S PUBLISHING BOARD: Natasha Boas, Kyle Bruck, Carol Davis, Brian Dice (PRESIDENT), Dave Eggers, Caterina Fake, Nion McEvoy, Gina Pell, Isabel Duffy-Pinner, Jeremy Radcliffe, Jed Repko, Julia Slavin, Vendela Vida. MAJOR SPONSOR: Mailchimp. PRINTED IN the United States.

DEAR MCSWEENEY'S,

I am writing to inquire about a job for my adoptive father, Mohammed, who is an unusual man and a remarkable polyglot. Formative years in Mumbai imparted him with fluency in Hindi, Urdu, Gujarati, Malayalam, Tamil, and English. As a Muslim with siblings across the Middle East, he picked up Arabic and Farsi, though it certainly wasn't faith or family that informed his postgraduate stint as a blackjack dealer and bartender in Paris, where he added French, Spanish, Portuguese, and German to his collection of tongues. It's all quite impressive and worldly—until you realize his aptitude for language has made him an insufferable Scrabble opponent.

After a recent trouncing that culminated in a thirty-four-point two-letter masterpiece, my triumphant patriarch mused, "Words are like families. You never know when you'll meet kin from a strange land, or when you'll be left a small fortune in a forgotten uncle's will." I don't know what he meant, exactly, but I do know the larger his margin of victory, the more likely he is to wax poetic. It's his delicate form of gloating, the boast of someone accustomed to loss.

He immigrated to the United States with the spirit of a starter of startups, but without any venture capital or novel ideas to foist upon the world. All he wanted was a place to hold court. He worked odd jobs, bussing tables and tending gas stations, until he could afford to lease a bodega in Spanish Harlem. It was capsized by unpaid rent before the GRAND OPENING balloons had the chance to shrivel. Didn't matter. More odd jobs led to more bodegas, the most successful

of which stayed afloat for little more than a year. Our living situation grew tenuous; we moved regularly from outer borough to outer borough, living in or near government-subsidized housing projects for most of my childhood. To my father, the infinite dialects spoken exclusively in the PJs made them the ideal home.

His businesses didn't fail because he lacked savvy, mind you. Common sense alone could have prevented those stores from shuttering. They folded because he was more interested in talking to his patrons than he was in selling to them. Everyone knew that their man Mo didn't subscribe to the shopkeeper's maxim, *If you're not buying, you're leaving.* Hell, you could post up at the front door, barring entry to a human hundred-dollar bill or Benjamin Franklin himself, so long as you had a story to tell. If your anecdote entertained, my father would show his gratitude by way of the store's inventory. A good joke, not a man-walks-into-a-bar joke but a *real* joke, one about a disappointed wife, perhaps, was worth one Mango Madness Snapple. For spinning a full-bodied yarn, replete with humor, tragedy, deception, and loss, you'd get a sandwich with your choice of fixings, a bag of salt-and-vinegar chips, and of course a Mango Madness Snapple to wash it all down.

At our bodega on Marcy Avenue, a charismatic regular known as Feet consumed his body weight in free food a hundred times over. (Feet's real name was Calvin, but the block called him Feet on account of his losing his only pair of shoes, counterfeit Air Jordan 4s, in a summer game of back-alley Cee-lo and proceeding to travel everywhere,

everywhere, barefoot in protest of the game's outcome, which he held had been rigged. His shoelessness continued well past reason, into December, because apparently "our toes are meant to touch the ground"; ergo, Feet.) From the storeroom, sitting on upturned crates with my homework, I heard Feet tell my father stories about his addiction and rehabilitation; about plying a prison guard with his sister's frozen tamarind juice for extra phone privileges; about bootlegging the first half of *Titanic,* sleeping through the second, and selling the tapes to tourists in Times Square anyway. Feet's audience of one laughed and later retold the stories at his dinner table, often as epilogues to his own verbal novellas. I realize now that Mohammed's many fluencies were symptoms of a yawning need to relate to something universal by finding himself in a stranger's lore. For whatever reason, he found exactly that in Feet's accountings.

In 2015, a month after Mohammed retired and moved to the suburbs of Atlanta, Feet died of an overdose. They hadn't spoken in a decade, as the bodega's solvency had been short-lived, as always, and Feet wasn't the type to stay in touch. When I phoned my father about his passing, words interrupted long silences. "That makes me feel lonely," he said, "and old."

Since then, I've tried to see him more. I get on the plane with printouts of a few stories I memorize for effect. Some are mine; others are from periodicals like yours. In keeping with tradition, once I finish the telling, he makes me a meal. (I like to think he'd feed me even if I didn't play the part of raconteur—you know, being his son and all—but I'd rather not try my luck.)

As an outlet that traffics in the kind of tales my father appreciates to the point of his own detriment, I believe you'd find him of much use. He would make for an excellent reader or an even better resident sandwich artist. You won't have to worry about salary, either; he'll happily agree to be paid in conversation. Trust me.

Whatever you do, don't play him in Scrabble.

Assalamualaikum, chaleureusement, mit freundliche grüße, and many thanks,
ZAIN KHALID
BROOKLYN, NY

DEAR MR. MCSWEENEY,

Not sure who or what's to blame—Martin Luther, cable news, or Japanese rocks. I haven't checked in for a while because I've become a little infatuated with my laptop's DELETE key. Lately, every time I get cracking on writing something down—a letter, an essay, the odd haiku—I edit it down to a blank page. There's so much yakking nowadays and all I crave is silence.

It might have something to do with Ryōan-ji, that rock garden in Kyoto. When I was planning my first trip to Japan a few years ago, I had intended to skip this austere collection of stones and sand because I was pretty sure I would never understand it. Then I was seated next to a half-Japanese woman on a plane, coincidentally an acquaintance of a departed friend, and she told me missing Ryōan-ji would be a mistake. And even though I was right and I still don't get it, I went and was so seduced by its emptiness that studying the history of Japanese gardens has become a real obsession.

What I respond to is the humility. Just rocks, gravel, moss, the occasional tree. There's also a kind of wisdom in how uptight these gardens are, the way they fend off nature. So much pruning. I once saw a gardener at the Kiyomizu-dera Temple dustbusting the leaves of a tree! I agree with these gardens: nature is chaos intent on murdering us all, so we measly humans fight back by raking gravel into parallel lines.

A while back a friend in New York City was texting me during the intermission of a Broadway musical he was real hopped up about. I happened to be sitting by a window in my Montana hometown watching a thunderstorm. I don't know what that means but it might mean something. Don't get me wrong. I still love musical theater. When I'm sad I cheer myself up by going on YouTube and watching the bottle dance from *Fiddler on the Roof*. But lately I'm just as bucked up by lightning on the Great Plains.

Possible non sequitur (though I'm not sure I believe in those anymore since everything really is related). This year marks the five hundredth anniversary of the Protestant Reformation. Even though my own Holy Roller mother will tell you I'm a godless heathen with nothing but an eternity of hell in my future, I still feel part of that tradition. Like a lot of things I'm interested in or affected by, the logical conclusion of Martin Luther nailing up his Ninety-five Theses on the church door in Wittenberg in 1517 is me and my nothingness. Protestantism was about getting rid of priests, cutting out the perfumed middlemen between a believer and her god. I wonder if he understood that once you give the priests the heave-ho, Jehovah

might end up in the same overcrowded dustbin.

When I was a child, my mom made my sister and me go with her to church three times a week—Sunday morning and Sunday and Wednesday nights. When I turned six, ABC, one of the three television channels available at the time, started airing a new show called *Charlie's Angels* on Wednesday night. I was immediately fascinated. I had always loved stories about women with jobs. I was also going through a Nancy Drew phase. Like, I adored Nancy because she always had things to do.

Because I wanted to be home to watch this show, I asked my mother if I had to attend Wednesday night church.

She said, "You don't *have* to attend church at all."

Okay!

"Oh, you're going to attend church," she countered. "We go there for fellowship and to learn. But you don't need that preacher to save your soul. All you need is your Bible. You are responsible for your own salvation."

On the one hand, this was a lot of pressure to put on a first grader. On the other hand, it was probably the most important, weirdly feminist moment of my life. She made me the preacher's intellectual equal and gave me the gift and weight of self-reliance. Not that I understood that at the time. Back then I sat through every Wednesday night service praying that said preacher's sermon would be short enough that I could make it home in time to at least catch the end of *Charlie's Angels*. But once you don't need the priest and you don't need the preacher, maybe at some point you stop needing the Bible and the deity described therein. And four decades later all you need from the universe is a little thunder and a lot of rain, a garden in Japan that you with your five hundred-year-old Germanic theological tradition will happily never understand.

Best,

SARAH VOWELL
BOZEMAN, MT

DEAR MCSWEENEY'S PREMIUM DEPT.,
Attn: Fulfillment Services

I am writing to thank you for sending me the package of premiums I checked off after sending in a contribution at the "Locally Sourced" level of membership.

The I BRAKE FOR WHIMSY bumper stickers and the set of Hal Hartley movie character shadow puppets arrived and were enjoyed by everyone in our shared loft/work/yoga/skateboarding/herb terrace space.

However, the Kathy Acker coffee mug has a cracked rim and when I tried to drink from it I spilled McSweeney's-brand Tanzanian peaberry all over my T-shirt with the recreation of *Guernica* done by kindergarteners, all three of which were also premiums included in my package.

I am sending these items back, along with a check so that my membership will be elevated to the "Disaffected Barista" level. Could you replace these items and include the Idea Notebook made from recycled Idea Notebooks from lower premium levels?

Thank you.

Sincerely,

PATTON OSWALT
HOLLYWOOD, CA

DEAR MCSWEENEY'S,

When my son Owen was nine I taught him how to drive.

Now he's twelve and writing an essay for school on driving rights. Driving, as we've discussed it, using high middle school parlance, is one of those privileges—like voting, drinking, working—"that society restricts by imposing a minimum age, below which young people are not considered competent." Owen's conviction is that there should be no minimum age for operating a motor vehicle, but a more rigorous driving test, open to all.

Clearly this is an attempt to get himself behind the wheel as soon as possible, though where he then wants to *go* I am not so clear about.

All this dates back to 2014, when we were living in West Texas, a place he still thinks of as home. In the last few years home-in-Texas has acquired an air of romance. Romance, for a twelve-year-old boy, means something like safety mixed with indulgence—and freedom from surveillance. (Though one of Owen's friends recently made a short autobiographical film called *The Sexy Mom and the Sexy Boy*—shot after shot of him surreptitiously recording his mom, and of his mom driving him around, making him dinner, being almost but not quite fed-up with him.) In Texas I taught Owen how to drive a 1942 Ford military Jeep. To maximize space on transport ships the government specified that these things had to have an eighty-inch wheelbase. Men drove them with their knees at armpit height. J. D. Salinger, a great empathizer with children and an army sergeant who stormed the beach at Normandy, comes to mind.

But for a nine-year-old everything is proportioned perfectly. After Owen got good enough to run through the gears and work the clutch without stalling we practiced reversing and three-point turns. I would shout the names of random animals and he would have to respond as though they were in our path. I would pretend that I was a general and he was my staff sergeant. These lessons took place on back streets and desert roads.

The landscape was so empty that on one occasion we hooked my belt to the steering wheel, held a stick on the accelerator, and sat together for a while in the backseat, chatting, unconcerned that any occasion for braking might occur.

It all became so routine that after a few weeks Owen actually said the words, "Dad, I'm bored of driving."

Now we live in Brooklyn. Here wheels do not roll without regulation, and he laments his lack of automotive opportunity.

My mom got him a hoverboard for Christmas—and they were immediately outlawed. I have a moped, and he can ride it well, but I can't justify letting him go beyond my line of sight. I let him drive the Jeep at times, but it's no fun getting stared at, dodging police, yanking to the curb when we see a squad car.

He may deserve a license more than a lot of people who are on the road legally. And yet, being twelve, despite three years of driving experience, in New York State he's obliged to wait another four years in purgatory.

Recently he built a rolling café, a sort of Lucy-from-*Peanuts* psychoanalysis stand on casters, which he and his friend Tosca, also twelve, and a rotating cast of

other children, often roll to the corner on weekends and operate as a juice and baked goods stand. They named it Nectar Café. It's even profitable. I got reimbursed for all the cooking and building supplies I fronted them. Tosca, more interested in the work aspect of youth rights, is currently applying for a permit to operate a food concession. Though a serious drawback to serving as base of operations for a kid-owned business is that they trash my kitchen. The rights and responsibility sine curves never seem to converge in my sink.

So when Owen and Tosca recently replaced Nectar's worn-out casters and repainted the stand I made a point of saying that they had to fully clean up their own messes. Tosca, hyperaware of laws and rules, got paint all over my sidewalk, and in response to my request that she be more careful replied that it was not actually my sidewalk, even though I had to maintain it, but the city's.

Shortly thereafter I noticed that a Papa John's Pizza deliveryman had parked his motorbike on the sidewalk and was helping her roll the repainted Nectar into my driveway on its new casters. He was a very short man with a thick Bangladeshi accent, getting paint all over his hands.

My girlfriend, Autie, and our friend Isaac were on the sidewalk. We thought Tosca had enlisted the Papa John's guy instead of us because she was trying to be independent and responsible.

"Poor Papa John's guy," one of them said.

In fact he had volunteered. And once he'd helped stow the café (technically a Papa John competitor) he disappeared into my backyard for a while. I was absorbed in hosing paint off what I naively considered my sidewalk.

When I finished I contemplated an abandoned Papa John's motorscooter and started to wonder what was happening in my yard. Was Owen striking a deal to use this vehicle? At which point the deliveryman came outside, gave me his business card, and rolled off. Then Owen emerged, shouting, "The Papa John's guy is a pervert!"

It took a minute to get the story, but it seemed the deliveryman had asked for Tosca's hand in marriage.

My reaction was to laugh—I was so relieved to let go of what I feared might have happened. And then I could not stop laughing. At which point Tosca emerged, told me that I did not respect the rights of women, and stormed off.

I called her parents, explained what I knew, and sent them a copy of the Papa John guy's card.

Her parents went to the chain's branch manager, who said, "I'm going to fire him. Do you want us to pay you money?"

They said, "No, we just want him to understand that he can't do that."

A school week later, driving Owen to a birthday party with Tosca, I got the chance to apologize for laughing.

Tosca's reply floored me: "When people are in a situation that's unexpected they don't really mean what they first do. So I forgive you, and by me saying I forgive you I really want you to feel forgiven."

Of the Papa John's guy she said, "He had worse English than I had understood." By which she meant he did not speak much. And then she explained what had happened:

He'd asked, "Are you married?"
She'd said, "No, I'm twelve."
He'd asked, "Can I have your number?"
"No!"
"I really like you."
"Okay."
"We be friends?"
"*No.*"

Contemplating this, Owen said, "I wonder if in his culture getting married…"

Tosca interrupted: "Me not being married by *next year* in a lot of cultures is just kind of obscene. Girls get married at eleven, twelve, nine."

In the intervening week, researching driving rights for school, Owen had also learned some of this. The age of consent—*i.e.* the age at which a young person is considered capable of choice in sexual activity—in most of Mexico is twelve.

Since *we* had, I asked Tosca, "Did *you* just learn all this this week?"

"*No,*" she said. "My mom's an anthropologist. I've known this stuff since I was eight."

Owen was full of empathy for a man whom he thought wanted a friend: "I feel bad for the dude. I mean, imagine moving to a country where you don't speak the language, and you don't have any friends. That was really brave of him."

Tosca, drily: "He probably has friends."

Owen: "But not many. I'm just saying that's brave of him to ask that."

All this intact empathy.

I was overjoyed and surprised that nobody, including the Papa John's guy, seemed to have spun out into the sort of situation that usually results in lawsuits, deportation, psychoanalysis. Hysteria instead of communication.

The state of South Dakota allows kids to drive solo at fourteen and a half. South Dakotans are the youngest motorists in the world. In a couple of years I'm planning to drive there over winter break, rent a house in in the city of Yankton, get a power bill to establish my residency, and allow Owen to take the driving test.

If he passes he can drive home, wherever that is.

SEAN WILSEY
BROOKLYN, NY

DEAR MCSWEENEY'S,

I am writing in response to a series of letters published in Issue 12 (December 2003) that debated the provenance of an unattributed short story submission titled "Gorilla Girl." I realize that fourteen years is a bit late, but I'm a slow reader.

Apparently, a fellow named Ryan W. Bradley answered a notice on your website regarding the story in question. He claimed that he had written "Gorilla Girl" in a drunken stupor and couldn't remember anything about it. The manuscript had been sent to *McSweeney's* by his friend, Jeffrey Brand, who hadn't read it. To complicate matters further, Bradley suffered a computer crash, destroying all evidence of his authorship.

McSweeney's editor Eli Horowitz was not convinced, and for good reason: these claims are entirely false. I can state this with the utmost confidence, because I am the author of "Gorilla Girl." I have no idea how my contact information was separated from the manuscript during the submission process, but I've taken the precaution of including my name, email address, and telephone number at the top of this letter, as well as at regular intervals throughout the text, in order to prevent a similar mishap.

[LETTER BY DAN MOREY, {REDACTED}@ GMAIL.COM, XXX-XXX-XXXX]

First, a little history. I initially wrote "Gorilla Girl" in the late nineties for a fiction workshop at Penn State. It was meant to be a comic Gothic/fabulist retelling of *The Taming of the Shrew*, *Gone with the Wind*, and other stories where men set out to "improve" or "break" women. My instructor told me the story (which features mild bestiality) might be good enough to enter in *Playboy*'s College Fiction Contest if I agreed to cut all the "cheap shots." These were gags with punch lines like "And then she ate it," "Your son the spanker," and "Tony Danza." At that age, I was unwilling to part with such gems, so the story was shelved.

"Gorilla Girl" didn't resurface until the dawn of the new millennium, when I rewrote it for Chuck Rosenthal's graduate fiction class at Loyola Marymount. This version was polished enough to win a cash prize at Loyola's annual literary awards and appear in the student-run journal, *LA Miscellany*.

[LETTER BY DAN MOREY, {REDACTED}@ GMAIL.COM, XXX-XXX-XXXX]

In 2001 I reworked "Gorilla Girl" yet again, expanding it to near novella-length. It was this manuscript that I sent to

McSweeney's. Being a pessimist, I interpreted your non-response as: "This abomination is not even worthy of a reply. P.S. You disgust us."

Shortly thereafter, my analyst sent me abroad to "decompress." Little did I know that as I sat in my favorite park in Shanghai, beside a statue of the great Ding Ling, waiting for inspiration (which, alas, never struck), there was a controversy raging back in the States over my perverse story. Incredibly, Alex Ross, an old friend from Loyola with whom I've only recently reconnected, saw Mr. Horowitz's online plea and recognized the title as mine, but misremembered the plot. He wrote to Mr. Horowitz, informing him that my "Gorilla Girl" was about "people (punk-rockers?) driving in a car and there was puking involved and maybe one of the girls had green hair or something."

So close. And so tragic. I understand that Mr. Horowitz grew obsessed with solving the mystery of "Gorilla Girl," and eventually had to resign his post due to mental instability. I can't help but wonder how differently both of our careers might have turned out had I been able to come forward at an earlier date.

[LETTER BY DAN MOREY, {REDACTED}@ GMAIL.COM, XXX-XXX-XXXX]

After the failure of "Gorilla Girl," I abandoned fiction for screenwriting, and spent many years perfecting a script for *Cannonball Run IV*. Unfortunately, my celluloid dreams were crushed in 2009 following the untimely death of Dom DeLuise.

Lately, I've taken to writing internet clickbait, a discipline my agent calls the future of the written word.

Here's my latest effort—the one for which I hope to be remembered: "Wow! Guess who died today? This really rich lady! Click here to find out if you're in her will. Oh boy!" Above this I have placed a photo of Mrs. Howell from *Gilligan's Island*. You wouldn't believe the hits it's getting!

Anyway, I trust this letter will provide some much-needed closure for your staff, your readers, poor Mr. Horowitz, and Ryan W. Bradley, whom I hope I haven't angered, as I've heard that people with alcoholic temperaments can be quite volatile.

Belatedly,
DAN MOREY
ERIE, PA

P.S. "Gorilla Girl," severely condensed for online consumption, appeared in the spring 2015 issue of *Menacing Hedge*.

P.P.S. If you're still keen on gorilla stories, I have a wonderful oulipian novel (nearly complete!) titled *Gorilla Summer* that has, amazingly, not been picked up by a major publisher. Now's your chance!

DEAR MR. MOREY,
I don't even know where to begin. All that was, what, twelve years ago? And yet it feels fresh, in part because I've been largely unable to function in the years since, plagued by the uncertainty, the betrayal, the overwhelming sense of failure. You extended a hand, Dan, and yet I was unable to grasp it. Instead, I was waylaid by the moist, sticky paw of Ryan

W. Bradley, and the stench is with me still, no matter how hard I scrub. "Gorilla Girl" sank into the shadows, and two lives were forever shattered.

And now this! Your letter was an unexpected thrill—I hadn't even dared to dream. But closure? It's pretty to think so, but no—it's far too late for that. Perhaps vengeance is the best we can hope for.

ELI HOROWITZ
SAN FRANCISCO, CA

DEAR MCSWEENEY'S,
Some time ago I went into the coffee shop near where I live. I ordered a coffee from the young woman with tasteful tattoos who works there. She was wearing overalls that day, and I decided to make a funny observation about that fact, because that is what I am famous for. And there is nothing weird about a forty-five-year-old man making jokes for a captive audience of one barista in her twenties, specifically about her appearance.

"You deserve an award," I said, "in *overall* excellence."

She didn't laugh. She took a long look at me and smiled gently, pityingly. "Nice dad joke," she said.

And that is how I died.

I had not heard the term *dad joke* before, which is part of why I was so adept at making them. But the moment she said it I knew she was right. The illusion that the young barista and I occupied the same reality vanished. I was a ghost to her, making a creepy joke from beyond the grave.

She gave me my coffee, and I thanked her for her service. I floated off into the void.

Now that I am dead I can reveal all my secrets to the world. Here is one of them.

A few years ago, when I was still on *The Daily Show* regularly, I was asked if I wanted to be made an honorary member of a humor society for college-aged children in another town. I am happy to join any club that will have me as a member, so I said yes, but the timing was awkward. The children of the humor society wanted me to come by their clubhouse in the evening for a ceremony. But I had a show the one night I would be in their town, plus I would be visiting my father, and I would have my own children with me.

"The only thing that would work," I said, "would be for me to come by the clubhouse on Sunday morning. You can adore me for a few hours, but then I need to go home." The college-aged children agreed.

I performed my comedy show and it went fairly well. On Sunday morning my dad drove me and my son and daughter to the part of town where the humor society for children had its headquarters: an old weird twisted brick building in an even older part of an old town. I asked my dad to entertain my kids for a couple of hours and then come pick me up and drive us all to the train station. And then I knocked on an unmarked door and went inside.

It was wonderful at first. The young men and women of the humor society could not have been nicer or, more importantly to me, more flattering. There were more young men than women (comedy is bad at this at all levels), and many of the men were wearing tweed jackets and ties and glasses. I had a certain look at this point in my career—Ivy-League pasty—and it was as if I had walked into a room of John Hodgman cosplayers, welcoming their god. They thanked me for coming and offered me whiskey. It was 11 a.m., but because I am still cool and young and relevant, I said yes, please. We mingled in their wood-paneled hall and I enjoyed talking with them about my very important and influential career.

I'm glad to report, McSweeney's, that one of the young Hodgman impersonators remembered fondly the advice column I used to write for McSweeney's Internet Tendency, "Ask a Former Professional Literary Agent." I explained to him that writing a letter for issue one of *Timothy McSweeney's Quarterly Concern* was how I got my start. I told him I had wanted to be a writer of serious short stories about people with deep feelings, but that McSweeney's taught me it was okay to be funny. I told him how profoundly that had changed my life, and I am certain he found this interesting.

We had a really good time as one whiskey turned to three and they showed me around their little clubhouse and liked me so much. This ceremony was fun. I was sorry I had a train to catch. Someone asked me if I had ever died on stage, and I said no.

Then they opened a secret chamber. I still remember the suddenness of it. We were in a corridor, laughing, and then there was suddenly a blank space in the wall leading to darkness. The president of the humor society turned solemn. He explained that now the real ceremony would begin, and he ushered me into the darkness.

I won't reveal all of what happened next. I went to Yale. I knew enough about collegiate initiation ceremonies to know that it would involve some embarrassing questions, candles or lanterns, self-revelations, and some confused waiting around in dark spaces. When I was finally led into the light I was seated before an obscure inquisitor. I was asked to explain the meaning of what I had just experienced.

I said I was not sure. I was told that this was the wrong answer.

It was getting late in the day now, and I was getting annoyed. But I always like to find the meaning in stories, and I also like doing well on quizzes, so I thought it over. To my surprise, the answer came to me as enlightenment.

"Well," I said, "I can only tell you what the meaning of this is *to me*." The inquisitor bade me continue. I felt like I was on the right track.

I told him how I had come to comedy late in life, and basically by accident. After publishing in *McSweeney's* I published a book of fake trivia that put me on *The Daily Show* as a guest; after that I was asked to be a contributor. It was a disorientingly quick process of about ten years, and so, on the first day I came to write for *The Daily Show*, I felt like a nervous fraud.

I told him how, standing there that first day on *The Daily Show*, I saw one of the faces I knew from TV. It was Rob Corddry, walking toward me down a long hallway. As I watched him approach, I remembered everything I had assimilated through the years about the culture of television comedy: that it was competitive, mean-spirited, and full of backbiting and sabotage. As Corddry got closer, I expected him to say something mean to me, or just punch me in the neck, because I was the new guy who had got here without earning it and he saw right through me. Or maybe he would just punch me for no other reason than that he was from Massachusetts.

But he didn't. Rob reached me and smiled and said, "We are really glad you're here." And no one ever acted as though that were not true. For the rest of my career at *The Daily Show* I found everyone to be ambitious, yes, but supportive and not interested in neck-punching or other humiliations. But I never quite escaped the feeling that I didn't belong there. Only now, now that I am older still than I was as I faced the humor society inquisitor, only now that I am dead, do I realize we never think we belong.

"Nevertheless," I said to the inquisitor, "I guess I felt like I always had some hazing coming to me. And now, here, in the most unexpected way and at the most unexpected time, I guess I'm getting it. And it's a relief."

The inquisitor held my gaze for a long time. There was light drifting in from a crack in the blinds. This was supposed to be nighttime, I thought in the silence. And then the inquisitor said that my answer was wrong.

I was a little mad now. "Look," I wanted to say, "this was fun. I have enjoyed pretending that I am in college again, but in fact I am a grown man. I had not expected to be psychologically tested by children today, but I have gone through it and found a certain truth in the experience, and now you tell me I'm wrong? No. *That* is the wrong answer, and someday you will realize this, but I can't wait around for that time because I am a grown-up with places to be. And also my daddy is picking me up at three o'clock sharp!"

But I did not say those things. I thought it through again, and after a couple more tries, I said the right thing. I won't tell you what it was.

After that the rest of the humor society emerged and feted me. We had a nice lunch of Thai food, and we were all friends again. It was fun. At one point the president told me that normally the final part of the ceremony would all be in the nude, but that they had decided not to do that because of my age and schedule.

I thanked him for understanding me.

In the first issue of *McSweeney's* I wrote a letter that brought my career in comedy to life. I am not actually dead now, of course. I live. But as our lives continue, they break across certain events into different lives, past lives, lives that feel lives away. I am writing you this letter now from the other side of fifty issues to say that the transition from youth to maturity, from one life to the other, is not always easy. But you have done a good job.

Also, I noticed that on the back of issue one you misspelled my name. It's HODGMAN, not HODGSON. Too late to fix it?

Thank you.

That is all.

JOHN HODGMAN
BROOKLYN, NY

DEAR MCSWEENEY'S,
I love internet comments sections. Lots of people with great ideas and we all gain a terrific education. But the one thing I can't stand is when someone, while making a political point knocking the other side for its ignorance, says, "Wake up sheeple." I worry that folks are going

to take that advice literally, like waking up sheeple is a good thing to do. It's not. Do not wake up sheeple.

I have been a professional sheeple rancher for four years now, since shortly after the government unveiled these majestic and unholy half-human, half-ovine creations to the general public for purposes of fleece, meat, and sport-murder.

In the precious few waking hours of their day, the sheeple tend to converse with one another, in simple declarative sentences, mostly about the weather at first but later in an effort to determine what kind of creatures they actually are. As the horror of realization dawns on them, their wee brains fill with such dread that they are rendered unconscious, a safety valve of sorts deliberately built in by the engineers hired by President Carter in the early years of development. The sleep period generally lasts about eighteen to twenty-two hours as the hybrid brain tries to resettle its monstrous truth into something approaching a settled state (the fleshy sacs near the ears are there to store extra deposits of Phenobarbital, should they prove necessary).

Then the sheeple awake naturally, not remembering the previous conversations, graze, stare at things, and begin to talk once more as the cycle repeats. It's their way. Not as God intended, but certainly as the engineers at Dow and Raytheon did.

Now, we get a few "progressives" up here at the ranch from time to time, attempting to "set the sheeple free" by telling them what's "really" happening. They think it's important that the sheeple know the "truth." And these folks get impatient waiting for the sheeple to wake up, so they, yes, wake up the sheeple. At that point,

because the sheeple's brains can't handle the toxic combination of neural signals, sedatives, and existential dread, this triggers a severe reaction wherein the muscles and electrical impulses turn inward and fiercely attack themselves. So fiercely, in fact, that the sheeple explode. And when some sheeple explode, the explosion wakes up the rest of the sheeple and soon it's like the goddamn Fourth of July. A friend of mine lost four hundred head of sheeple that way. Bits of hair and meat and wool and skin all over the field.

Some people ask why I'm even in this business, tending to such a large herd of very stupid, incendiary beasts that logically have no right to exist and are possessed with such a noisy and dispiriting reproductive process. Fair question. For me, it's the fleece: the magnificent stringy, oily, clumpy hair that I shear from them every few months. The versatility of this product means I can make rugs, seat cushions, and all the clothes I wear. It's profitable and, once you get used to the oils, a tolerable way to spend time.

So leave them be. Don't wake them up. It kills them. And only God has the right to kill them. And even though He probably should, He hasn't done that yet.

Sincerely,
JOHN MOE
ST. PAUL, MN

DEAR MCSWEENEY'S,

I write out of the concern you're bound to have, particularly on Sundays, that perhaps you've gone about it all the wrong way. I consider Sunday the midlife crisis of the week. You would think it would fall on a Wednesday, but no, Sundays are when you can matter-of-factly allocate hours, plural, to sit in a bay window and stare pensively out at what you wish were a body of water but is definitely the bluntness of scaffolding.

But aren't we all just beings encased in scaffolding, waiting to unearth our brand-new renovations at some unknown future point with a giant ribbon-cutting ceremony slash Facebook post? These are the types of thoughts you get on a Sunday. As you may gather, they are indulgent beyond defense.

During a recent navel-gaze, my brain attempted to deconstruct compliments. I have reached something of an impasse with compliments. They are shifty things, appearing altogether different from various angles. As a comedian* who regularly digs around in my mind's landfills for buried neuroses and idiosyncrasies worth exploring further, I hardly know where compliments received fit in. For a while I was cataloguing them very diligently in my email drafts folder, where they remain in a document innocuously marked NICE THINGS.

I decided that whenever I was feeling low and my demons were having a block party I could open up my drafts and peruse some of my better moments. Generally, one's drafts folder is a graveyard of stunted attempts at connection and commitment. Mine is a real who's who of unfulfilled

professional obligations, personal relationship détentes, and a three-word reminder to *make dentist appointment* written solely in the subject line. One draft simply has the letter *a* in the TO: field. Who the hell is *a*?! We'll never know. What we do know, however, is that Peter Diffler** once sent me a "Great job on this podcast" email, and into the NICE THINGS it went. Is this what it's come to? I'm stockpiling self-esteem blips like acorns for winter?

I will say that there's something manageable about compliments in stasis. I generally can't accept a compliment in real time without the immediate reflex to volley back. If I can't think of something to ping-pong the other way, I feel constipated. How dare you appreciate my humanity if I can't return the simple favor? Thus, these positive pupae get stuck in a purgatory where I can't absorb them but I also can't let them go. It's like I'm collecting tokens I can never redeem for prizes. It's a set of missed connections I sift through on occasion, wondering who this girl is that these people are talking about.

Lately, I'm less likely to waffle on the praise. I don't do it as a favor to the other person but as one to myself. *Take the compliment*, I impress internally, like a sniper directed to *take the shot*. I focus on the words and appreciate that someone took the time to say them in this strange, brutal world. It isn't even the words themselves so much as the rareness of generosity with no expectation in return. If nothing else, it's a chain of garlic for a case of the Sundays.

Your friend,
APARNA NANCHERLA
BROOKLYN, NY

---

* I am not happy about starting this sentence in this way. To state one's profession so offhandedly feels arrogantly casual to me. Though, as you can see, I purposely kept it to force personal growth's hand.

** Name changed to protect myself? Peter? You?

AT NIGHT

by ETGAR KERET

(Translated by Sondra Silverston)

AT NIGHT, WHEN EVERYONE is asleep, Mom lies awake in bed, eyes closed. Once, when she was a little girl, she wanted to be a scientist. She longed to find a cure for cancer, the common cold, or human sadness. She got excellent grades and had a very neat notebook, and in addition to healing the human race she wanted to travel to outer space or watch a volcano in action. It's hard to say that something went wrong in her life. She married the man she loved, works in the field that interests her, and gave birth to a sweet little boy. And yet she can't fall asleep. Maybe it's because the man she loves left to pee an hour ago and still hasn't come back to bed.

At night, when everyone is asleep, Dad walks barefoot to the balcony to smoke a cigarette and add up his debts. He works like a horse. Tries to save. But somehow, everything costs just a little bit more than what he can afford. The neckless man from the café already lent him money once and soon he'll have to start paying him back, but he has no idea how he can do that. When he finishes his cigarette, he hurls the butt from the balcony as if it were a rocket and watches it crash into the sidewalk. It's not nice to dirty the street, that's what he tells his son whenever the kid drops a candy wrapper on the ground. But it's late now, he's very tired, and the only thing on his mind is money.

At night, when everyone is asleep, the boy dreams exhausting dreams about a piece of newspaper that sticks to his shoe and won't come off. Mom once told him that dreams are the way our brains tell themselves things, but the boy's brain doesn't speak clearly. Even though that annoying dream recurs every night, smelling of cigarette smoke and wet with stagnant water, the boy doesn't understand what it's trying to say. He tosses and turns in his bed, knowing deep down that at some point, Mom or Dad will come in and pull his sheets tighter. Until then, he hopes that the moment he manages to peel that piece of newspaper off his shoe, if he ever does manage to peel it off, a different dream will come.

At night, when everyone is asleep, the goldfish comes out of the fishbowl and puts on Dad's checked slippers. Then it sits down on the living room couch and zaps the TV. Its favorite programs are cartoons, nature films, and CNN, but only when there's a terrorist attack or a photogenic disaster. It watches it all without sound so as not to wake anyone. At about four, it goes back to the fishbowl and leaves the damp slippers in the middle of the living room. It doesn't care that Mom will have something to say to Dad about that in the morning. He's just a fish, and if it's not a fishbowl or a TV screen, he couldn't care less.

DETAILS

by CHIMAMANDA NGOZI ADICHIE

DEAR OYIN,

Have a safe flight. I can't think of what else to say. That's not true. Of course I can think of much else to say, but I don't know if I should say them. I don't know if you want to hear them. We didn't talk about the after, because you didn't want to talk about the after. Maybe we should have talked about the after. Anyway, have a safe flight.
CHISARA

HEY CHISARA,

I wasn't looking forward to coming back to America. Still, it was nice to see the very clean and very shiny Atlanta airport, the escalators sliding with ease and the toilets flushing at the wave of a hand. As I waited for my bag, I smelled dried fish. I hate that smell. I hate dried fish. I always know which airport carousel has the bags from Nigeria because I just follow the smell of dried fish. Why do Nigerians bring so much dried fish? Nigerians are the one group of people in the world who love their food but don't celebrate or proselytize it. Nigerians will arrive in a foreign country and their first hope is to find Nigerian food—or something as close as possible to Nigerian food. Yet all the Nigerian restaurants I know here are sad kiosks, with the skeletons of chairs and tables. No ceremony, no poetry. They push your food onto plates and push the plates to you. Nigerians don't take friends to Nigerian restaurants. It doesn't occur to them. They love their food enough and don't much think that other people might love it, too. Or maybe don't care if other people do.

How are you?

OYIN

OYIN,

Why is your email about dried fish? (And why didn't we talk about the foods we hate?)

CHISARA

DEAREST CHISARA,

First of all, I'm sorry. I reread my email with your eyes and I saw its underlying glibness. I wrote it on my way home from the airport, feeling a mix of things, longing for what I left behind, and disoriented to be back.

I thought about what you said that day in Silverbird, after we bought popcorn. That I like details, too many details of inconsequential things, because it is a way for me to hide. You actually said "deflect and evade and hide" and I wondered why *hide* was insufficient, and I felt guilty of one crime more than I had committed. But you're right, although I do truly like details, in addition to using them as camouflage. I remember also thinking or maybe realizing that you are a bit of a bully, and—shame on me—I found it exciting. Exciting and frightening. I felt something similar when you asked me, "What do you want?" that night. You knew what I wanted but you wanted me to say it. You forced me to confront my own desire. It upset me and exhilarated me. What do you want me to say? A part of me wanted

to, and still wants to, wait this thing out in silence. Or in small details of small things. Like the jar of bath salts that I am looking at right now, as I type while seated on the toilet. It's on a ledge by the Jacuzzi bathtub we hardly ever use. My husband bought it some time last year. He had attended a conference, and got it from the spa of the fancy hotel he stayed in. He brought it back in an elegant bag, the jar itself engulfed in soft layers of the smoothest, daintiest milky paper. It smelled of honey. I like honey (I should for someone whose name means *honey*, ha). From time to time, my husband and I have talked about using the salts, using our tub. But we never have. Showers are so much more efficient, and that tub just seems like too much work. I am looking at the bath salts now and suddenly wondering—what would I do about them? What would I do with them? There is so much intertwined in a marriage, so much tangled, so many lives braided together.
OYIN

OYIN,
I am sorry, too. I know I shouldn't push you. I don't want to but I also really want to. So, the bath salts. I tried to imagine them. All I could see was you and your husband in the tub. Even that word *intertwined* has a strange ring for me. Is this what you want me to think about? Are you trying to say something to me? Are you sleeping with him already?
CHISARA

CHISARA
It is unfair of you, to ask me that question. And unfair to misunderstand me.
OYIN

CHISARA
One week of silence. Please write to me. Please. I miss you.
OYIN

MY DEAREST CHISARA,
The truth of my life is that I have never wanted the things I am supposed

to want, and yet I tried to want them. I have never truly liked the things I am supposed to like, and yet I wanted to like them. My not liking these things, not wanting these things, was a failure to me. Proof that I lacked something or lacked in something. When I was coming back to Nigeria two months ago, I would never have imagined you. And now I think of how profoundly changed I am, how three weeks with you and around you has left me a person with new skin.

When you asked "What do you want?" that evening, I could not answer not only because it was easier to hide in silence but because I did not, and still do not, have the language. Can you please try and understand this? We are both fragile. Very fragile.

OYIN

DEAR OYIN,

I've had malaria the past week, although that is not the reason for my silence. I am not one of those people who gets malaria often—I remember when I was growing up, people just assumed once they felt unwell that it was malaria which always made me wonder what if it's something else and they are slowing dying of it?—so when I do get sick it is always quite serious. For three days I was shivering in bed and my teeth chattered and my joints ached and my stomach churned. Do I sound a bit like you? I'm trying to. This hiding-behind-details thing might not be so bad after all.

I saw a doctor and took medicine and drank a lot of Lucozade. Why do people think Lucozade is medicinal? It's just sugar. But all my friends who came to see me brought Lucozade with them and I love it anyway, so now there is the carbonated sweetness of Lucozade eternally on my tongue. Eniye brought fruits, but my stomach didn't feel up to oranges and bananas. She asked about you. I must be imagining things, and imagining that there was something about the way she asked, but really why would she ask about you? She introduced us for goodness' sake. She knew you first. (But she doesn't know you best! Sorry, I could not resist that.)

Also, Toyosi was here when Eniye came, and Toyosi was saying something about the Single Women fellowship in her church (she said she's tired of going because the pastor's assistant always sees negative "visions" about her life and she doesn't think marriages that happen from church last long anyway) and Eniye just turned to me and asked, "How long has Oyin been married again?" I started wondering what the connection was between you and what was being said. Did you meet your husband in church? One of the many things I don't know. But even if you did, her question was still strange. I told her you had been married for four years and I looked her in the face with a dare in my eyes. Maybe she saw us that evening in Silverbird. Or maybe she meant nothing. Maybe her thinking is, Chisara and Oyin just happened to really get along and became closer to each other than to me, the friend who introduced them. Besides, I have to remember that stubborn willful obliviousness of my people. To her and to many like her, this is a harmless image: two women holding hands as they come out of the theater in Silverbird. Which is a good thing of course.

I'm well now and went back to work yesterday. My boss said I lost weight and he hopes I regain it quickly. His words: Don't let this malaria take your fine shape o. He's banker-smart and not bad-looking and wears a stupid bow tie to work on most days, the kind of man who, if he knew, would tell me that being who I am is a "waste" of a beautiful woman. He's been leering at me since I started working in that bank. I've been opaque to him since I started working in that bank. But yesterday I wanted to talk to him (don't ask why). So I asked him if he was happily married and he replied, "It depends on what you mean." And then I asked him what he would think if the person he loved was married and told him about the jar of bath salts in their marital bathroom. At first he stared at me with something like hope, as if I was trying to tell him that I liked him, and then when the part about the jar of bath salts sank in, he just stared blankly at me, as if the malaria had affected my head and I was a little off. Maybe I am a little off. After all, I am saying the things you don't want to hear.

CHISARA

CHISARA,
You're angry with me. Please don't be.

Yes, I met my husband in church, at a fellowship for young professionals. It is one of the many things I want to tell you. I want to tell you about the foods I hate and about everything else. I am going to find a way to come back to Nigeria in the next month. So we can sit down together and talk. And hold hands. And more.

Yesterday morning I broke the jar of bath salts. I just picked it up and let it drop. It shattered on the tiled bathroom floor. I told him it had been an accident.

Which of the many memories of us do I want to dwell on? I ask myself this question every day.

OYIN

OYIN,
I wish you hadn't told him it was an accident.
CHISARA

THANK YOU FOR
YOUR PATIENCE

by STEVEN MILLHAUSER

THANK YOU FOR CALLING customer service. All agents are currently assisting other customers. Please stay on the line and your
call will be answered in the order in which it was received. *Pause.*
Thank you for your patience. Please stay on the line and a representative
will be with you shortly. *Pause.* Your call is very important to us and we
appreciate your patience. Assistance is just a moment away. You don't have
to keep saying the same thing over and over again. I'm not an idiot. *Pause.*
Thank you for calling. Please be assured that your call will be answered as
soon as possible. Just pick up the phone. I've got better things to do than
stand around all day waiting for you to pick up. Yoo-hoo! I'm right here!
Stuck in the kitchen. Dropped off my daughter at pre-school ten minutes
ago. It's my free time. Sun's out. You need my account number? It's here in
front of me. Just pick up. Pick up. We're sorry to keep you waiting. Please
do not hang up and redial, as this will only further delay your call. Oh,

you're good. Is that what you do? Read people's minds? Fine, I'll give it another minute. Whatever it takes. You want me to be patient? Is that what this is all about? Patience? Don't talk to me about patience. I'll give you patience. I've got patience coming out of my ears. But hey, you know that. We're good at waiting, you and me. It's what we do. Me and you, girls. It's what women do. Boys take, girls wait. Put *that* on your bumper. Thank you for calling customer service. All agents are currently assisting other customers. Please stay on the line and your call will be answered in the order in which it was received. You'll make me scream. I swear you will. Is that the plan? Make her wait? Make her scream? The waiting room or the nuthouse? Oh, right: patience. A little practice is all it takes. Fifth grade. God, Tommy Edstrom. Does that ever happen to you? Standing around minding your own business and look out, you're back in the old neighborhood. Fifth grade. I wasn't thinking of boys yet, not in that way. But I was aware of them. There was this one boy in my class, Tommy Edstrom. I'd see him looking over at me sometimes. Tommy Edstrom. Thank you for your patience. Please stay on the line and a representative will be with you shortly. Blue eyes, and these blond lashes, even though his hair was brown. He hung out with boys on the playground, but he'd look over at us girls. In class he was always polite, friendly. So what happened is this. On the last day of school, he comes up to me and asks if he can walk home with me. No boy had ever asked me that before. At first I couldn't understand why he wanted to walk home with me. Why would Tommy Edstrom want to do that? It didn't make sense. But I—Your call is very important to us and we appreciate your patience. Assistance is just a moment away. I could feel something inside me, an excitement. We walked home. The same walk I took every day, past the same old houses, but now they all looked different, like I'd never seen them before. They looked, oh, I don't know. Alive. Every shingle, every window, alive in the sun. I remember a baseball lying in the grass. The creamy whiteness of the leather, the red stitching. Grass stain like wet paint. At my house he followed me into the living room. Shook my mother's hand. I could tell she liked that. He stood talking to her a little before we headed upstairs to my room. You know what we did in my room? Thank you for calling. Please be assured that your call will be answered as soon as possible. You know what we did? Try and guess. You'll never guess. No, not that. We set up my folding table and began working on a five-hundred–piece puzzle. Big old ship with sails on a choppy sea. He was very good at puzzles, Tommy Edstrom was. He asked me about the books in my bookcase, right above my favorite stuffed animals left over from when I was a little kid. *Anne of Green Gables*. I loved that book. He said he liked to read. Asked me if I ever went to the movies. At five o'clock he said he had to go home. My mother gave him a ride. Me sitting in back hoping he'd turn around. At the door of his house—We're sorry to keep you waiting. Please do not hang up and redial, as this will only further delay your call. At the door of his house he turned and waved. That was the beginning of summer. Tommy Edstrom. Each day I waited. God, did I wait. I don't know whether I was waiting for Tommy Edstrom to call me up on the phone or just show up one morning in my backyard. Like a squirrel or a blue jay. Or maybe I'd bump into him when I walked to the bakery down by the stream to pick up a sliced rye for my mom or some blueberry muffins hot out of the oven. Can you fall in love in fifth grade? Did you? Age ten going on eleven? I don't know if I was in love with Tommy Edstrom. Maybe I was in love with the houses in the sun. The baseball in the grass. All I know is that I wanted to walk home with him again. Thank you for calling customer service. All agents are currently assisting other customers. Please stay on the line and your call will be answered in the order in which it was received. That sentence doesn't sound right. Do you even know what you're saying? Tommy Edstrom. I kept waiting for him that summer. One evening I rode my bicycle out to his neighborhood, way across town. When I got to his street I saw an old woman sitting on a porch, looking at me. She had a bony white cat on her lap. The whole thing gave me a funny feeling. I turned back. All summer long I waited. I knew, but I kept waiting anyway. End of August I was already thinking about the first day of school. What if Tommy Edstrom had moved away to another town? What if Tommy Edstrom—Thank you for your patience. Please stay on the line and a representative will be with you shortly. The first day of school, there he was.

He was friendly, polite, just like before, but something was different. His hair was combed back in a new way and his eyes had a hardness to them. On the playground he hung out with a crowd of tough sixth graders. Collars up. Belt buckles on the hip. He didn't ask me to walk home with him that day. He never did again. I could tell he'd swerved off in some other direction. And though I knew it, the way you know things like that, I still waited for him to come up to me after school and ask if he could walk home with me, the way he'd done back then, a long time ago, in the fifth grade, when I was young and innocent. If you know what I mean. Are you still there? Are you listening? Your call is very important to us and we appreciate your patience. Assistance is just a moment away. Assistance is ten years away. Doesn't it make you sick? A job like this? How about getting a real job? What are there, three of you? Two? Hard to tell you apart. The Patience sisters. You know what you could do? You could put out a CD. The Patience Sisters, singing "Assistance Is Just a Moment Away." Hit the charts big time. But watch it, girls. Someday somebody won't be able to take it anymore. They'll sneak up behind you: a hand on your mouth, knife across the throat. Blood soaking through your blouse. Onto your sports bra. Or how about a needle in the arm? Wake up in a dark place. Hands tied behind your back. Duct tape over your mouth. Jeans around your ankles. You'll see. Just keep it up. Just you keep making me wait. Thank you for calling. Please be assured that your call will be answered as soon as possible. Spring Dance, junior year. Maplewood High. I wasn't one of the popular girls, but I wasn't unpopular either. I had friends. We went shopping in town, hung out together on our back porches. Rode our bikes to the beach, played badminton in our backyards. I wasn't what you'd call pretty, but I wasn't bad-looking. Good eyes, straight teeth. No cheekbones, but what can you do. I had friends who were boys, but no boyfriends. It was all right. I didn't worry about it. Did you worry about it? Then came Spring Dance, junior year. I was invited by—We're sorry to keep you waiting. Please do not hang up and redial, as this will only further delay your call. Invited by a boy in my history class, Gary Pearson. It was the first time a boy had wanted to be with me since Tommy Edstrom. Do you know what I felt? Relief so strong I didn't know what to do with it. It bothered me, that relief. Had I been standing around waiting, all this time? One of those tight-sweater girls who spend all day doing nothing but thinking about boys? Another dumb blond, and I wasn't even blond? More of a you've-got-to-be-kidding-me brown. I began looking at Gary Pearson in a new way. I don't mean at his body. Though you know, he did have a nice body. I liked the way he'd roll back the sleeves of his shirt twice and push them up a little, so you could see his wrists and the beginning of the muscly part of his forearms. But looking at him was more about figuring out who he was, this boy I'd known in Maplewood High for almost three years, this boy who for some reason—Thank you for calling customer service. All agents are currently assisting other customers. Please stay on the line and your call will be answered in the order in which it was received. This boy who for some reason had made up his mind to invite me to the Spring Dance. What did he see in me? He must've been trying to decide. Picturing me in his mind. What excited me wasn't what you think. Not kisses, touches, naked bodies. What got my heart going was the thought of some connection between me and this boy, this Gary Pearson, some closeness that had nothing to do with skin but with something deeper, untouchable, something that—listen to me! Can you believe it? I don't know what's gotten into me. Talking away a mile a minute. But it was like I'd been missing something all this time and now, at sixteen, I was walking home again with Tommy Edstrom, who'd been keeping me waiting all these years. Or something like that. I don't know. Something like that. Something like that. Thank you for your patience. Please stay on the line and a representative will be with you shortly. God, do you ever listen to yourselves? Do you? Same old song, over and over. Round and around and around we go, where we stop, nobody knows. And what's the message? Shut up and wait. I'll wait, all right, but I sure as hell won't shut up. I'm good at waiting. I waited for the Spring Dance. I saw him every day, Gary Pearson. He was friendly, an easygoing smile, but it was never more than that. Sometimes we talked about the dance. He'd just gotten his driver's license, he'd pick me up at quarter to eight. That was it. He was always rushing off to track practice, tennis practice, this practice, that practice. The night of the dance he drove up to the house in his father's Buick. Walked up to the front door and handed me a red rose. Complimented my dress. Your call is very important to us and we appreciate your patience. Assistance is just a moment away. The Spring Dance. Who knows what I was waiting for, the night of the Spring Dance? It wasn't what you're thinking. Oh, maybe off to one side of my mind. But in the center I was waiting for something to happen in my life, something that would push me away from what I was. That baseball in the grass. The sort of push you'd want if you were unhappy, but here's the thing: I wasn't unhappy. Can you want something, even if you're happy? How does that make sense? At the dance we danced close, but not closer. When we sat, we talked. I was having a good time. But I was also waiting for something. Waiting for what? Maybe for the night to show me what it was. The dance ended at midnight. He asked me if I'd like to—Thank you for calling. Please be assured that your call will be answered as soon as possible. He asked me if I'd like to take a ride in the car. I said yes. He drove us one town over, where there was a small parking lot looking down over a lake. You could see the lights on the other side of the water. I realized the night had been leading up to this moment. Here I was, alone in a car with Gary Pearson, the night of the Spring Dance. He started talking. He was tired of this town, he said. He wanted something bigger. He was planning to go to college in a big city. Manhattan, Chicago. Sometimes, driving around with friends at night, he'd think: There's got to be more. He felt I was someone he could talk to. We're sorry to keep you waiting. Please do not hang up and redial, as this will only further delay your call. He told me about his plans, his dreams. He said he liked talking to me. Said I was a good listener. And then something happened, in that car. It's not what you're thinking. It's never what you're thinking. What happened was this. As Gary Pearson talked, I felt a little shift inside me. I'd been feeling a kind of closeness to him and then I wasn't feeling it anymore. He was talking about himself. He was talking and talking about himself. He was like somebody studying his chin in a mirror, turning his head this way, that way, every which way. It would've been better if he'd stuck out his hand and grabbed a handful of breast. Oh, I'd've knocked his arm away. But it would have been something. I just wasn't there, in that car. You know what he did? You know what Gary Pearson did? Thank you for calling customer service. All agents are currently assisting other customers. Please stay on the line and your call will be answered in the order in which it was received. He pointed through the windshield at the moon. I looked at the moon. It looked like a moon. He said the moon didn't even know he was alive. He said the moon would still be there when he was dead. I tried not to glance at my watch. When he was done talking he turned to me and said he guessed it was time to head home. There was a question in his eyes. I said I guessed so. At my house he walked me to the front door, thanked me for the evening, and bent toward me. I turned my face and he kissed me on the cheek. In school he—Thank you for your patience. Please stay on the line and a representative will be with you shortly. In school he was the same as always, friendly and busy. Sometimes we talked in the halls. Never about the dance. He was always rushing off somewhere. I didn't want him to call, but I waited anyway. Even when we don't wait, we wait. That summer he sent me a postcard from Wyoming. He said he liked seeing a different part of the country. In a P.S. he wrote: "I'll never forget the spring dance." At the end of summer his parents shipped him off to some prep school in Massachusetts. He called me once and talked for an hour. I never saw him again. I know what you're thinking. I know exactly what you're thinking. Your call is very important to us and we appreciate your patience. Assistance is just a moment away. You're thinking, Poor girl! Nobody loves her! Boo-hoo! You're idiots. This isn't about boys. You think everything is about boys? I don't even know why I'm talking to you. I know you. I went to school with you. Small-town girls with small-town ambitions: hook your man, make a baby, grab that house. Split-level ranch on a quarter acre. Maple tree out front. Waiting for your hubby to get home from work. And what about me? You want to know my story? Is that what you're after? The story of my life? My life doesn't have a story. Or maybe it's a story everyone's heard before. Small-town girl graduates from high school, goes on to college, finds work, ho-hum. It's not what you want. You want pain. You want glamour. You want failure. You want death. I can't give you that. I can give you just one thing. Just one little thing. A little secret. Thank you for calling. Please be assured that your call will be answered as soon as possible. As soon as possible? Really? As soon as possible? I wanted to be done with high school as soon as possible. All senior year I waited for college. I was tired of popular girls and unpopular girls and Spring Dances and Gary Pearsons. I wanted something new. Have you ever wanted something new? College. There's not much to say about it. I slept with a few boys, read a few books. More books than boys. Another one for your bumper: MORE BOOKS THAN BOYS. That about sums it up. That doesn't sum it up. Listen, college was all right. I grew up a little. But all the time I was still waiting for something. Not for a man. That would take care of itself. But something. Sometimes I found myself thinking about Gary Pearson, talking in the car. There's got to be more, he said. There's got—We're sorry to keep you waiting. Please do not hang up and redial, as this will only further delay your call. There's got to be more. Was I turning into Gary Pearson? Maybe I needed to hitch a ride out to Wyoming, jump on a plane to Paris, join the Peace Corps and save lives in Africa. I didn't do anything. Don't get me wrong. I wasn't unhappy. But I wasn't exactly happy either. An in-betweener. That's what I was: an in-betweener. The good thing about college? I met people who had passion. Not that kind of passion. I mean passion for theater, passion for math. Only a few, but still. You could see it. You could smell it. Was that what was wrong with me? Not that anything was wrong with me. But I wanted something. I was waiting for something. Not unhappy. Not one of those. But short of the real thing, if you know what I—Thank you for calling customer service. All agents are currently assisting other customers. Please stay on the line and your call will be answered in the order in which it was received. But why would you know what I mean? You've got it all figured out, haven't you. Here's a question for you. Have you ever thought of killing yourself? It's not that hard. A rope around the neck. They'll have to cut you down. Be sure and comb your hair carefully. And take your time choosing the right dress. Oh, and don't forget: fresh underpants. That's very important: fresh underpants. You don't like rope marks on your neck? There's always the bottle of sleeping pills. Easy as pie. Car in the closed garage. Breathe deep. I'm getting tired now. My ear hurts, even though I keep shifting to the other one. I want to tell you something. One more thing, before you pick up. Because you will pick up, won't you? I've been waiting a long time. It's a little secret I have. Just one. Thank you for your patience. Please stay on the line and a representative will be with you shortly. Not that kind of secret. How come that's all you ever think of? Is that your own little secret, out there in your house with the baby and the bird feeder and the sunshine coming in through the kitchen window? Your husband's probably doing it. Why not you? Is that what you want from me? Well, give a listen. After college I lived at home for a year, temping at a nonprofit. Then I took a job on a newspaper, rented an apartment in town. I liked my work. I learned a few things, dated a few men. Then it happened. Are you ready? Are you ready for this? I met someone. A good man. I loved him and he loved me back. I married him at thirty-two. And you know what? I'm still in love with him, after six years. Are you disappointed? Of course you're disappointed. A story with a happy ending. I've let you down. I can feel it. Your call is very important to us and we appreciate your patience. Assistance is just a moment away. Not even a juicy tidbit you can sink your teeth into. No red-hot affair with the guy next door in his black nylon running shorts and sleeveless T. No arguing over who does the dishes. No troubles in the ol' bedroom. Talk. Laughter. Things feeling right. No, I'm happy with the way things turned out, happy as a lark. Are larks happy? Only sometimes, when I'm walking downtown on a sunny day, or say I'm sitting on the back porch, when the sun's gone down and the sky is that shade of blue you only see just before night, there ought to be a name for it, a feeling comes. Do you know that feeling? It's like a shadow falling across your heart. Or say it's like finding something in a drawer. It's something you haven't seen before. Thank you for calling. Please be assured that your call will be answered as soon as possible. A small wooden thingamajig, a little larger than a thimble. Set on a small block of wood. You don't know what it is, that thingamajig. If you could just figure it out, something would calm down inside you. You could stop waiting. Does that sound crazy? It's hard to say what I'm trying to say. It would be nice to lie down and close my eyes. But then I might not hear you, when you pick up. Something happened to me, two months ago. I've never told anyone about it before. It's my little secret. It won't take long. Are you still there? Hello? We're sorry to keep you waiting. Please do not hang up and redial, as this will only further delay your call. It was the middle of the morning. My daughter was at pre-school. I drove to the supermarket. We needed a few things, a half gallon of milk, fresh veggies for dinner, a can of spray for a stuck window. I like supermarkets. They give me a sense of freedom, you know? Everything changes, aisle after aisle. It's like being in one of those big-city zoos: here come the polar bears, right after the monkeys. Of course, I know every aisle by heart. But you keep seeing things. Shouldn't I get those cherries, two dollars off, today only? What about that package of macaroons? Do I want a package of macaroons? When was the last time I had a macaroon? Do I even like macaroons? I always go up and down every aisle, just to make sure. There were plenty of people around, pushing their carts, stopping, reaching up. And then, who knows why, I put some things in my cart that I didn't really want. Maybe it was because my cart looked a little empty. Have you ever done that? Just a few things. Thank you for calling customer service. All agents are currently assisting other customers. Please stay on the line and your call will be answered in the order in which it was received. The sight of those extra boxes in my cart, I don't know, gave me a good feeling. Who knows why? I began pushing my cart down the aisle, stopping along the way, reaching out for cans of soup, jars of mustard and relish, boxes of cereal. Dropping them all in. By the time I was done with two aisles, my cart was almost full. Who knows why you do what you do? Do you know why you do what you do? My cart had one of those wobbly wheels, so it wasn't all that easy to push. I didn't care. I just wanted to keep doing what I was doing. Thank you for your patience. Please stay on the line and a representative will be with you shortly. I was feeling excited. I wanted to see how much the cart could hold. I told myself I'd put it all back the second I was done. I kept sticking things in, shoving a jar of salted peanuts between two boxes of pancake mix, adding bottles of cranberry juice and packages of tortilla chips. The fuller it got the more excited I felt. One aisle later, my cart was heaped over the top. I mean way over. Something fell onto the floor. I scooped it up and jammed it back in. I knew it was time to stop but I also knew that if I stopped now I would never forgive myself. Your call is very important to us and we appreciate your patience. Assistance is just a moment away. I was in the next aisle. I began taking down packages of English muffins, fitting them in. Whole wheat multigrain bread, packages of seeded rye. I came to boxes of crackers and began putting them on top. Cheddar cheese crackers, sea salt crackers, heart-healthy crackers with those little red hearts on the box. The pile was up to my chest, my neck. Some lady at the end of the aisle had stopped and was looking over at me. I wasn't pushing the cart anymore. I was just piling things on. Higher and higher. Have you ever done that? A man in a green uniform was walking toward me. I could see his pants flapping against his legs. I began pushing the cart away. Thank you for your patience. Please be assured that your call will be answered as soon as possible. The cart was too full for pushing, but what could I do? The man was coming toward me. I could see the high pile shaking a little. Do you know what that's like, the shake before the crash? You hardly notice it at first, but you can see it growing, like there's a living thing inside. And then it all came down, boxes and jars and cans and bottles, smashing against the floor, rolling along, splitting open. A lovely avalanche. It was horrible but lovely, lovely. The man in the green uniform was coming closer. I've never told this to anyone, not even my husband. And you know what? We're sorry to keep you waiting. Please do not hang up and redial, as this will only further delay your call. You know what? I didn't care. Isn't that the strangest thing? I didn't care. Let them arrest me and throw me in jail. Let it all come crashing down. But you know what? Nothing happened. I offered to pay for it all, but the manager said no no, it's all right, not a problem. They didn't want any trouble. Just get her out of here and clean up the mess. They thought I was crazy. Do you think I'm crazy? Who does a thing like that? My life is good. I have what I want. Not many people can say that. Can you say that? All you can say is please be patient, please be patient, please be patient. I'm as patient as they come, but sometimes. Sometimes. I'm tired now. I'm not angry at you anymore. For keeping me waiting. You can't help it. It's who you are. But you know, I'm done talking to you. If you pick up, I'm not saying anything. Not another word. Thank you for calling customer service. All agents are currently assisting other customers. Please stay on the line and your call will be answered in the order in which it was received.

NANCY, ALL
TOO NANCY

by JONATHAN LETHEM

I

MOST OF US HAVE experienced the inkling that there is a world behind the world.

NANCY © GUY GILCHRIST. REPRINTED BY PERMISSION OF ANDREWS McMEEL SYNDICATION FOR UFS. ALL RIGHTS RESERVED.

2

The supposition that our reality is a vast clockwork construction, made of multiple subjectivities, can become an obsession—giving way to conspiracy theories, or sensations of paranoia or solipsism: that belief that only we ourselves are real.

3

Such anxieties are often deepened when we confront the fundamental mystery of the Other—and our inability to leap across the breach between ourselves and any other person.

4

Yet too mystical a view of consciousness is offset by the fact that we live embedded in an indifferent and natural environment, one more often brutal, homely, and fallible than embracing or sublime.

5

Any self-centered view of reality is humbled at an early age by encounters with irrefutable evidence of our parents' lives before we were born—this comprises an almost fathomless realm of mystery.

6

Esoteric visionary flights are also checked by our routine engagement with a universe of imperfect artifacts, which present unceasing opportunities for acts of coping and management.

7

Our carnal appetites also embed us in the material world, desires agitating our bodies toward a greater number of enticements than we possess limbs with which to grasp.

8

These flesh-envelopes we inhabit possess a certain theatrical aspect. Even the shyest among us functions as a performer in the theater of the social matrix.

9

On the other hand, if our social selves are a fiction, we are not the sole authors. Often, when peering out from behind a mask, we can only guess what faces others have drawn for us.

10

We arrive into a world already cluttered with attitudes, expectations, and assumptions. A huge amount of authentic human freedom is earned by simple gestures of refusal and negation.

11

The encounter with oneself is a lifelong pursuit—a mirror stage that never ends.

12

When we consider that our selves seem to be born anew each time we wake, life may seem a series of endless rehearsals behind a curtain that never actually rises—a strangely liberating realm of suspended judgment and infinite possibility.

13

Reconciliation comes in the acceptance that the worlds of reality and illusion, mind and matter, are inextricably mingled and interdependent—two sides of one coin.

14

From time to time such observations may strike us as complete enough that we can brush aside metaphysics and get on with the business of daily life without succumbing to such preoccupations.

15

Nevertheless, any given supposition tends to be dwarfed by an uncanny awareness of our elusive proximity to matters beyond the grasp of any language, including my own in this present undertaking.

TO ~~WHOM~~ MR.
JULIUS CRAAB IT
MAY CONCERN*

by ISMET PRCIC

KNOW IT'S THE PITS now that you collect this letter from me to you of me writing that I am very sorry a bucket was kicked by your mother in her full house in Portland.

It is very hard when somebody's motherbuckets get kick in the whole globe, especially to us.

---

* The original letter is written in pencil on a single sheet of computer paper, filled in completely with miniscule print. The text has sporadic punctuation and no regard for paragraphs. We have chosen to publish each sentence in its own paragraph for easier reading and we added punctuation where we deemed it necessary. Words in Bosnian are reproduced to the best of our ability as they appear on the page.

The following newspaper cutout was clipped to the letter:

> The extent of the problem isn't clear—city officials couldn't provide specific numbers, including the total number of "zombie homes" in Portland—and solving it would require navigating a complex paper trail of ownership records, mortgage debts and lien payments. But during a City Council work session Tuesday morning, Mayor Charlie Hales signaled Portland will take a more aggressive tack in dealing with landowners who let homes slide into disrepair and become havens for squatters or drug use.
> —Luke Hammill, *The Oregonian*, April 5, 2016

Both documents courtesy of Mr. Julius Craab of Park City, UT.

Receive my sorry from me about your deadness.

Too, receive my sorry of King's Tarzan English (Tarzan, King of monkeys, joke) but I find only two dictionaries to look: *The Dictionary of Clichés* and *Straight from the Fridge, Dad: A Dictionary of Hipster Slang*, this two books.

I use words from this two books that make sense to me and hoping that you will hear in your brain what I think in my brain.

It will not be all roses, like you say in America, but keep your shirt on, like you say too.

I understand that the words from two books don't mean *beechilly* what they say.

For example, in library I type in Bosnian word for something, like a tree I don't know in English, like *bukva,* and find in Latins that it is called *fagus sylvatica*, then I type *fagus sylvatica* and internet tell me the name of the tree in English is *beech*, and I know that you will know now what I mean when I write beechilly because *bukvalno* in Bosnia means stupid and dull, like dumb beech tree.

In ex-Yugoslavia the joke is: How to make Bosnian? Make bear sex the beech tree, joke.

There is no spelling, I am afraid, in my Bosnian language but if I make mistake receive my sorry please if I write *bitchily* or *beachily.*

I understand that it makes you different, and how, and so far and so far.

You don't know me, I am sure.

My name is Ekrem Goljo and I was living in 6323 Skidmore Street with my beloved but now I live in the bush behind Casa de Flores apartments and the full house of your good mother when I play my cards right.

I am on my first legs again, respectively, contrary to popular belief.

People in America think, a man from Balkan half-island, no English, he beat his beloved, and slaughter chicken in bathroom wash space, and yell and drink alcohol and don't shaves neck, I know.

Line of black where hair on chest stop and hair on neck is shaved, and golden bling on there to pull on hair, ouch.

I, thank you, shave neck and have no blings.

Now that I left my beloved and have to grasp the nettle with bare hands, in America you say that.

Grasp the nettle when you're on last legs.

We say: I sex hedgehog in the back.

But no, I'm good now, on first legs.

I have not seen hedgehog yet in Portland but I catch pigeon and squirrel, to eat not sex (*Gluho bilo*).

Squirrels are fat and picky in Portland.

There is mind-hurting old woman across the street from your good mother buy peanuts to them, they eat better than me, the church mouse.

So I eat *them*, natural meat.

There is a good book they call *Meat* by this Scottish and he have pictures how to peal squirrel.

You cut skin in the middle of squirrel, put your fingers in between meat and skin on the inside and pull like arm-exercise of springs in the morning, simple.

I have tent in the bush and fire pit of your good mother to use when it is cold, she give me.

I am snug like a bug in the rug, which is funny to say on top of voice.

There is nettles in the bush and young top of nettles I put in soup when they grow in spring and summer like my mother show me in war (po' man's C Vitamin).

I cook all my foods in the fire pit and never drink your brown shit Coca-Cola in my life.

You Americans are peculiarities.

Too, I was cook to my beloved but now I play possum from her.

It is sad, I will tell you.

When it's not cats and dogs I hang around Wellington Park for children and dogs and old people pretending to run but going very slow.

Why you let fat people drive in invalid chairs in America?

That is when first time I seen your mother, and she carry big branch of tree and sweaty.

It is very pretty, she says to me, but truth be told was just branch.

Truth be told she smell like she was in the grip of the grape, drunk like Earth, I am sorry to tell you.

But she very nice, not alcoholic, just woman who drink, like my mother.

I carry her branch to the house but holly shit there was no room for branch, everything full: boxes, pillow, textile all rumple everywhere, *memli soba,* pot and pot of green foods on top where you can't see no carpet, and books on books on books to the roof and little on the side, like the guilty tower of Pizza in Italy.

Can't see the house from all the trees.

But she give me white shpritzer and I see how much the house is full, and we drink outside.

She says the house was filled with hashishars and smackheads and sad young bums of Jehovah's witness which they run from home for tattoos and birthdays, but she run them all away.

Survival of the fittest.

She ask me about my neck in the woods and I don't understand but I tell her I am from Bosnia and she says she has you in Utah, her son Julius, who has business with Bosnians and ask me if I know Jovo but she can't say Jovo surname.

Receive my sorries, but why Americans ask question like this?

Maybe it was much too many shpritzer but I feel afraid when she ask, because to her it is very easy to say *Do you know Jovo?* but for me it is very hard.

Jovo is Orthodox name and Ekrem is Muslim name, two sides, usually.

I didn't say that my father was hosed down with many bullets of the Orthodox neighbor guard in the assemble building in brick factory when the maniac Orthodox soldier (who was my teacher of shop in elementary school) with a knife wanted to see how long he can stab my father to die slow.

Milk of human kindness, that neighbor, for shorting my father's pain.

I didn't tell her I didn't know if your Jovo was like him or he was like maniac.

So I smile and say good, we have something together.

Receive my sorry that I didn't say her truth.

You can be scared that I am Muslim, or you can't, but I swear I am not ferocious.

I don't bend five times in a day and when I am scared I pray Arab words but it is like abraka-dabraka, like in a book for children.

I eat pigs when I was in Bosnia and Orthodox maniacs still try to kill me because they think I don't eat pigs.

Now I don't eat pigs because who can understand maniacs' brain?

Your good mother is Christian and I was happy to neighbor her.

She one time complain how when she was a little baby her father got always a goose for Christmas but they close the wood factory job and she never eat goose any longer.

But I see goose, many many goose, in one park across the autoway where there is basketballs and small lake and people moving slowly.

In the middle of grass on the beach of the lake slow people in white clothes stand with spread eagle legs and move their hands all slow and walk on eggshells.

I see that goose lay near the slow people, not afraid.

So at the dawn's early light I go and stand with stick and move slow like on eggshells until I am close and then *duh!* I kick the goose with stick in the head and put it speedy in the rucksack and I'm out of there!

I give goose to your mother for Christmas but she scream and says blood, blood and you can't eat goose from Canada, I don't know how she know goose is from Canada.

But in Bosnia war we eat sparrow and pigeon and crow so I know it was hard to her because goose was not in the store before.

But I make it in the fire pit and it was good.

I like white meat of chicken and it was peculiarity to see that goose from Canada have black meat where chicken have white meat.

Too, my beloved is Christian and it is how we come to America.

America didn't want just Muslim husband and wife or just Orthodox husband and wife or just Catholic husband and wife to come to America.

But if Muslim husband and Orthodox wife go to the American embassy they say good, come.

I got married with beloved because I didn't want to go fight anymore and because all her people go out before.

We went to school together, not boyfriend and girlfriend first, but just school.

They send us in Phoenix, Arizona in the desert with cactus and everything the same color.

Take winter people and play with fire to put them in hotness in Arizona and take hotness Somali people and put them on ice in Minnesota.

Who gives jobs to people make plans like this where to send people?

In Arizona we fight all the time.

We come to Portland because her cousin show her how to work with computers and my beloved is very smart with numbers, flying fingers.

I cut sheep throats on farm and live in bloody butchery with Mexicans and Dominican Republicans and Democrats Republicans of Congo.

When we have pause in butchery we eat fast and then we play football in the field and mud like children, rain or shine, goal is door of barn.

The ball is not football ball but pointy ball like egg and American managers take it some time in their hands like goalmans, and run all around like chicken and throw it from one to other, speaking fast Englishness, laughing.

Not good kind of laughing but behind back laughing like here's the hand under the hole in buttocks, like we say in Bosnia: *Evo ruka al, ispod shupka!*

My mother, who drinks, she had a recitation about farting in the olden school times that she always says, and I, child, remember it.

She says don't repeat in school because of dirty laundry.

It's hard to repeat in English but I do my best.

"Ho Shi Min's troops

Attack your butt.

Chief skirmish are

Around your hole."

It always bust my stomach in laughing.

But anyhow, all this laughs is not worth a hill of beans because, you know.

I have to tell you about your mother now.

She's nowhere to be found.

I knock on back door, one day, two days, and clock alarm in the house is so boring, all the time like flies, and I can't sleep.

Receive my sorry to say, but I break window in the back door and right off the bat I thought I could smell rat and I was right; it was your mother, smells to high heaven.

I know this smell from Bosnia, when a lot of people exploded, hither and yon people pieces, and they clean the street, and there was containers of trash smelling too, but the people smell was deep, in my brain.

It hit bellow the belt of my heart and understanding.

I don't know if it was her heart or brain, but her carpet I see is green, good carpet.

In American TV children do this in snow when they lay down in it but I can't find the word in my two books.

She was on her back and spreading eagle with arms and legs on green carpet, but decent, thank God.

She had eyes close and her face was not like I saw in Bosnia, surprised in the negative.

She look like asleep for days but a little stiff and not natural.

But it happens when soul left us and we become stiff like furniture.

The Oregonian paper scare populace, say zombie home everywhere.

I'm pleased to say that your mother not a zombie; she a good egg.

I moved my tent to by the wide spot of the road, where people drive and don't walk, and leave me alone.

I can't stay behind your mother anymore because I'm scared but I walk by her house pretending to be recycle man and there was people there in beekeeper suits like in outer space taking all her stuff in orange plastic sacks.

Receive my sorries but I take the fire pit and Garfield blanket from the extra room with the dolls.

And all the wine and other bottles.

And medications that I know.

And I took the branch that start our friendship to remember her.

I know you don't see from eye to eye but I must say to you the only clean place of your mother house is the picture of you.

It's easy to remember.

I stop calling my mother because it is hard to say to mother that I escape from motherland because I don't want to die, and I lie to myself and say it's because I believe in future.

It's hard to say to my mother that I lie and marry beloved not for beloved but because I am scared.

I lie to myself and still say in my brain that my tent is extraordinary in the US of A, that sky is the limit, that who knows what the future will bring.

But sometimes, in the night, when cars go by fast, I know that future only bring old things back, like war.

History repeats itself, but only badness of history.

Any goodness history, like the branch, Ekrem has to work hard to keep in life.

Old good things we have to work to keep to heart, remind in brain.

Old bad things keep us, show up close to heart and close to brain anyway, even when we would kill to forget.

Receive my sorries forever, I don't know how to write what I mean in my brain, in realness.

Sta da ti kazem, brate.

Jednu nogu ispred druge, kazu ovd'e, cak i kad si u invalidskim kolicima.

Mi smo samo ljudi, i k'o tak'i, mi smo dobro ruzni, al' smo dobro glupi.

Sta nam fali, jel'.

Postovanje,
Ekrem Goljo, zvani Eko

SEPTEMBER 14

by HEIDI JULAVITS

TODAY ON THE WAY to Edith Wharton's house I got a speeding ticket. I was on the Taconic Parkway, which from the name sounds relaxing and beautiful but isn't. The trees closed in on either side. It was like driving through a straw. The sun shining above the straw registered as a good reason to be depressed, because somewhere else, but not here, people were really happy. I wanted to get off the Taconic as quickly as possible, though this wasn't the reason I was speeding. I always speed. Once you start speeding it is impossible not to always speed, because you grow accustomed to the world moving past you at a certain clip. Sealed inside a car, you're unaffected by wind resistance. It's all about the blur quotient. The degree of blur. You can get addicted to the calm this blur bestows. I am driving too slowly when I notice individual leaves. When the landscape gets crinkly and sharp, and the world wants too much of my attention, I grow crabby and exhausted. I am (this is not what I said to the police officer who pulled me over) but I honestly am *more* apt to get in an accident when I'm driving slowly, because there's just too much to see.

So I was speeding and I was pulled over. The cop was a young man, as they always tend to be in relation to me these days. How to play this? I tallied my advantages and disadvantages. I wasn't driving my usual car. I'd borrowed a very fancy Swedish car from my in-laws. This put me at a disadvantage. This cop, whose annual salary was probably equivalent to the cost of the car I was driving, I wouldn't blame him if he made certain assumptions, and unconsciously/consciously desired to fine me for being a person I was only pretending to be. So the first thing I said to him was, "This isn't my car." I tried to explain, too, that this car was so much fancier than my usual car, which was not at all fancy, and so much slower.

No change in his attitude. He asked me if the address on my driver's license was correct. It was and it wasn't. The address is my Maine address, because I have a Maine driver's license, and Maine plates on my usual car, and I'm registered to vote in Maine and was born in Maine and plan also to be buried there, but I pay taxes in New York, and work in New York, and am called for jury duty in New York, and technically live in New York. I didn't want to out myself to this upstate cop as a person with a summer house (which we can afford because we sublet our city apartment for a profit, though it was unlikely I'd have time to get into the pyramid-scheme particulars of my finances with him), but nor did I want to risk not receiving the fine they'd eventually send to me, because sometimes official mail does not get forwarded, and then I'd fail to pay that fine, and my license would be suspended in New York.

Where, again, I technically live.

I decided to risk it. I told him the Maine address was correct.

Then there was the business of finding the registration. Actually, first there was the business of cracking the safe that was the car's glove box. My in-laws' car is designed for people without any preconceived notions about cars. The ignition is not where the ignition should be. (It's between the seats.) The glove box is also inscrutable. It has no latch. It does have a regular keyhole but I had no regular key. I tried to think like a Swede. I felt around the exterior of the glove box. The glove box was curved and resembled a woman's lower body in a plastic pencil skirt (if that woman were lying on her side), and the act of my feeling and feeling the smooth flank of the glove box while being watched by this young man in a uniform made me really uncomfortable. My hands started to shake. I thought, Don't let him see you freak out! But then I thought, What if I did? What if I let my hands shake even more? What if I were so obviously scared of him? Would he let me off?

I am forty-four years old and I had never tried this. I have never acted helpless and in need of saving. Maybe because until recently I was pretty confident that I was hot enough to flirt my way out of this type of situation. Now I am not so sure.

So I decided to act scared. My voice got tremblier. I opened the glove box, finally (it turns out you *push* on the keyhole with your finger: it was a fake lock that proved as effective as a real one), and shakily flicked through the papers inside, and acted like I had no idea what a registration looked like, and handed him receipts and other random slips of paper for his perusal. Was this the registration? Was this? Finally I found it. He returned to his car. I waited for the verdict. Then I started to rethink my scared strategy. He'd have pity on a scared girl, or a scared old lady, but would he really have pity on a scared middle-aged woman? His mom wouldn't react this way! She'd have more pride and self-control! I regretted that I hadn't tried to flirt with him. But might not that have backfired too? His mom wouldn't try to flirt her way out of a speeding ticket!

The cop returned to the car. I was composed, neither flirty nor scared. I was just a neutral person by then, a person without a plan. He gave me a ticket. He called me "ma'am."

FEAR OF LOOSE TONGUE

by LYDIA DAVIS

PLEASE BE KIND, RON, she says—
no mention of *anything*
that may or may not have occurred
at Hamburger Mary's.

OPPORTUNISTIC SEED

by LYDIA DAVIS

SHE HOLDS THE DOOR for him as he carries a case of wine into the house.

A seed floating on its bit of fluff takes the opportunity to enter the house behind him

(though this will not turn out to be, for the seed, a good move).

TWO MAYORS AND A WORD

by LYDIA DAVIS

THE FORMER MAYOR OF our village is publicly upset with the present mayor.
The former mayor objects to the use of a certain word
by the present mayor:
It contains an added superfluous negative, he says,
and has no place in a village document.

The present mayor quickly concedes the point,
though with a smile whose meaning we cannot read,
and corrects the word.
(The word in question is: *irregardless*.)

PHILOSOPHICAL QUESTION POSED
BY STRANGER IN PAMPHLET

by LYDIA DAVIS

WILL SUFFERING EVER END?

Would you say:

   yes?

   no?

   maybe?

PLEASE CLEAN THE KITCHEN

BY DAN KENNEDY

Look, I'm not going to lay some cutesy guilt trip on you about how we're not here to clean up after you and all of that mumbo jumbo. Fact is, if you want to leave stuff lying around in here and not clean up after yourself, then that's what you're gonna do. But check this out: I knew a guy named Tim. And the thing about Tim is he was such a god-damn downer—I mean, to be clear, he wasn't, like, actually sad or actually depressed. He wasn't in difficult straits or circumstances, but his whole demeanor was a stoop and a shrug. Hey Tim, we got tickets for this concert, wanna go? (He shrugs. Never mind that it's his favorite band.) Hey Tim, you can borrow my motorcycle if you want while I'm out of town. (Tim slouches for a hunched moment then lurches into his trademark shrug.) That was everything with Tim. He was the kind of guy who would shortcut doing the dishes, not even wash the backs of them, but he would act like he totally washed them—and he lived alone in a studio apartment! The only person he was lying to was himself. So it was basically that old cheating at solitaire thing. And we all got to talking about it. And we realized Tim never made his bed, always left stuff lying around, never quite knew where things were or what he was looking for. Read that last part again. Feel that on a macro level, not just the level of unmade beds and dirty dishes. Hey, do what you want, clean up after yourself or don't, nobody can control you but you. But I swear to god, in this life you're either moving closer to cheating at solitaire or further from it. This isn't between you and me, or you and us, or us and them: it's between you and you. Also, I see the good intentions in you and I think you get what this sign is saying. You're one of the good ones, I bet.

DELIVER ME

by SHERMAN ALEXIE

ACCORDING TO THE PJ PIZZA employee handbook, each delivery driver was required to wear an official PJ Pizza royal blue polo shirt with a PJ Pizza patch on the right breast pocket—a patch that included the embroidered restaurant name and motto "PJ Pizza: When You Wish for Deep Dish," and also an embroidered caricature of Harold Middlestaff, the founder, owner, and manager.

You might ask why the restaurant was named PJ Pizza instead of Harold's Pizza or Middlestaff's. You might also ask why Harold dropped the possessive and called it PJ Pizza instead of PJ's Pizza. The answers to your questions are contained in the employee handbook: "PJ is *not* a singular entity. Instead, PJ Pizza is the full name of our restaurant. PJ Pizza is the *only* proper name of our establishment. PJ Pizza is our identity. Therefore, PJ Pizza will *never* be known as PJ's Pizza. Employees are required to use the full name, 'PJ Pizza,' and will be reprimanded if they refer to our restaurant as 'PJ's Pizza,' or the diminutive 'PJ's.' Employees are also required to politely, but firmly, correct any customer who mistakenly refers to our restaurant as 'PJ's Pizza' or 'PJ's.' To reiterate, our restaurant, the finest pizza place in Spokane, Washington, will now and forever and ONLY be known as 'PJ Pizza.'"

Based on that particular entry in the PJ Pizza employee handbook, you might assume that Harold Middlestaff was an obsessive-compulsive dickhead. And you'd be right. But he also employed two assistant managers who rose from jobs as dishwashers. Moreover, one of those dishwashers-turned-assistant-managers was a mostly unhappy man named William, who, over the years, transitioned into being a mostly happy woman named Cameron.

So, yeah, Harold Middlestaff was a progressive obsessive-compulsive dickhead.

I delivered PJ Pizza's deep-dish extravaganzas for three years. I began the job as a part-time driver, at the same time I began community college as a part-time student. I made it halfway through the first quarter of school— sleeping through English and history classes—before I dropped out and asked Harold Middlestaff for more work shifts.

"You're my favorite kind of person," he said. "A smart guy who doesn't like books."

As a driver with three years' experience, I grossed almost $625 a week. Unlike many other restaurant workers, we didn't collect tips at PJ Pizza. After the state passed a law that raised the minimum wage, Harold Middlestaff shrugged his shoulders, obeyed that law and then some by paying slightly more than required, and charged a 15-percent service fee to diners instead of encouraging tips. That simple move seemed to balance the books. PJ Pizza stayed in business partly because of Harold's financial skills, but mostly because we did indeed make the best pizza in Spokane. We were in high demand. Harold gave his employees most of the money collected from that 15-percent service fee. So, after getting my share of that cash pool, and after paying federal, state, and city government taxes, and various other work-related fees, I earned $1,956 a month. Poverty wages, basically, even for an unmarried person living alone in Spokane. I could only afford to rent an attic bedroom in a boarding house. Though calling it a boarding house makes it sound like my landlord was a 1950s eccentric artist—an elderly widow who painted in the backyard and made blueberry scones for her Merchant Marine renters. In truth, my landlord was a corporation that bought old houses, performed a minimum amount of repair and remodel, and rented out inadequate rooms to the inadequately employed.

That company's motto should have been, "You can hear your housemates fart all night long but our low prices will never be wrong!"

On a Sunday, during a particularly crazy shift where I'd delivered twenty-two pizzas and put nearly thirty miles on my car, a battered Nissan that seemed to have more room for the pizza-warming sleeve than it did for me, I delivered a bacon and spinach pie to Anna, my girlfriend, at her parents' home one block outside of our advertised delivery zone.

Usually, she only ordered pizza when her mother and father were gone. And usually, Anna and I would leave the pizza on the kitchen counter and run upstairs to enjoy quick mid-shift sex in her bedroom.

But things had changed. She greeted me at the door and did not usher me inside.

"Listen," Anna said as she stood on the small front porch. "I'm joining the Navy."

"What?" I asked.

"I've joined the Navy," she said. "I ship out in ten days."

"Wait, what?"

"I'm leaving," she said. "I'm sorry."

"Hold on, hold on," I said. "When did you decide this?"

"I've been thinking about it for a while. I signed up a few months ago."

"And you're just telling me now?"

"Well," she said. "I wanted us to be happy before I left. I still want us to be happy. We have ten days. Let's make them good ones."

I wasn't sure what to say.

I had many cousins and uncles who'd served in the U.S. Armed Forces. But half of Anna's family was a trail mix of peaceful hippies who wanted no part of any violence and the other half was an arsenal of conspiracy theorists who were convinced they'd eventually be going to war *against* our country.

"I don't understand," I said. "Why is this happening?"

"I need to do what's best for me," Anna said.

"I thought you loved me. I thought we were in love."

"We are in love," she said. "But the Navy will pay for college."

She was still pissed at me for dropping out of school.

"Come on," I said. "I said I was sorry for quitting."

"I showed you the numbers. College graduates make more money than non-graduates. *Significantly* more."

Romance was easier before everybody could google everything.

"Hey," I said. "I know garbagemen who make more money than lawyers."

I didn't know if that was true. I hadn't googled it. But it sounded great.

"But Jeremy," she said. "You don't want to be a garbageman or a lawyer. All you want to do is deliver pizzas."

"This is only temporary," I said.

"Temporary, temporary," she said. "You're always going to be Temporary Jeremy."

She sighed, stepped inside her house, and gently closed the door on me. That was more painful than if she'd slammed it shut.

"I still have your pizza," I shouted.

"Keep it," she shouted back.

We drivers used our personal cars to deliver pizzas. Harold Middlestaff paid for the gas we used during work, based on odometer readings, and for regular car washes and detailing, to maintain a professional look. But Harold Middlestaff did not pay us for basic engine maintenance or for any repairs.

We also paid for our own insurance.

Things are added to things.

Things are *compiled.*

And trust me, you want to be the one compiling and not the one being compiled.

I met Anna when she was walking her dog, Darla, in the park. I didn't have a whole lot of extra money for entertainment. I couldn't afford Netflix so I binge-watched people instead.

"Cute dog," I said to Anna as she walked by with her five-pound mutt.

"Yeah," Anna said. "And she knows it."

"She does prance," I said. "She must be a show dog. How did you train her to walk that way?"

"She walked like that when we got her. She's a rescue dog. We got her from the Humane Society."

"So she's a girl with a mysterious past," I said.

"Darla loves old ladies," she said. "So we think maybe she was owned by an old woman who died. And then she must have run away because they found her living by the Little Spokane River. Her hair was so dirty and matted, they had to shave her bald."

"Wow," I said. "She's pretty small to have survived on her own."

"Yeah," Anna said. "You'd think that would mean she's smart. But she's not. I mean—she's not dumb. She's just average, I guess."

"Average but cute," I said. "Just like me."

Anna smiled.

Harold Middlestaff gave one free PJ Pizza polo shirt to each delivery driver. We were expected to buy at least one more shirt. Some of the drivers bought three or four extra shirts to make sure they always had a clean one ready for work. Harold sometimes gave surprise five-dollar bills to drivers who were exceptionally clean and diligent and organized. A tiny bonus. It was a wink, a pat on the back, enough for a venti mocha at the Starbucks down the block. Harold Middlestaff loved a spotless work shirt in what was a messy job.

"If you look good," he always said, "then the pizzas look better."

But I thought it was a waste of money to own more than one shirt. Those polos cost thirty dollars, which seemed like a lot for something probably made by toddlers on a dictator's private island in the Pacific Ocean. There was no washer or dryer in my boarding house so I hand-washed my polo shirt every night in the bathroom sink. Sometimes, I wore my polo into the shower and scrubbed it with the same shampoo and soap I used to clean myself.

Sounds goofy, I know, but it cost $5.50 to wash and dry a load of clothes at the self-serve laundromat. There's no way I had the money, or the time, to properly wash my shirt on a daily basis.

So, okay, sometimes, I'd come home tired and toss my dirty PJ Pizza polo to molder on the floor. Sometimes, I'd stagger home utterly exhausted and fall asleep in my shirt. So, yeah, once in a while, I'd wear an unwashed shirt to work. Of course, I would first do some spot cleaning with a bar of soap. And, to mask my body odor, I'd roll deodorant directly onto the fabric of the shirt. When it stank the worst, I'd apply two or three coats of Speed Stick to my armpits and also to the shirt's armpits. Sometimes, depending on my mood and the weather, I'd wear a shirt that hadn't been fully washed in three or four days. Eventually, I'd stink so bad that Harold Middlestaff would lend me a new polo to wear, but only for that one shift. He'd always take it back and would charge me a dollar for rental and laundry.

One dollar here, one dollar there. Harold Middlestaff knew how to count better than I ever did.

A few minutes after Anna told me she was leaving me for the Navy, I sat in a shopping mall parking lot, eating the bacon and spinach pizza in my car and wondering about my future. How could I keep Anna from joining the Navy? Or, if I couldn't stop her from enlisting, then how could I maintain a long-distance relationship? She'd be serving on a ship where there'd be a few dozen women and hundreds of men. What could I do to keep her faithful?

I realized that I needed to prove how much I loved her. I needed evidence. I needed something real and substantial. I needed to propose marriage. So

I googled "engagement ring" on my phone, saw that I couldn't afford anything, and changed my search to "budget engagement ring."

Walmart was selling a one and seven eighths–karat silver sapphire ring for fifty bucks. The ring looked decent in the photo. It was cheap. Way cheap. It seemed to be the cheapest engagement ring in the universe. Only fifty bucks! Who couldn't afford that? What kind of romantic loser couldn't dredge up five ten-dollar bills? Me. I couldn't afford it. I didn't have an extra fifty bucks. Payday was two weeks away and Anna was leaving in ten days.

Shit.

"Where have you been?" Harold Middlestaff asked when I finally returned to the restaurant.

"Traffic," I said.

Harold Middlestaff thought I meant car traffic but I was talking about *emotional* traffic.

"If you run late like that again," he said, "I will dock you an hour's pay."

I lost a few hours of pay every month because of my chronic lateness. It might not have been legal to punish a worker like that, but it seemed morally fair, I guess.

"You've got five home deliveries waiting," he said. "And one corner."

Our delivery area included the rich neighborhoods of Spokane's South Hill and the poor areas along the East Sprague corridor that were busy with used car lots, pawn shops, legal pot stores, middling ethnic restaurants, dive bars, and massage parlors. East Sprague was also the working grounds for most of Spokane's street prostitutes.

On my first night on the job, I took a customer call from a loud woman.

"Honey," she said. "I need one of them veggie calzone things. Small size."

"Okay," I said. "What is your address?"

"Corner of Sprague and Roy."

"Yes, ma'am, but I need the specific address—the house number, please."

"Oh, honey, you must be new. I won't be in no house. I'll be standing on the corner of Sprague and Roy, right by that check cashing place."

"I don't know if I'm supposed to deliver to people standing on the street."

"Don't worry, baby, Mr. Middlestaff knows all about me. I've been a customer for years."

So that was the first time I delivered directly to a prostitute. Her street name was Betty Shoes. Her real first name was probably Elizabeth but who knows about her real last name. I probably delivered thirty or forty small veggie calzones to her over the years. I delivered to other prostitutes, as well, but Betty Shoes was always the loudest and kindest. And then she stopped calling. I didn't like to think about the terrible reasons why she might have gone away. I hoped she'd left the streets for a job like mine—demoralizing and low-paying, yes, but not so damn dangerous and unhealthy and naked.

"Come on, Jeremy," Harold Middlestaff said again. "You've got five home deliveries. And one corner."

"For Betty?" I asked.

"No," he said. "Sorry."

He put his hand on my shoulder. I don't know how much he truly cared about Betty or her vanishing. But I was fairly sure he cared about how much I cared.

"Now get your ass moving," he said. "And put on some deodorant. You stink."

Hustling out of the store with the pizzas, I tried to smell myself—to get a sense of how much I reeked. But, scientifically speaking, humans are unable to accurately gauge their own funk. Oh, you can recognize your own scent and you can also recognize that you need a shower or three, but the true nature of your most epic stench will always elude you. It's a primitive form of self-protection, I guess. After all, how could our distant ancestors have crowded into small caves if their noses weren't immune to the prehistoric miasma?

I shoved the pizzas into the warming sleeve sitting on my car's passenger seat and dug through my glove compartment looking for something to mask my body odor, finding only a half-filled tin of mints. So I crushed the mints with my thumbnail, poured a little bit of water into the tin, shook it hard for a minute, and created a minty-smelling paste that I rubbed into my armpits and onto my lower back. And then I sucked the minty residue off my fingers so my breath wouldn't smell so much of bacon and spinach.

Some cleansing ritual, huh? Who says we ever stopped being cavemen?

A month after I started at PJ Pizza, I delivered three extra-large, extra-cheese pies to a dorm room at Gonzaga University, and was surprised when a guy from my high school answered the door. We weren't friends or anything. My high school had almost three thousand students but this guy and I had shared a few classes together and said hello in the halls.

"Hey," he said as I handed over the pizza. "Don't I know you?"

It had only been two years since we'd graduated. His name was Edward. He was good at math and science. And he'd been on the debate team.

"Jeremy, right?" he said.

He was a handsome guy. Kind eyes. He smiled. Happy to see me, though we were both way too young for nostalgia. I wanted to smile back. But I suddenly felt so much shame that I almost vomited. I wasn't ashamed of my job—work is work, after all—but I was ashamed that I hadn't even applied to any four-year colleges. I'd known I didn't have the grades for a place like Gonzaga, but I may have had a shot at Eastern Washington or Washington State University. Maybe. I didn't even try. I'd never been on the official college track, but I'd also never been told I wasn't college material. I guess, when it came to school, I'd always been somewhere in the in-between.

"You're Jeremy," he said. "From Shadle Park High. It's me, Edward. Don't you remember?"

"Sorry," I said. "You must have me confused with somebody else. My name is Harold."

"No," he said, still smiling. "You're Jeremy. We had Current World Issues together. And Geometry."

"My name is Harold Middlestaff, Jr.," I said and walked away without collecting money for the pizza.

*   *   *

We were required to put twelve pepperoni circles, no more and no less, on the small pizza. Sixteen on the medium. Twenty on the large. And twenty-four on the extra-large. Or maybe it was ten, fourteen, sixteen, and twenty. Or maybe it was something else. I was always forgetting. I sometimes had a tough time remembering numbers—remembering them in order. So, sometimes, I'd put on the wrong number of pepperoni circles—or too many ounces of cheese or scallions or pineapple—and Harold Middlestaff would catch my error during one of his regular spot checks.

"Jeremy," he asked me once. "Why does this keep happening?"

And I said, "Pizza making is art, not science."

Harold Middlestaff laughed, but he still docked my pay for the cost of the extra ingredients.

At other times, he also docked my pay if I didn't put on enough ingredients.

"That's a lesser pizza you made," he would say. "That's a pizza you settled for."

Anna read books.

She had a library card.

Sometimes we went to the library together. I'd use the free computers to surf the web while she looked for something good to read.

She liked books about other countries. Novels, sometimes. But mostly history books. And travel books, too. She liked to look at maps.

She'd put her finger down on a map, sound out the name of a country or city, and ask me to guess at what might happen in that place.

"What kind of dances do they have?" she'd asked. "What kind of musical instruments?"

Once, I said, "I think all musical instruments are based on the same basic idea. It's not like discovering a new animal or something. Everything is basically a drum, flute, or guitar, right?"

"Fuck you," she said.

After I delivered the five pizzas to five houses and delivered the corner pizza to a prostitute I didn't recognize and who didn't know of any street worker named Betty Shoes or what might have happened to her, I wondered again how I might obtain the fifty bucks I needed to buy the engagement ring for Anna. I briefly thought about robbing a convenience store. I knew a few guys who'd worked the Circle K down the street from PJ Pizza, so I knew how the stores worked. And I figured it would be a relatively safe crime. Well, I wouldn't rob the place where I knew people. They might recognize me, even if I wore a mask, and it would be rude to rob and scare friends. But it would still be fairly safe to rob a more distant store staffed by strangers. After all, I would only be armed with my loud voice and an imaginary gun. And I knew that corporate employees—the guys who worked at 7-Eleven and big places like that—were legally required to cooperate with robbers. I also knew those guys didn't give a shit about their corporate overlords. Those workers wouldn't try to heroically defend the cash register. They wouldn't risk their lives to confront me. I didn't want to risk my life, either, so I wouldn't rob one of those independent stores where the owner worked the graveyard shift. That kind of dude would protect his store, his property. His hard-earned money. That kind of dude might kill me. So I'd rob a 7-Eleven. I also knew that 7-Eleven workers only kept a small amount of cash in their tills. They regularly dropped most of their bills into a time-locked safe. So it wouldn't be a big-money felony. I wouldn't be stealing a dramatic amount of money. I just needed fifty bucks for the ring and maybe another fifty to justify the risk. Maybe I'd use that extra cash to buy a new shirt and tie. I'd wear that new shirt when I proposed. It was beginning to sound like a possibility, like unarmed robbery was something I could pull off. And since I would only commit the crime once, and would wear a mask and shirt I'd bury deep in the woods somewhere, there was little chance I would ever be identified and arrested.

I wanted to google the statistics for unsolved convenience store robberies, but I realized that's the kind of internet search that might lead me to getting identified and arrested.

Yeah, a criminal mastermind. Like all of the criminal masterminds sitting in jail.

So, instead of committing a felony, I texted Anna a row of heart emojis.

But she didn't text back.

I waited and waited and thought maybe I should throw my phone off the Maple Street Bridge into the Spokane River. Maybe suiciding my phone would solve all of my problems. My phone bill ate up 10 or 20 percent of my income every month so it would certainly solve some of my economic problems.

And then I saw three people—two women and one man—pushing an old station wagon into the parking lot of an abandoned Chinese restaurant.

I was named PJ Pizza Employee of the Month only once in three years. It was a month where I managed to wash my shirt every night. I was a conscientious delivery person for thirty consecutive days. I delivered my pizzas politely and efficiently. I treated my co-workers with kindness and good humor. I even made Harold Middlestaff laugh three or four times.

"You keep working this hard," he said, "and maybe you'll be working in the front office with Cameron."

It was rumored that Cameron made thirty dollars an hour. That sounded like a fortune. I wanted to make that kind of money. I wanted to be Employee of the Year. Employee of the Millennium. But, damn it, I couldn't even defend my crown as Employee of the Month.

In any case, I don't think I won that month because of my work habits. Mostly I think I won because of my consistent but brief loyalty to a fresh shirt.

For winning, I received a small trophy and sixty dollars in cash.

Jesus, does the money ever arrive when we need it the most?

I don't know why I pulled into the parking lot of that abandoned Chinese restaurant. And I don't know why I stepped out of my car and approached the two women and one man who'd just pushed that old station wagon into the lot.

One of the women was tall. One was short. The man looked like a trailer park sex symbol who'd started shoplifting cigarettes in second grade and had never stopped. I knew Anna would have never left a guy who looked like him. He was probably the kind of guy who could make her orgasm. She'd never orgasmed with another person. Only by herself. And only with a battery-powered toy. She couldn't even orgasm if I used the toy on her. She still loved sex with me, she said, but I had my doubts. How could I not have my doubts? I did my research on the internet and tried all sorts of moves. I tried to be emotionally and physically honest. I tried to communicate. I tried to be the kind of man who was good in bed. I'd been good with other women, I think. But nothing seemed to work with Anna. But I wasn't going to give up no matter how much I doubted myself.

But, at that moment, on that night, my greatest doubts magically took the form of a denim-jacket-and-jeans dude in a Chinese restaurant parking lot.

"Hey," I said to the trio. "Is that really a wood-paneled station wagon? I haven't seen one of them on the road in—well, I don't know if I've ever seen one of them actually moving."

"Yo, genius," the tall woman said. "This one ain't moving, either."

The man smirked. It was too damn rehearsed. Like he'd perfected it in a mirror before he'd tried it out in public.

"It was my mom's car," the short woman said. She wiped tears from her face. "She gave it to me before she died."

"I'm sorry it's not working," I said. "But it's a lot easier to fix those old cars than the new cars these days. New cars have enough computer power to take you to the moon."

"What are you?" the tall woman asked. "Some kind of college brain?"

"No," I said. "Just a pizza man."

"Okay, pizza man," she said. "Do you know how to fix cars?"

"No," I said.

"Then what good are you?"

"Not much good at all," I said. "But I guess I can give you a ride somewhere?"

I instantly regretted offering them a ride. I regretted pulling over in the first place. I regretted my sad attempt to use crushed Altoids as deodorant because I smelled like somebody had taken a shit in a cup of mint tea.

I regretted that I didn't make lists. I regretted that I never paused long enough to seriously consider my decisions. I regretted that I didn't know how to *ponder*. And then I realized that I ponder all the time. I just don't know how to ponder *well*.

"Are you a serial killer?" the tall woman asked me. "I bet you're a quiet pizza man until you smell pussy. And then you start killing women. Is that who you really are, pizza boy?"

"Okay, wow," I said. "I'm just trying to help. So, yeah, I think I'll get back to work now."

I'd become one of those men who were intimidated by bluntly sexual women. I couldn't handle the reversal in expected gender roles. I was small. What the hell was I supposed to do or say? I exhaled, turned, and walked back toward my car, but the man rushed over to me, put his arm around my shoulder, and whispered to me.

"Hey, dude," he said. "I'm sorry she's being so tough. But you got to help me out. I just met her tonight. I met her at the strip club. She's a stripper, dude, and she was taking me back to her place to do it, man. I'm going to bang a stripper. Come on, dude, this is a dream come true. You need to give us a ride. So I can ride her. You get it? Tell me you get it?"

"Well, where's your car?" I said.

"Dude," he said. "I got laid off. I sold my car. I took the bus to the strip joint."

I laughed.

"Dude," he said. "Don't judge me. It's public transportation and I'm the public. So you don't get to judge me. You're a fucking pizza man."

"I'm sorry," I said. "You're right."

"All is forgiven, dude, if you just give us a ride."

"But to where? I'm working."

"Hey, Misty," he said to the tall woman. "How far is your place?"

"I live in Post Falls," she said.

"We live together," the short woman said. She leaned against her mother's station wagon, almost like she was hugging the car. Is there anything more depressing than the *whirr-whirr-whirr* of a shitty car that won't start? We live in a country that treats cars like Catholic saints. So what can you do when your car can't even perform the simple miracle of starting its engine?

"I don't know, man," I said to the three of them. "Post Falls, Idaho, right? That's across the state border. It'll take like an hour to drive there and back, and I'm working."

I was nervous. The trio didn't seem dangerous. But how many murder victims have thought the same thing about their murderers? I wondered what struggling actor would play me in the *Forensic Files* TV reenactment of my violent and completely avoidable death.

"Hey, Ted Bundy," the tall woman said to me. "I'll pay you to give us a ride."

"How much?" I asked.

"How much you want?"

I thought about Anna. I thought about her blue eyes. I thought about how she liked to read aloud to me. I liked how she would sometimes stand naked on the bed and excitedly read to me about some amazing animal—a blind spider that only lived in one cave on one island near Japan. And I thought about how, maybe, it was far more important for me to love Anna's voice than to love her body. And how maybe it was more important for me to pay attention to the things she chose to read to me than it was for me to give her orgasms. I thought about how I don't know shit about shit. I thought about the price of that Walmart engagement ring.

"Fifty bucks," I said. "I want fifty bucks."

"Shit," the tall woman said. "You think I'm rich or something?"

I stood tall, nearly as tall as her, and said, "I think you're pretty. Beautiful, in fact. I think you're a beautiful stripper so that means you probably have at least fifty one-dollar bills in your purse."

I felt like an asshole for talking to her like that. It was disrespectful. But I wanted that money. I needed that fifty dollars.

"Okay, Dahmer," she said. "If you're so smart then tell me how old I am."

"I don't know. Why does it matter?"

"Just take a guess at my age."

"I don't know," I said. "Thirty?"

"You're a big liar," she said. "Give me a real answer. How old do you really think I am?"

"Forty," I said.

"I am forty-three," she said. "I am already a grandmother."

"Okay," I said. "What does that mean?"

"It means I'm an ancient bitch stripping on a Sunday night in Spokane fucking Washington. So how much money do you really think I made tonight?"

"Wow," I said.

"Wow what?" she asked.

"Wow, you just kicked my ass with some real economics."

"Damn right," she said. "I can give you twenty-three bucks right now and I'll give you the rest when I break open my piggy bank."

"Your piggy bank in Post Falls?"

"Yeah, Lee Harvey," she said. "Take us to Post Falls and you'll make some real money."

"Okay," I said. "Let's go."

I once tried to apply for food stamps but learned that I was only considered a low-income earner.

"But not low enough?" I asked.

"People in official poverty get partial benefits," the clerk said.

"Official poverty," I said.

"Yes," she said. "And people in deep poverty get full benefits."

Sometimes, *counted* means you matter, but most times it only means you're another number.

After I threw the pizza-warming sleeve into the trunk, the tall woman handed me twenty-three one-dollar bills. It was a smooth and neat stack of bills. No matter the job, you have to take at least a little pride in the income, I guess. Then the tall woman climbed into the small backseat with that dude and noisily dry-humped him as I drove toward Post Falls.

The short woman sat in the passenger seat and fumed. I guessed she wasn't a stripper. She seemed too plain and shy. And I also guessed that being roommates and friends with a stripper—with the kind of stripper who ended up in backseats with greasily handsome and unemployed customers—often put her in uncomfortable situations.

I didn't want to make too many assumptions. But then, she caught me making assumptions and made some assumptions of her own. She leaned close to me and scowled.

"I am not fucking you," she whispered.

"I hadn't planned on it," I said.

"Why?" she asked. "Because I'm not like her?"

"No," I said. "I have a girlfriend."

"They always have wives and girlfriends. It doesn't matter."

"I'm sorry," I said. "I just want my money and then I'm going back to work."

"Whatever," she said.

Harold Middlestaff was married to a woman named Mary Norman. She'd kept her maiden name. So I guess that meant her name had never been a maiden name. They had no kids. But they did have three cats and two dogs.

"No," Harold Middlestaff said. "They are not my children. Or my substitute children. We didn't want children. Not even metaphorically. We own cats and dogs because we wanted to own cats and dogs."

The tall and short women lived in a duplex on a dark and isolated street that was only technically in Post Falls. It certainly looked like a place where idiotic pizza men went to die.

"Yeah," I said. "I'm going to wait out here. You can bring me out the rest of the money."

"Are you scared?" the tall woman asked.

"Yes, I am," I said. "Just get me the rest of my money and then I'll go."

The tall woman leaned close to me, so close that I could feel her hot and sour breath on my neck, and said, "Hey, give me back my money."

"Are you going to mug me now?" I asked, though I was more sexually aroused than afraid.

"No," she said. "Give me back my money and come inside. And I'll strip for you instead."

"Dude," the man said. "That's the best offer you will ever get in your whole life."

"Fuck this shit," the short woman said. "And fuck you, pizza man. You are an ugly fucker."

Then she roared out of my car and stomped into her house. She'd hurt my feelings. I had the urge to run into the house and tell her that she was ugly, too. But she wasn't ugly. And neither was I. We were something less than pretty. We were average. And in an ordinary situation, that woman and I might have been friends or lovers. At least we would spend our entire lives loving and being loved by people who looked like us.

"Come on, dude," the man said. "You get to watch my skinny woman get naked. And then you get to fuck the fat one. It's the full meal deal."

"Hey," the tall woman said and slapped him. "Don't talk about her that way. She's my best friend."

"Okay, okay," he said. "My bad."

"So, hey, School Shooter," the tall woman said. "What's it gonna be? You want me or do you want the cash?"

I considered my options. I had no moral objection to strippers or stripping, to the noun or verb. Or to any kind of sex work, in person or filmed or streamed to the internet. As long as we're talking about one or more consenting adults. And I have certainly watched plenty of porn, not as much as some of my friends but more than some others. As with most things in my life, I am average at porn consumption. But when it comes to going to strip clubs with groups of friends, I have to admit that I am completely baffled. Why do a bunch of straight guys want to pop simultaneous erections? And I'm not homophobic. I appreciate the erotic logic of gay men who want to enjoy synchronized boners, whether or not they use them on one another. But what's in it for straight men? I mean—there's nothing mysterious happening. A naked woman (who may or may not be straight) dances on a stage and the audience of straight men gets sexually aroused. That's two plus two equals four. It's not interesting to me. It's not enticing. So, yeah, in another reality, I might have enjoyed a solo strip show by this tall woman—by Misty—but I didn't want to be sexually aroused anywhere near that dry cigarette butt of a man who seemed way too eager to be sexually aroused near me. This was the dude who rode a public bus *alone* to sit *alone* in a strip club. That was pretty damn baffling, too. Or maybe it wasn't baffling at all. Maybe everybody is the same kind of lonely as everybody else. Maybe everybody is exactly the same *amount* of lonely as everybody else. Maybe straight men travel in packs so they can share their baffling and foolish loneliness.

Or maybe I just decided that watching a beautiful grandmother stripping in her duplex living room in Post Falls, Idaho, was the loneliest thing in the world. Maybe that shit would have won the Olympic gold medal in Lonely.

And what about that short woman, the roommate? Jesus. I didn't want to add to her misery. She'd obviously and justifiably decided to hate me. I just wanted my fifty bucks. I just wanted to drive back to my job. I just wanted Anna to change her mind and tell the Navy to fuck off. Or wait, I was happy that the Navy existed. I was happy they protected me. I didn't want them to fuck off. I only wanted them to tell Anna to stay home and accept my imperfect love.

"Listen," I said to the tall woman. "I just want the rest of my money. And then I need to go back to work. Though I've probably already lost my job."

"Are you sure?" the tall woman asked. "I move real good."

"I'm sure," I said.

"Okay, okay," she said. "Your loss."

She and that lost and pretty man stepped out of my car and walked arm in arm toward the house. The tall woman didn't look back, but the man looked at me, smiled, shook his head, and said, "Thanks, dude."

I waited ten minutes for the rest of the money.

And then I waited ten more minutes.

I knew I wasn't going to get the rest of the cash. I should've been happy for the extra money I did receive.

And then the short woman pulled back the curtains and stood in the front window. I guessed her friend would be apologizing to her in the morning. I guessed there had been many such apologies. And the same number of forgivenesses. And their relationship would keep working like that. Until the moment it stopped working. Until there were a thousand apologies and only 999 forgivenesses.

The world isn't fueled by fire or wind or water. The world runs on resentment.

I waited a few more minutes for my money and then I drove back to work. When I pulled into the PJ Pizza parking lot, I noticed that Harold Middlestaff had sent me a bunch of text messages.

Where are you?
Where are you?
Where are you?
Where are you?
Where are you?
Okay, now you're fired.
Don't come back.
I'll mail you your last check, minus the cost of your last six pizzas and the warming sleeve in your car.

I sat in that parking lot and counted my money again and again. I hoped the act of counting would turn twenty-three dollars into fifty dollars. I was hoping for paper alchemy.

I cried.

But then I stopped crying.

I realized my pain was only worth a few moments of tears.

Then I texted Anna a row of emoji ships.

And then I texted her, *Bon voyage.*

And then I texted her, *See you next life.*

And then I walked into PJ Pizza with only the smallest hope that I could win back my job.

THE DEATHS
OF HENRY KING

SELECTED DEMISES

by JESSE BALL AND BRIAN EVENSON

(Illustrations by Lilli Carré)

1

HENRY KING WOKE WITH a hammer partway through his head. Someone pulled the end of the hammer out of the hole and then brought it down again, causing Henry's body to shake a little all over, especially at the extremities.

2

Henry King was asked to meet a friend in a park. He went there and was killed. That same day, a bit later on, someone left an envelope on his doorstep. It wasn't a very fancy envelope, yet neither was it the absolute cheapest kind.

3

Henry King signed a piece of paper that said, *I want to die*. On 42nd and 5th a bus ran him over and he was so unremarkable, even at that moment, that a dozen more cars hit him before anyone thought to stop.

4

Henry King was burned to death in a house fire although many others were saved. "There is still someone in there," said the Fire Chief.

5

Henry King fell from an open window. A girl was telling a joke about a platypus. It was an extremely funny joke, and many kept laughing, even when they saw what had happened.

6

Henry King stayed late at the factory. His legs were caught in the machinery and it embarrassed him. The factory was sold by the owner that night and no one ever came back onto the premises, leaving Henry to death by starvation.

7

Henry King accepted a drink from a wild-eyed girl underneath a bridge. Some minutes later, she was rolling over his body and removing an antique watch, the gift of his grandfather.

8

Henry King climbed a ladder and then it began to rain. By chance all the rain went into his mouth and he drowned before he could fall.

9

Henry King couldn't breathe. His throat had closed. He ran to the window and waved to someone outside. He slapped at his neck and chest with his hand. He waved to someone else who waved back and even smiled, yes, smiled.

10

Henry King was deep in a mine when the workers' canaries started to perish. Soon the canary in the cage on his belt, it, too, perished. He had time to do one last thing.

11

Henry King ate six and a half pounds of glass before bleeding to death. "I believe that's a record," said his friend.

12

Henry King fell down the stairs in a building nearby. There wasn't a mark on him. "You would think he had survived," said a girl.

13

Nobody knew how Henry King had come to be in Little Chute during the Great Wisconsin Cheese Festival, nor why, when the giant wheel of cheddar broke its moorings, he did not at least try to jump out of the way.

14

Henry King realized mid-leap that the other building's roof was in fact much farther away than he'd realized.

15

All that remained of Henry King after his fall from the balloon was a Henry King–shaped dent in the ground. Soon that was gone as well.

16

Henry King discovered that the inside of Henry King looked like any meat one might buy at a butcher's shop. He smiled wryly, and perished.

17

Henry King wore a special shirt for people who may be one day kidnapped. This made him more comfortable in day-to-day life. He bought special shoes for people who need to survive short falls. He wore an actual helmet. He covered his crotch with a semi-articulated neoprene-and-steel codpiece. This odd appearance was sufficient to provoke a mob in Buenos Aires, where he was killed while attempting to enter a soccer stadium. Thirty people stood on his head until it was flat. They left his body alone.

18

"Heinrich König?" asked the man with the expressionless face as he pointed the Ruger LC9 at his skull. "Henry King," corrected Henry King, shaking his head. But the dark-suited man had already pulled the trigger.

19

Henry King must have taken a wrong turn somewhere, for he was not to be found among those who had successfully navigated the river and now floated on in the lake, cans of Schlitz balanced on their bellies. Instead his tube popped and he was swept along by currents and bashed by rocks until his corpse was caught in a backwater. It lay there bloating in the company of his own can of Schlitz, which, thanks to the water, was ice-cold.

20

The bottles in the cellar were delicately balanced. Removing the '45 Château Margaux brought all the other bottles cascading down on Henry King. He lay there half-crushed and badly cut, dying, stinking of expensive wine.

21

It was a mistake to try to separate the two fighting pit bulls. Henry King was fairly certain both of them bit him repeatedly, but was in no condition to ascertain which one tore his throat out.

22

Henry King died of the kissing disease. Those he knew preferred not to speak of it.

23

Henry King played a game called Clouds and Jewels with the cooks in a sinister Chinese restaurant after the usual mahjong game was over with. Clouds and Jewels, as they called it, involved eating small bits of one thing disguised as another and guessing what was what. At least that's how the first cook explained it to the detective, as they stood there in the harsh fluorescent light of the kitchen, looking down on Henry King's corpse, where it rested beneath the filthy card table. "I know what you mean," said the detective, carelessly.

24

"Henry" King, in reality Henriette, leaned her musket against one wall of the dilapidated French fort, removed her regimental coat, laid her cocked hat on a chair, and shook out her long hair. What will history think of me? she wondered. At that moment a French light infantryman who had been disguised as a pair of candlesticks stood up on the table and shot her through the face with an outdated heirloom arquebus: some sort of matchlock, one might say. That a man who would disguise himself as a candlestick should have such a weapon... it is inevitable, thought Henriette, and promptly perished.

25

According to twelfth-century parish records, the King had been accosted by a smiling man who claimed his name "to be a reverse of thine own, sire. Thou art King Henry, and I am Henry King." King Henry's response was to have Henry King beheaded.

26

Henry King seemed to have been turned to stone. There was a great deal of consternation among his neighbors: half believed he had been petrified, the other half believed he had made a statue of himself and then left town. Discussion became argument and argument became fisticuffs, and in the brawl that followed, Henry King, or his representation, was knocked over and broken to pieces.

27

Henry King went to Hokkaido to see the cherry blossoms. Never mind that there are better ones elsewhere; it was to Hokkaido he went. And, quite simply, the visit was too much for him. Even these so-to-speak Hokkaido cherry blossoms, they were too intense, too perfect, too redolent of life's equal measure of splendor and strife: he collapsed on the spot, clutching at his chest. "I confess!" he cried, beginning a sentence he would never end.

28

Henry King, world traveler, sat staring at his plate. There was, he was fairly certain, a snout, a foot as well, a gummy ear edged with a thread line of dark bristles. If they can eat it, it must be all right, he told himself, and dug into the meal that, months later, would end up being the death of him.

29

His last memory as Henry King was the stick coming down toward his face. It was followed as if without transition by the smiling face of a nurse, but by then he had lost track of his name and never quite managed to retrieve it.

30

Henry King was an extra in an Andy Warhol film in which the twenty prettiest girls in New York City climbed up a ladder and fell off into the East River. The last one fucked it up really badly so Andy Warhol said get the next prettiest thing on the set up that ladder pronto and Henry King was next prettiest but couldn't swim. They made him go anyway.

31

"Henry King, you say," said the grizzled old man to the investigating officer. "He never told me his name but I suppose it must be him. You'll find him at the bottom of that," he said, and pointed with the stem of his pipe to the edge of the ravine.

32

In the dream Henry King was thrown free of the car and, though badly injured and comatose for weeks, managed to survive and go on to marry, have children, and have grandchildren, finally dying peacefully at a ripe old age. In reality, Henry King, asleep at the wheel, was killed instantly when his car crossed into the other lane and struck a semi head-on.

33

The phone call came late at night. "You've been activated," said a flat, expressionless voice. "Excuse me?" said Henry King. "The puppy is out of the crate," said the voice. "But I don't have a puppy," said Henry King. There was a long pause. "Incorrect," said the voice. "You will be terminated." "Terminated?" said Henry King. "Hello?" But the line was already dead.

34

At security, Henry King found he had forgotten to bring the note from his doctor, and had his inhaler taken away. On the plane he was seated next to a woman trained as a nurse, and when he began to have trouble breathing she did her best to talk him through it. "Breathe through your nose, honey. Breathe through your nose," she kept saying in a voice so calm and so relaxed that he was surprised, when he opened his eyes, to see so much fear gathered in her face. His breathing grew worse and worse. An emergency landing was made, but by the time they touched down he was already dead.

35

Henry King felt his way along the crack in the bathroom wall. He slowly wormed his finger into it, though doing so stripped his finger to the bone. His hand followed, then his wrist, then his whole arm. To make the rest of his body fit, he had to pound it flat by beating the body repeatedly with a cast-iron pan. After that, though, it was easy. Before he knew it he was back behind the crack. But it was too dark to see what, if anything, was there, and though he had managed to work his way in, he did not have the same success working his way back out.

36

The path wound slowly along the narrow spit of land and through undergrowth and trees. Here there was a damp earthy smell and there the woody tang of eucalyptus. Henry King could see the waves below, the sound of them more distant than he felt it should be. A path led down to a beach but was blocked off with police tape and a warning. He ignored both. At first the going was easy, then more difficult, then the sides of the path crumbled and gave way and Henry King began to scramble back up. And then the whole path went, and he along with it.

37

Henry King rode the glass elevator up to the thirty-first floor so that he could look out and see the lights and the enormous Christmas tree in the square. In the brief pause between when the doors opened and when the doors closed again, he could not help but imagine what it would be like to fall from this height, to go tumbling down the side of the building and flash into the ground below. It came to him so vividly that for an instant he felt he was living hand in hand with his own death. Then the doors closed and he rode the elevator down again and walked home alone.

INTERNAL LIFE

by CORINNA VALLIANATOS

O UR NEIGHBOR'S CAR IS large and shiny, its seats like padded pedicure chairs. I would never drive a car like that, but I spend more than two hundred dollars on shoes and cry when my husband discovers the charge on our credit card. Oh my god I love this gun, our son said the other day, playing a video game, and I said, from the doorway, I feel I've lost my grasp on this family. Hot wind shakes the spear-shaped seeds from the female ash tree onto our yard. Friends invite us to dinner and introduce us to the other guests, a couple and their three children. The woman has the best job in the world, our friends say. Can we guess what it is? Hotel room reviewer, our son says, and they say no though that *would* be good. Astronaut trainer, puppy walker, flower sniffer, like, for perfumes? They're shaking their heads. Give up? She makes stuffed organs, they say. We don't understand. Yeah, like anatomically correct stuffed lungs, uteruses, hearts, stomachs. She sketches them out and gives them personalities, approachable ones, mostly. Then they're manufactured—the details get a little fuzzy here—and shipped all over the place. Hospital gift shops and gynecologists' offices, preschools. We make interested noises but I'm distracted. I guess the heart is ballsy and unsubtle and the liver's a hard worker, but what about the spleen? Its dignity's in its unknowable quality, it seems to me. Grilled swordfish is served. Children laugh and scream. Our host gets drunk and the conversation bends toward candor. The question of why we have just one child arises and when I tell them that my blood formed a clot that stretched from my pelvis to my knee they seem so relieved. That there's a reason, I mean. And anyway, I say, I didn't want to subscribe to the cult of motherhood, and they nod, they nod, they like this phrase. The stuffed organ maker's daughter calls our son Daddy. Daddy, Daddy, she says, running to him and encircling his waist with her arms. He is twelve and she is six. She presses herself against him and he laughs it off for a while but she won't let go. Finally he removes her roughly and I scold him for it. The stuffed organ maker tells us that at school her daughter gets so nervous about seeing him she has to throw up. Her husband leaves with their littlest and later we drive her and her other two home. Our son rides in the hatchback, where we allow him to remain even after they debark. The pinprick shine of dashboard lights. The body's shapes waiting inside. I can feel them sometimes, soft and slippery, delicately indefatigable.

THE LACE SHIRT

by CARRIE BROWNSTEIN

I AM NEITHER GLAM nor glamorous. During the early days of my band, Sleater-Kinney, which if you don't know plays pretty heavy music, my look could best be described as "business casual." For many years I paired an electric guitar not with black boots or heels or a leather jacket or skinny jeans, but with a pair of saggy-assed slacks from Banana Republic and a button-down shirt a few sizes too big. If I wasn't twenty-four years old with dyed black hair shouting angry lyrics, you would have thought, What's my bank teller doing on stage?

But back in my youth I did have one brief run-in with glamour. It happened in middle school, which is an inopportune time for glamour. I mean, I wish I could have considered my pimples a glittery constellation and my greasy hair a champagne waterfall. But that just wasn't the case.

How I got to the glam part is a little circuitous.

As a kid, I was obsessed with soap operas. I would watch them every summer. For the two and a half months I was on school break this was my schedule: I tanned in the mornings using Hawaiian Tropic SPF 2 oil; flung myself headfirst down homemade water slides made from tarps, garbage bags, and garden hoses; came inside the house for tuna salad stuffed in pita bread; then grabbed a Popsicle and a Crystal Pepsi and sat down to watch three to four hours of TV. *The Young and the Restless*, *All My Children*, *General Hospital*, and *Days of Our Lives*. I was so crazy about *Days of Our Lives* that when a character named Kayla temporarily lost her hearing and her boyfriend Patch (because he had an eyepatch) learned sign language, I also learned sign language. Patch literally signed the song "The Rose" by Bette Midler while tears streamed down his face, and so—because I had to—I signed "The Rose" to my family over dinner while pasta sauce dripped down my chin.

I also asked my dad to take me to an auto show. Not for the cars—I couldn't care less about cars—but to meet another actor from *Days* (which is what us fans call it) named Drake Hogysten. He played Roman. He was actually the second actor to play the character of Roman, which I think is common on soap operas. Later, the original actor came back and we were supposed to act like we didn't notice. At the auto show, I got to sit on Drake Hogysten's lap and get my picture taken with him. I tried to make small talk by saying things like, "I love you." Then it was my friend's turn. She was blonde and named Kim but Drake called her Kimmy, which made me mad because it seemed for a second like they might end up dating.

In Seattle, near where I grew up, we had a local talk show called *The Brian Tracey Show*. During the height of my soap-opera obsession, Brian Tracey announced that he was going to dedicate an entire week to *Days of Our Lives*, and each day a different actor from the show would be a guest. I asked my mother if I could get out of school early and go to one of the tapings. Knowing my propensity for melodrama in the face of refusal, she said yes.

The day arrived. I was buzzing. This was my first time ever being on a TV set. While about a hundred of us sat in the studio waiting for the show to begin, a PA asked each of us to write our name on a piece of paper. There would be a drawing later—for what I did not know, but I assumed a mug or a sweatshirt, or maybe a signed headshot.

Then the show began. The guest from *Days of Our Lives* was Judy Evans, who played Adrienne. For those of you keeping track, she was Patch's sister. (And probably also his mom; I have no idea.) By the way, I looked this up: Judy Evans is *still* playing Adrienne. Actors stay on these shows literally until they die. It is very stable employment.

I don't recall much about Judy's interview except that she was nervous and kept leaning over to the host, and he would take her hands and reassure her. And I thought that, like all soap stars, she was beautiful.

After the segment with Judy ended, Brian Tracey brought out his next guest: a woman who ran a store in Los Angeles to which movie studios donated props and costumes. The proceeds went to charity. The store owner put Brian in a leather jacket that had been worn by Rosanna Arquette in *Desperately Seeking Susan*. This garnered a huge round of applause from the audience. Over in the Pacific Northwest we weren't used to seeing film artifacts like coats.

Then Brian Tracey said he was going to pick a name from a glass bowl and that someone in the studio audience would be the lucky recipient of another item of clothing from the store. Cool! Ally Sheedy's oversized sweater from *The Breakfast Club*? The stone from *Romancing the Stone*? Absolutely not. Instead, the item was an off-the-shoulder lavender lace crop top that Cher had worn in one of her exercise videos. In case you didn't know, in the eighties everyone had an exercise video, kind of the way people have sex tapes now.

So Brian reached his hand into the jar, and even from my seat three quarters of the way back I could tell it was my name. Sixteen letters, the last three smaller because I'd run out of room. My stomach dropped. Then it happened: he read my name. The camera whipped around. The audience cheered. I stood up and covered my entire face with my hands, and waited what felt like eternity for an announcement that we had gone to commercial. "Cut," someone yelled. I breathed a sigh of relief. But that wasn't the end of it. A producer walked up to our row and asked that I come down and stand next to Brian for the final segment.

Nervously, I walked down and shook hands with Brian, who handed me Cher's lace crop top. I thought, Is there somewhere private I can change? Am I about to be partially nude on TV? I was thankful I'd decided to wear a bra that day, which I didn't quite need—the empty cups slid around my flat chest like a car on an icy road. They told me to put the top over my own shirt. Phew.

But let's talk about my own shirt. What I decided to wear was a rayon blouse. Every section had a different color. Blue on one half, green on the other, a red sleeve, a blue sleeve, and, just for fun, a purple collar. I looked like a package of gummy bears. But my shirt was just the warm-up act to the actual freak show: my hair. Recently I had begged my mother for a spiral perm, which to her credit she had advised against. But I *really* wanted one. And then about five minutes after I'd gotten one, I decided I didn't. I came home from the salon and began vigorously combing through it. The method was only partially successful. What I was left with was about an inch of straight hair near the root, dark from my greasy scalp. And the rest of my hair was a triangle, damaged and dry from the chemicals, about as soft as a bale of hay. The ecology of my hair was so varied that it could host both desert and sea animals. It also elicited concern from my mom's friends, who more than once I overheard asking, "What's wrong with Carrie's head?"

So there I was in the last segment of the show, standing next to Brian Tracey while he bade everyone in the audience and at home farewell. With his arm around me, I stared directly into the camera, frozen, in hopes people might think I was a mannequin or a doll you do CPR on. Not knowing what to do with my face, I held a smile the entire time, until the corners of my mouth shook the way your stomach does during sit-ups.

Then, mercifully, it was over.

I went home. Back to my ordinary life. I returned to school the next day.

Instead of cementing my affection for the genre, my experience on *The Brian Tracey Show* cured me of my obsession with soaps; I no longer associated them with escape but rather with entrapment and humiliation. I had lived through my own five-minute melodrama and realized that I wasn't cut out for it.

But what I did have now was this Cher shirt. This seemed like the real prize. I'd broken up with *Days of Our Lives* but in its place found something more exotic, more intriguing, more glamorous.

There aren't a lot of opportunities for a twelve-year-old to dress up in a see-through lace top, so I didn't have an occasion to wear my new shirt. Every once in a while I'd picture an event for which it would be appropriate. I had always thought that if I ever got to attend an award show like the Grammys or the Emmys I would wear an IZOD polo shirt with a matching cardigan sweater, but maybe this would be better? Or perhaps there would be a slumber party and I would surprise my friends by turning up looking a little sexy, and they would wonder, Whoa, where has she just been? even though I'd probably be coming straight from soccer practice.

I kept Cher's top in my closet next to my Esprit and Generra and J.Crew. I didn't have anything else lavender or lace. It stood out. Every once in a while I'd put the Cher shirt against my nose and breathe in. It didn't carry my own scent the way my other clothes did, and I inhaled the fabric the way you do an item of clothing left behind by a lover in the early days of courtship. I wondered if there was something this shirt could tell me. About Cher, about the world outside my suburb, about my future, about myself. Mostly the shirt smelled vaguely of sweat, but I was afraid to wash it. I worried that all its magic and potency would disappear, that it would assimilate into my household, into my parents' impending divorce or my mother's illness, into my own sense of loneliness, instead of being what it was now, something that could save me from all of it.

This lace shirt stayed in my closet all through high school. It seemed to wink at me when I opened the door, as if to say *not yet, but soon*. Somehow, by just being around, this lace crop top formerly owned by the mercurial, dazzling enigma that is Cher gave me a sense of possibility. When I felt sadness or doubt, it was a glimmer and a glow I could check in on.

I didn't feel like I could display this glamorous object outright. I never wore it, not once. But what is remarkable about something glamorous is that it's always in conversation with our secret self. We can summon it in all its beauty and strangeness, in the way it stands in for hope or longing. I think everyone has a little piece of glam tucked away, in their closet, perhaps, and sometimes simply knowing it exists is all we really need.

LITTLE BIG HORN

by THOMAS McGUANE

AUDREY AND I DROVE in a four-door clunker that would have perfectly served a State Farm insurance salesman from Ohio through what I think of as the old Midwest: small colleges on the only hill in town; farmhouses with neglected woodlots and haunted outbuildings like the writhing structures in Burchfield paintings; towns that had lost their caregivers but were still inhabited by the old making their way along unrepaired sidewalks to a post office they hoped would not be taken away; ostentatious courthouses with pigeons in empty windows and vacant doorways. I'm not sure Audrey cared about this heightened pathos. This was her last trip before law school and she wanted to keep it light.

"That was a bank," said Audrey. A tattoo parlor now. Audrey had a tattoo, a little one, rarely seen. I'd seen it. I don't know who else had. She got it in Prague. "How about it? Something for your neck?" Across the way was a cannon, fetched home from the Civil War, leaving the bodies in the ground down south. My thoughts lingered on the soft blue skies and clouds of Ohio that must have once successfully cheered these little places. A roadside marker celebrating the optimism of Johnny Appleseed just seemed cruel now. Audrey, fanning herself with the road map and staring at yet another evangelical church, asked if Jesus was making these people fat. The harder light of the Dakotas would be less melancholy, fewer people to fill the air with their vanished hopes. We'd be there soon. The windshield and satellite radio would press everything but the flattened images of landscape into the background. I don't know why I felt this way. Perhaps it was a foreboding based on leaving home and the whole idea of Idaho, my final destination.

We had only taken one long road trip before and it ended in disaster. I think she may be claustrophobic, but in any case she went on a rant about absolutely everything. This was one of those autumn-in-New-England trips and the truth is neither of us was very interested in anything about New England, especially the little towns and churches. I remember a lot of Halloween shit in doorways, so that's when it was—November, and no sunshine. We started by arguing about what to have on the radio and it went on to some sort of irrational abhorrence of New England itself, altogether ridiculous considering that we knew zip about New England, but we couldn't stop arguing. In a chowder joint near Portsmouth, New Hampshire, road-weary and tired of talking, I asked Audrey how she felt about the witchcraft trials and—thinking I was referring to her—she blew sky-high. I said, "That's it, I'm driving home." And Audrey said, "Hasta la vista." And I left, car and all. I so seldom feel actual rage that I might have been a tad pleased with myself. Anyway, the gauntlet was down; anyway, she had credit cards. The next stop was to have been Salem but if she figured that out I never heard about it.

A short time afterwards, she went off to Europe with a sly frat boy from Dennison. They made several stops before coming home: Versailles, the Hermitage in Russia, Prague, and a Battle of the Bulge tour that must have been a real hoot. The only evidence of the trip I ever saw was a photograph of Audrey and Mr. Slyboots in front of a German tank. I took her back, though we don't say that these days. Perhaps Audrey returned herself to me. Do such things clear the air? Hardly, but we were doing quite well, considering.

I was on my way to my new job in Boise, but on the way we would stop in Montana to visit old friends Niles and Claudia, who were joining us on a trip to the Little Big Horn battlefield. Our shared pasts seemed a big part of our lives and maybe they'd restore some of the excitement of earlier days. I suppose it was my idea that we needed restoration. Audrey had little interest in the visit, and anyway from Boise she'd be flying home to school and we'd have to find a way to work it out. Time with friends from more ardent days would help to carry us over.

In college, Niles and Claudia were hard-partying style mavens who seemed to live on the edge of disaster. Now it was woodstoves, homemade clothes, and life off the grid. Niles acquired arty found things like an iron lung decommissioned from a medical museum in Youngstown, Ohio. They were each from different parts of the upper South, Niles from a family of recently risen professional people—two doctors and a judge—and Claudia from old, landholding, jobless bourbon aristocrats and dilettante politicians with ancestors in the Confederate Congress. Sometimes when they talked about home and their "people" you sensed that Claudia thought Niles's family were all toadies no matter what they'd achieved, while Niles thought Claudia's people were parasites who had pauperized themselves with alcohol, horses, and quail. Sometimes Claudia made up stories about the sources of Niles's family's wealth, the most far-fetched being that they had made a fortune by patenting an African-American folk remedy for stool softener, the only family in West Tennessee with a porta potty in their coat of arms.

Audrey and I, pallid Midwesterners, spent less time partying and more time in bed in our garret above the knitting store with its view of the tire repair shop, practicing as much safe sex as schoolwork allowed until it seemed condoms were driving our test scores. My father and grandfather were anxious for me to join their fading iron ore business and from time to time sent their viceroy, an alcoholic CPA with tobacco-stained teeth, to urge me to "take advantage of my advantages." The old mine would barely provide a living. I needed a job.

The Black Hills were lovely out of nowhere, and after resisting roadside invitations to powwows, cave tours, and cliff diving, we stopped to eat at a café with a handwritten menu and Cinzano awnings. We had the luncheon special, called Aces and Eights after the cards held by Wild Bill Hickok when he was killed, elsewhere known as a cheeseburger with fries. Soon back in our car, we drove in silence for nearly a hundred miles. Then Audrey said, "It's not travel, it's not anything."

"Go ahead and roll down the window."

"Let's see if there's any reception." I was daydreaming about Claudia and her air of mischievous promise. "Prick-tease with a drawl," Audrey once said.

We crossed the Montana line and it looked the same as South Dakota. We knew that it got better up ahead but so far our impatience compressed everything. We drove as though we were beating our heads against the same freeze-frame and Audrey wasn't taking it well. She leaned against the door and moaned. She nodded to herself and asked, "Is that the arms of our Lord behind those clouds?" She fluttered her lips with her forefinger to suggest derangement.

Niles had gone on to graduate school while Claudia worked answering the phone in a nail salon, but she still said "Yay!" a lot. And "Boo!" I thought it was cute, Audrey not so much. We watched the presidential elections together and every time Tim Russert put up a card representing voting results from one state or another, Claudia yelled either "Yay!" or "Boo!" By the time we learned who the new president was, Audrey and I were ready to jump out of our skins. We just wanted one of these goobers to win and get us out of our misery. Every other night Russert praised his father, Big Russ, who was a saint, wise, generous, self-effacing. After one too many anecdotes about Big Russ's goodness, Claudia drawled, "If big Russ doesn't fuck the babysitter, I'm gonna kill myself." One more election and Audrey would be a lawyer and in two more a judge; Niles and Claudia would be back in Tennessee with other people by then. Nothing we could possibly have imagined.

Audrey was at the wheel as we turned in at their mailbox, and I was riding shotgun with a huge bag of caramel corn on my lap. It had rained a little and the dirt road up to their house, mostly dark except where overhanging trees had kept it dry, was cut into the side of a hill and wound upward until it suddenly opened to a clearing that gave onto a view of the valley and the scattered small town below. In the middle of the clearing stood their house, an old bungalow with various modern appurtenances: attached greenhouse, solar panels, and, flapping away, the customary Tibetan prayer flags. A weather vane on the roof seemed to have been modeled on Sputnik, spinning around without pointing anywhere.

When you haven't seen people for a long while, even old friends, dauntingly precise adjustment is required, something akin to acting. The struggle to get out of my side of the car caused me to upset the generous sack of caramel corn. Audrey cut her eyes at me. But by now Niles was on the porch, I was standing in the caramel corn, and Audrey was calling out that I had made a big mess as usual. Claudia stood a pace behind Niles so that she could gaze directly at me. I felt Audrey's elbow.

Niles viewed our arrival without enthusiasm. Claudia stared in the middle distance. Audrey muttered from the safety of her open car door, "What on earth is going on here? They're staring at us. Let's appear puzzled. Show them your puzzle face!" We strode up and hugged them as though whatever was missing would be replenished by the vehemence of our greeting. We squeezed away at the lifeless couple, then held them at arm's length like two fish we had just caught. Niles, head thrust from the neck of his turtleneck, said, "Here's the news: Claudia and I are not getting along. We thought we could sort it out before you got here but, well, we didn't." Later I would picture this thrusting head and high-colored face. "Doubtless," Niles continued, "Claudia is as vexed with me as I with her." Mystified by Niles's diction I asked what we should do about the caramel corn. I just couldn't think of what else to say.

"We need space," recited Niles. His turtleneck suggested a maddening jauntiness. "If you could take Claudia with you it would do us both a world of good. Would you consider it?" He smiled in the off-center way of comedians who wished to convey that they weren't sure this was a joke. "Would you? Pretty please?"

"Why not?" said Audrey. It didn't sound like Audrey. It was just a squawk and seemed directed at me. She knew as well as I that we were hosed. I kept nodding without saying anything.

"This is friendship," said Niles, discovering some lint on his woolen carpenter's vest. He frowned skeptically, as if his own observation had been foisted on him, then smiled abruptly. "Guys, I can't believe you're doing this. As I recall, your last road trip went badly." I looked to Audrey for a response but it was not forthcoming.

We went back down the same highway, heading for the Little Big Horn battlefield. Claudia, in the back seat with her small suitcase, said, "We'll be fine. Niles is a bore but I'm used to it. People like that come out of nowhere." To lighten the atmosphere Audrey swapped moisturizers with Claudia, who then touched the end of her nose in thought. "Honestly, we've just been in that awful place too long. An audience of one, the shack nasties. Too many books, especially that long one about the Danube. Ask me anything about the Danube." She turned to me and asked if my teeth were mine while I recalled "The Blue Danube Waltz," thinking it would contain a hint about where the fuck the Danube was. "They seem brighter than before. Niles collects stuff no one wants. He thinks that if he dislikes something it will soon be valuable. He moved the iron lung into the living room. He gets in it and thinks about the stock market while it breathes for him. Audrey, how would you like ten years with a premature ejaculator?"

"Is that an Indian?" asked Audrey of the hitchhiker standing beside the Canyon Creek on-ramp. Best to ignore Claudia, who was playing around in her purse.

"Native Americans don't dress like 'Indians,'" said Claudia. "That's a hippie. I realize it was an awkward question." She swept her lips with a tube of ChapStick.

"Do they still have those?" Audrey asked as she picked caramel corn from the floor mat. I think she meant hippies.

"They do here," Claudia said.

"It's too hypothetical."

"You have to spot them before it's too late. Eliminate the ones in cowboy hats. Then move to the turtlenecks, car buffs, and southern new money."

Audrey, wincing slightly, experienced this as noise. Finally she asked, "Claudia, you and Niles, how big of a deal is it actually, would you say?"

"Honey, it's as big as I need it to be."

We had arrived: motel, vacant lot, chain link, Walmart bags in the lilacs. I secured adjoining rooms and keys. We took Claudia to the café at the Trading Post and ate tacos made with Native American fry bread and buffalo burgers. We were right across from the battlefield where Sitting Bull had made so many beautiful memories. Claudia and Audrey discussed leaving home, letting me scrutinize the four Frenchmen at the table near the service entrance, including one who'd bought a war bonnet in the gift shop whose mock eagle feathers from assorted poultry were now fluttering under the ceiling fan. Claudia gazed at us. "Are you two always this happy?"

"That's a joke, right?" said Audrey.

"You just seem a bit complacent. To me. But what do I know?"

"We long for complacency."

The sudden widening stare from Audrey alerted me to possible danger.

Claudia said, "Hey, I was just reaching out. Is all it was." She now wanted to buy something for Niles and made a detour through the gift shop, returning with a Custer's Last Stand coffee cup wrapped in tissue. She held it against her cheek and smiled at us. "*Complacent* was a poor choice of words."

"You want to make it a little clearer?" said Audrey.

"No, Miss Audrey, I don't. I'll leave it at that. Just another chapter. It's so nice we've grown up. Do you remember the crazy stuff we used to do?"

"No."

"Oh," said Claudia and held the Custer coffee cup very still. She smiled at the odd silence in the room and said, "So that was then, and this is now?"

We paused before saying goodnight, moths batting around the lights at our doors. In the parking lot, an elderly Native American in an oversized and tattered suit coat lit his companion's cigarette. He waved away the smoke and she smiled at him. It made me happy to notice it. Once in our own room, Audrey sat heavily on the bed and said, "I'm taking her out. Where did she come up with this so-called complacency?"

I said, "She's confusing it with contentment." It was utter bullshit. When placating Audrey, I could lay this stuff on with a trowel. I don't know why I bothered, because when I look back, there's the Native American in the suit coat waving away the smoke and Audrey and I are just getting used to the idea that we were hardly meant for each other. I must have provided a relief, because the rest of the trip was much more fun. We packed up, checked out, and headed to the Little Big Horn battlefield in our quiet car, so quiet in fact that I turned on the radio and listened to cattle prices while we drove. We strode out onto the battlefield in the fresh morning air, the smell of prairie, a sky streaked with altocumulus clouds. Among the headstones where the troopers of the 7th Cavalry fell, we came to the very spot where Custer had died and where his small headstone was, remarkably, no bigger than anyone else's. Claudia read the inscription, looked up, and cast her eyes across the battlefield. Audrey and I were lost in our thoughts.

Really, it's all good. I hated Boise (it took three years) and went home to the badly shrunken family iron ore business and somehow made a living only slightly smaller than the one I'd made in Boise. One year I managed to ignore a ton of parking tickets and ended up in Audrey's court. "You again!" she said and threatened me with an ankle monitor. I paid the tickets.

THE SURE CURE

by DIANE WILLIAMS

DID BRACE HER with one hand, but my daughter is remarkably agile and well-balanced.

What I had done in the first place, in the park, was to pull down her trousers and put her up there on the low wire fence post. Anyone—and there were many on the pathway—could pay her mind while she obediently squatted to urinate.

In future, this cynosure will stand her in good stead. In the present, she hardly needs my help.

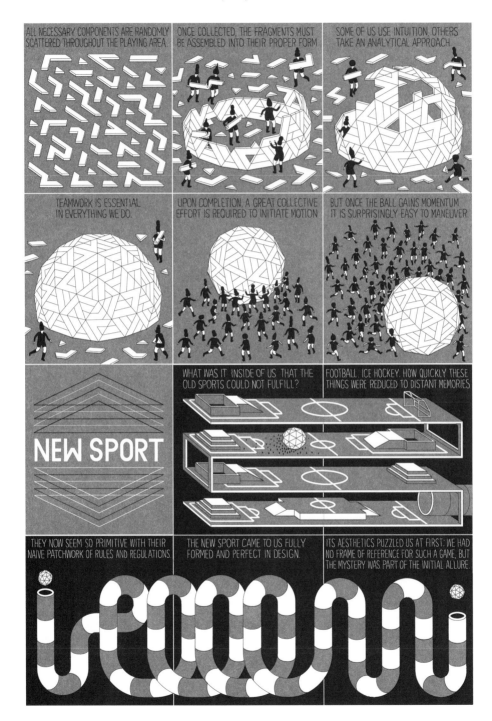

ALL NECESSARY COMPONENTS ARE RANDOMLY SCATTERED THROUGHOUT THE PLAYING AREA.

ONCE COLLECTED, THE FRAGMENTS MUST BE ASSEMBLED INTO THEIR PROPER FORM.

SOME OF US USE INTUITION, OTHERS TAKE AN ANALYTICAL APPROACH.

TEAMWORK IS ESSENTIAL IN EVERYTHING WE DO.

UPON COMPLETION, A GREAT COLLECTIVE EFFORT IS REQUIRED TO INITIATE MOTION.

BUT ONCE THE BALL GAINS MOMENTUM, IT IS SURPRISINGLY EASY TO MANEUVER.

NEW SPORT

WHAT WAS IT INSIDE OF US THAT THE OLD SPORTS COULD NOT FULFILL?

FOOTBALL. ICE HOCKEY. HOW QUICKLY THESE THINGS WERE REDUCED TO DISTANT MEMORIES.

THEY NOW SEEM SO PRIMITIVE WITH THEIR NAIVE PATCHWORK OF RULES AND REGULATIONS.

THE NEW SPORT CAME TO US FULLY FORMED AND PERFECT IN DESIGN.

ITS AESTHETICS PUZZLED US AT FIRST: WE HAD NO FRAME OF REFERENCE FOR SUCH A GAME, BUT THE MYSTERY WAS PART OF THE INITIAL ALLURE.

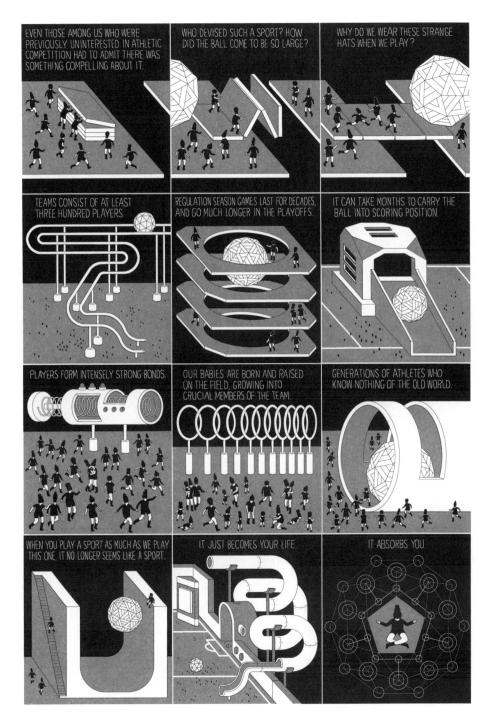

RAFAEL CLAIMED TO HAVE
A BOREDOM DETECTOR...

by DORIAN GEISLER

Rafael claimed to have a boredom detector. He claimed it was in his soul. He was six.

Rafael learned about the soul from Jude last Sunday while eating a doughnut and talking about his grandfather in the basement of the Presbyterian Church on E. Washington.

When his mother told him to finish his science homework (a research project on a species of manta ray common off the shores of southern Florida) Rafael went 'Beep beep!' and then said, in a perfect monotone: 'Boredom detected.'

His mother, always a quick-witted woman, said: 'Careful, there, Rafael, or I will have to take that boredom detector away from you.'

Rafael responded: 'You can't. It's in my soul.'

Dorian Geisler's collection Flowers of Anti-Martyrdom *is available now from McSweeney's.*

TEN COMMANDMENTS

HOW TO SPOT A HOAX

by KEVIN YOUNG

I

LATELY, I'VE BEEN THINKING a lot about hoaxes. Been writing about them, too. But whenever anyone asks what I'm working on, I'll say, *I'm writing about liars*. While not a lie exactly, this isn't the whole truth; hoaxes aren't simply lies, but lies with explanations. Or, to quote disgraced cyclist Lance Armstrong, "one big lie... repeated a lot of times." Despite what we might think, the hoax isn't an accident, or a slip of the tongue—just as plagiarism isn't simply forgetting to cite a source. The hoax is rather a kind of coded confession, revealing not only a deep-seated cultural wish but also a common set of themes—or feints, or strategies—that add up to a ritual. This is why we often are not just fooled, but made fools of, by the hoax—indicted by its revelations, not of what's true but of what we truly believe.

2

Not quite as American as apple pie, the hoax is as American as George Washington's not-really-chopped-down cherry tree. Or better yet, as American as Joice Heth, the black woman who P.T. Barnum in all likelihood bought, pretending she was the first President's nursemaid. This would have made her over 161 years old. When she died Barnum had her dissected in a medical theater, charging admission, and used the revelation of her normal advanced age—her having been a hoax—to further his first successful humbug, launching his long career of successful humbugs. In short, Barnum made even the revelation of the hoax part of the hoax.

3

The hoax has changed. Despite the horror of Heth's end (and servitude), earlier centuries like the eighteenth used the hoax to honor; the nineteenth used it as humor. Since the twentieth century, the hoax has become a figure of horror. Our current hoaxes go to extreme lengths to manufacture pain, to be believed in extremis. The modern hoax is about suffering and, worse, pretend pain: this dulls us to real tragedy, and to each other; and, equally troubling, to the power of actual art.

4

The hoax often emerges as a reaction to the unimaginable. What actually happened proves hard to believe—which is not to say hard to prove—and the hoax takes over. Whether in the case of honor killing or modern slavery or the troubling spate of recent fake Holocaust memoirs, hoaxes replace actual, powerful experiences with fake ones that are tidier and tamer, yet wilder and *worser*. Facts overwhelm us; fantasy proves more relatable exactly because it is hard to believe: someone writes a book pretending both to be Jewish and to have survived the Holocaust by traveling with a pack of wolves across Europe. Whether the Holocaust or slavery or child abuse or addiction, hoaxes take the difficult and make it easy to digest. Hoaxes also make actual messy history, both personal and public, more muddled than it really is. The results give, for instance, Holocaust deniers only more fuel, even as many of the hoaxers claim to be identifying with the pain they essentially plagiarize.

5

The hoax is about race, plagiarism about class. This is because race itself is a made-up thing pretending to be real. That doesn't mean it doesn't have real consequences, like the hoax. When confronted with the contradictions of race and racism (which the hoax conflates, seeing color instead of culture) the hoaxer reaches for the grab bag of clichés—from the fake Indian to the tragic half-breed to the magic Negro to the holy hustler—all in order to convince us of what we already, secretly, think.

6

Like art forgery, the hoax doesn't wear well and tends to look ridiculous quickly. Once revealed, it can be hard to believe anyone ever thought the awkward painting was a Vermeer, or that anyone believed that white girl with the faux-ghetto accent was really a member of a black gang. Though deceptive, hoaxes aren't exactly hidden—indeed, there's no such thing as a private hoax. At its most artistic, say in Edgar Allan Poe's many hoaxes or in the work of my favorite fake poets, the hoax's public nature becomes something akin to a popular form to be played with. But most hoaxes, like forged paintings, aren't meant to stand on their own: they are plagiarisms of another's strong style. The hoax shortcuts or plagiarizes the personal struggle that characterizes great art.

7

The hoax is contagious, while plagiarism is addictive. Both seem catching, until caught. Is there a cure? I haven't found one exactly. But in seeking the complexity and cold comfort of art instead of the easy solutions the hoax offers, we might help spot the hoax in action, if not before it starts. If the hoax can't be helped—and occasionally helps keep us on our toes—hoaxes do seem to flourish in particular times, whenever art and our own judgment of truth and art recede.

8

Our current time—once the Information Age, giving way to what I call the Age of Euphemism—is especially vulnerable to the hoax. Our era's embrace of truthiness and "faction"—fact meeting fiction—is a sign, side effect, and symptom of our own fragmented, factionalized culture. And even selves.

9

The hoax undermines both art and the self, oddly reducing each to autobiography even as it performs its fakery. It often does this through the exotic other, or a dark double, or a tricky trio, which only reinforces the self as superior to all others. Real art invents, which is to say, takes into the self things that aren't it—or aren't obviously, at least—making claims on us that are its own. Such claims are not based on autobiography, or backstory, or, strictly speaking, money; this last seems the hoaxer's and the plagiarist's chief aim.

10

You will swear not to tell the truth, not the whole truth, nothing like the truth, so help you. The hoax's worst, unoriginal sin: dismissing the power of art to move us and denying the breadth of the self.

JORDAN TELLER

by SHEILA HETI

T HE TERRIBLE WILL OF the man who longed to be my first lover was complicated by the fact that he was my cousin, which only made the love stronger, and made me want to put my hands all over him. I was never attracted to him—I admit, I never even knew him—before we were stuck together, his family and mine, northeast of the north pole, but that is when we fell into some kind of love for each other (or was it just me?), a real sincere erotic infatuation, all of which was heightened by precisely that disgust for each other, in the way that cousins can be disgusted by each other, in the way that siblings often are. Of course, I was disgusted by almost everything he said. He really was objectively an unappealing man.

I would see him speaking to my little brother, who was about eight at the time, and it would make me so mad—how little he knew and how little he cared! But he would put his mouth to mine in real passionate kisses, and my hatred of him, and my boredom with him, and most especially my embarrassment about him—made ever greater because I had chosen him—would be, in a heap of indistinguishable shame, intensified and smothered by the power of his kisses, which weren't especially great kisses, but were made that much more fantastic and will-melting by the fact that he, Jordan Teller, was my cousin. What a man, I would think, he really must be, in order to put me, his own cousin, under the spell of his positive masculinity. Of course, I never did get a chance to find out just how great he was, or whether he could fuck or not, because all we did was kiss, and we only did it a couple of times, and none of it was all that open-mouthed. So naturally there was very little I knew about him for a fact, sexually. Would I have even wanted him if he weren't my cousin? It's next to impossible to tell.

There was something funny about the sky that winter (or was it summer? there was lots of night, that time of year), which is partly what caused us to fall into whatever love or lust was visited upon us, I am sure. It was too peculiar and too beautiful not to have been totally responsible. The sky was almost on fire—and it was not just the northern lights, which is a spectacle in itself, but the very speed at which the stars twinkled in the sky, as though they were all going off in their own terrible, climactic orgasms. They popped like flashbulbs, the large ones held in silvery pots, as they flickered on and off.

We had to keep my brother busy, and we did, by tossing a ball and hoping he would run after it and bring it back, but not too quickly. We tossed it far that time of year, then sat on the steps with our parents asleep, waiting for morning, excited and simply feeling very bad (at least I did), and he would touch me on my mouth with his mouth, and that would light up more than just the sky, which was streaked with pink and all sorts of colors. That was the only time we felt any sort of love or lust for each other. In the daytime he was working on his memoir, and it was really awful. It was very clichéd and there was no way I could love a rather ugly, memoir-writing man in the daylight. Only at night, with the night sky on fire, leaving shadows of pink on that blackest earth—that darkened carpet—could I love my cousin with the fat lips and bad hair. Only when night was out.

As I said, during the day he was working on a very conventional memoir! He had just got the idea for it that summer (or was it winter?)—but it was nothing that could make me love him any more than I already did. Did I love him? Maybe not. But the degree of shame that existed between us was a kind of perfection which contained precisely the perfect degree of horror to make him a magnet for all that was wet and longing in me, the fact of which (there being anything wet and longing in me) I would not have admitted before, and in fact had absolutely no notion of with my rather tepid previous boyfriend, who loved me, but was not, I see this now, a blood relative.

When we first got the idea of kissing into our heads, the memoir was just an idea in *his* head. But by the time we had kissed and loved each other a third night—*loved?* no, for there was a kind of antagonism in it all—he had already composed his two and a half perfect sentences, which he would repeat in his head and aloud to me. Just the perfection of them and the tedious nature of what they revealed is what I disliked so much. That he would even think there was an audience for such a thing! But this innocence is partly what made me so attracted. The ego that would conceive of such a thing was, that summer or winter, the very ego that would steal my heart. I do not claim I fell in love with an angel, or anyone I would have approved of back home, where my sensibilities were more alert, and tempered, besides, by my friends, whom I could never have brought such a dough-faced man before. But as it was, it was just his family and mine, and the fact that such an ugly cousin could steal all that was wet and longing in me—the sheer novelty of it—pulled me into deep, bewildering kisses in those moments when my little brother was fetching his ball, and the bright light of the stars flickered on and off like a signal to us below, as we sat beneath that widest sky, all lit up for the first time ever.

It was a certain quality of his—one that made me wonder *what on earth is this quality of his?*—which made me so attracted to him. It's hard to explain, but a quality which is not a quality but which puts in one's mind the idea that there *is* some quality which needs to be pinpointed before any further progression can be made, is perhaps the most alluring quality a man can possess. This quality might have been seen as arrogance in the city, but it was not arrogance, for despite the fact that he had a memoir on the go, it was not so self-congratulatory, from what I could tell from his two nearly perfect sentences. Jordan Teller was not an especially arrogant man. Neither was there a happiness he carried around about being JT. I cannot say precisely what quality of his made me fall in love with him, but I was happy to find it in a man while being stuck in a house in the northern plains, with no other woman around to make me either have to hurry him up and cement it, or let him go out of sheer embarrassment at having any sort of wick in me that could be lit up by such a slouch, by a man as immature as him. That summer (or was it winter?) might never even have happened if there had been even one woman around to say, *What a loser,* which would have turned me off him completely. Or had there been even one young man, whose repulsive nature was equal to that of Jordan Teller's (though I can't in all honesty say he was repulsive—quite the contrary) this would at least have forced me to compare my darling JT to him, and allowed me to assess him finally and for all time as a real slouch. Or had there been even one boy whose beauty was such that the sun shone directly from his skin, tanning me to a crisp in his presence, I would have thought, *That Jordan Teller really is a poor candidate of a man.* But as it was, there was nobody around to shift in one way or another my feelings for JT. Certainly my mother and father did not talk about his various qualities, nor did anybody gossip about how ridiculous the first two lines of his memoir were (*were* they even ridiculous?); had there been even the slightest bit of criticism about him, it would have turned me off him completely, but nobody—the especially peculiar thing was—spoke about him at all, not once. I did keep my ears open, and was really starving for some opinion of him one way or the other. Had my mother helped me out by snuggling me close to her in her bed and letting me speak my feelings, something might have changed—yet how could I have done such a thing with a mother such as her? So it was that before me was a man untouched by the suggestive presence of any other man or woman, and that quality which caused me to wonder *what on earth is that quality?* might just have been our proximity to absolutely nothing that strange time of year.

*   *   *

There were two ways he got into my room that summer (which I'm beginning to think it was—summer). My room was in the basement with two shuttered windows leading in from the street, so if I ever got home late at night from wandering about (it wasn't always so cold) I could sneak in through the window—just push open the shutters and pull myself through. Not far from the windows was the back door to the house. I kept the door to my bedroom locked when I was inside, but I unlocked it when I went out—for instance, when I went with my mother for a walk. Although we seldom walked, we sometimes did. He got into my room at least twice, I won't say more; one time through the windows, and the other time through the door.

When I came into my room, Jordan Teller was sitting there on the washing machine. It startled me so much to see him sitting there that I screamed. I screamed when I saw him, looking two ways: first so handsome and desirable, like everything my whole body cried out for, so that I nearly fell on the floor from the sheer joy of knowing someone who could make my blood run in such a way. But then, upon seeing that small smile upon his face, that ugly memoir-writing smile, I felt horror that JT was such a troll, midgety and fat with greasy hair. I wouldn't have it this way, him coming into my room whenever he wanted. I ran at him screaming, *Get out!*

Despite my attraction to him, you will know it for the truth when I say that very soon after, he began taking me up the ass, making me hold myself open for him, on my bed, while my mother paused outside the door, calling for me to go with her somewhere, to pick something up or drop something off. Then he would do it in the night, gripping me so close that I could not get away, my door ajar, so that anybody walking by could see. The terror this put in me—that somebody might see us doing this thing—was even more awful than the fact that he forced himself into my ass. That is why I screamed when I saw him on the washing machine. That is when it hit me, how things were going to be.

*　　*　　*

There was one Sunday when we were walking back from the shore—Jordan Teller and I, holding hands and looking up at the sky, the waves black and my hair black with ice. We were walking, making prints in the snow, and he turned to me and looked into my eyes and said that I reminded him so much of his mother, it was impossible for him to do anything but retch at the sight of my face. There was nothing to say to this, so I did not say anything. I continued walking, focused only on my walking. I had been staring at him for three whole days, and so lovingly, wondering what movie star he reminded me of.

Sometimes I wonder if the connection I felt with Jordan Teller was only within myself. Now that I look back on it, I can't imagine that he gazed at me with love even once that whole summer. Or if he did, it was only to glance away at something else a moment later.

Jordan Teller was in his world, and I was in the world of Jordan Teller, and these two worlds were far apart.

The first time I saw Jordan Teller, he was working on the docks, pulling up fish and gutting them by the shore as I came over on the tiny boat with my mother and father and brother. At first I did not know it was my cousin I was seeing—I had never seen him before. My family is introverted, and we do not associate with other people much, not if we can help it. Though I do remember one time when we crossed the street.

We were pale children, quiet little ghosts. My parents had no friends and discouraged us from having any. People taint you, my parents said, though they never explained to us how. One would think, looking at them, olive-skinned and so well dressed, that they were a glamorous couple with glamorous lives. But it only seemed that way, for my parents were turned towards their own insides. People have the power to change you, my parents said, which is a very bad thing. They made efforts in our upbringing to keep me and my brother separated, he in one room, me in another, tapping out sounds on the wall. The rare times I saw him, he seemed to me like a doll, like a creature from another planet.

When we were twenty feet from shore, my mother said, *That is your cousin.* Imagine my surprise. My very own cousin! I didn't know I had one, and I was instantly overwhelmed. How human—to have a cousin. My insides felt entirely exposed. It was too fantastic to be true.

How can I compare my life to anyone else's life? It's a good question. Especially since I have barely known anyone else. But I think there is a porousness to people, a real porous quality that lets anyone seep in and out; a great and spongy willingness to let other people play inside them—a jelly weakness, not caring one way or another. Knowing all this from my childhood on, how could I let my cousin mark me, and go and leave his scent inside me? For now I smell different than before. Animals react to me differently since Jordan Teller came inside. My insides are no longer purely my own.

There we were, lying on the sand, the wide, bruise-yellow sky overhead, our hands folded behind our heads, and no electricity between our bodies, yet every part of me was twitching with fear, nothing was relaxed. My family will say they saw nothing. But they should have known. They should have come to tear us apart! He fucked me up the ass in the middle of the night! With my bedroom door wide open! Yet not a sound from anyone.

Now I cannot find my way home. I think there was a blue sky once, and a bright yellow sun, and a moon overhead; that we were on the sand below, looking out at the waves. That is how I think of him—as sandy water, slipping out from between my toes. Then he was behind me, then he was in front of me, pressing himself into my skin. The memory of a person makes them not like a person at all.

Jordan Teller and I went walking one day. We used to walk, that's all we did, me and my beautiful cousin, down the frozen beach. Me and Jordan Teller—there was never a dull moment. Except when we were sitting together, entirely bored to tears. In fact, now that I think of it, there were many dull moments. Nothing to do and nothing to think about. There we were, day in, day out. The adults were dull as rocks. Sometimes JT would pull me close by my shorts, and stick his thumb underneath them, stick his thumb in my bum, and there I'd be hovering, just looking around, burning up inside. I know that happened more than once, by the seashore, just him and me together.

There were terrible sounds, and thunder from the sky, and big massive bodies being flopped into the ocean, cannon bombs and all the other tragedies that happen at sea. It happened right before our eyes, so many miles off, it seemed like another world almost. Often we would sit and watch these terrible masses being dropped from the sky. We wouldn't say anything, just watched as they were dropped into the sea and made a tremendous splash. The waves would be huge—first we'd feel them small, washing up over our feet, then much larger until they were tidal waves, great wide arms coming up from the sea to grasp us where we were. At these times we'd hurry back. Or I'd hurry. JT would head back slowly, not even turning to see if the waves were still approaching. His way of moving, completely unconcerned, was as if nothing could harm him.

One time he pushed my head into the sand and yelled at me to look— *Did I see it? Did I see it?* It was a used tampon of mine. It had only a spot of blood, and was wedged between some stones. I don't know how it got there. It was puffed and bloated, wetted by the sea and me. Obviously I had done something horrible, this was no surprise to me. I bent down and picked it up with my fingernails, and stood and turned around, carrying it in front of me, not looking at his eyes. I felt his weight and his heaviness, the broadness of him behind me. Then I began walking away, and as I walked, ashamed, I wondered what to do with it. I just didn't know what to do with it. I ended up walking with it all the way back, and placing it beneath my pillow.

*   *   *

A dog drowned when we were up there. The dog that had become Jordan Teller's dog. There were two packs of dogs that began coming for food. The brown dog with the white ear was Jordan Teller's. It happened that he would leave his pack whenever he saw Jordan Teller. He must have smelled something in him, just like I did, and the three of us would walk. Or Jordan Teller would walk and the two of us would walk behind. The dog never looked at me, and I never looked at it. Jordan Teller barely acknowledged the dog. There we were, following Jordan Teller to the sea, all along the shore.

One day, a huge and heavy bullet was dropped into the ocean, a few miles from land. JT had been sitting on a tree trunk that was hanging over the water, while the dog and I were lying on the sand, a little ways apart. I was looking one way—frankly I was bored. I think JT and I saw the bomb at the exact same moment. It came, and a huge gasping tumble rained down on our heads and our entire bodies, and carried us swirling into the tide, into the dark and heavy waters which sucked us back from shore, then deep into the sea, then spat us back on land again. I was screaming when I emerged, unable to open or close my eyes. We had been flipped and hurdled and pulled upside down, until finally we were tossed in one strong blow onto the wet and sandy beach, Jordan Teller first, me next, landing on my shoulder. When we dragged ourselves up, out of the tide's reach, and looked around, the dog was gone, he was nowhere to be seen. When Jordan Teller realized his dog was dead, he began pulling at his hair, running around in circles, crying out for his pet. I didn't even know he cared about the dog! When I finally touched his arm, I felt the fire in him had gone out. I sat quietly on a little grassy patch, and waited, amazed that something meant anything to him at all.

I began having terrible dreams, dreams of words only, no feelings attached. Tedious, thick novels of dreams, dusty novels of words. I would wake up exhausted, unable to function the entire day from the groaning in my brain. Perhaps my parents, with all their notions about keeping me from influence, had this devious plan in mind all along—first they decided to isolate me forever, then they set this man upon me, who they told me was my cousin, to teach me a lesson which I wouldn't know the purpose of for many years to come. In moments, I wanted to rush up to my mother and father and scream at them that they must know! How could they not! He was fucking me in the ass every night! It was impossible for me to say anything. But my hatred at them for doing this, once it was there, was always there.

I don't know what possessed me to go to him in the middle of the night. I only did it once. I usually slept straight through the night, or else he visited me. But one night I woke at three in the morning, just opened my eyes and sat straight up. No one was around. I lay back down and tried to sleep, but I was wide awake. So I got up out of bed. I was wearing a long nightgown and I put my slippers on. I found myself walking around my room, then I grew tense and excited. Everything was silent and I felt scared and giddy. I smiled to myself. I would pay a visit to Jordan Teller. I let out a giggle, then covered my mouth with my hand, but I was still grinning. I slipped out of my room and hurried down the hall, pausing for a moment at his door to listen in and make sure he was asleep. Then I pushed open the door and rushed all the way across his room and jumped into bed beside him, and in that instant a huge fist came out and pummeled me in the chest. I folded in two, hit my nose on something hard, then fell onto the floor. Jordan Teller was leaning over me, his whole body blue, lit by the moon streaming through. His eyes were fiercer and more sinister than I had ever seen. His teeth seemed pointed, too. He growled at me that *the fucking bitch had cut off his ear, had eaten his fucking ear!* I ran out of his room, down the hall and into mine, and, crying, slammed the door shut. I lay there quivering with fright. I couldn't sleep. I kept on waiting for him to come down the hall and throw open the door. At around six in the morning, when the sky started to turn lighter, I finally fell asleep. The next day he barely looked at me. I did ask him, a few days later, whether he ever talked in his sleep. We were eating outside, at a picnic table. He handed me his corn to throw away, and I did.

*   *   *

Women in love have no time limit. I have seen it happen, or heard of it perhaps—two women, in a washroom. From one of them: *If he doesn't ask me within twenty minutes*... (tying a sweater around the waist of her dress). But she's obviously lying. Women in love have no time limit. The men can take forever. There is no going, there is no coming. There is no in between.

I think few women are ever in love, or have ever been in love, the way I was with Jordan Teller. With Jordan Teller, there was no time limit. It went on and on and on. There was no beginning after the beginning. It just went on in one straight flow. I saw him with the fish, then it never stopped. Nothing had to be done, nothing had to happen, he never had to open his door, never had to touch me—it would have been enough. Like a woman in love, I had no time limit. I had none.

Jordan Teller was an absolute necessity for me. At times he would stay in his room and keep his door closed. Those days were absolute torture. I felt lost, there was no hope. I brooded about, hanging around, wondering when he'd emerge. I would try to distract myself. I would take walks up and down the shore, go to all the places where we had gone. I would throw a ball to my brother, but it wasn't the same. Once I rapped lightly on his door and heard a groan. I turned away, walking down the hall, sadder than before. The beautiful kisses between us were dead, they were long in the past. There would be no more kisses again. We never talked about it, he never said why, he never told me a thing. I had given him everything that was mine, but he thought I had given him nothing. But I had loved him! I had given him everything of myself! But he thought I had turned him away. I don't know why he thought this. I had given him every feeling I had gathered before we met. But he thought I had given him nothing. It wasn't true. I had given him everything. And I already knew that after Jordan Teller, I would have nothing to give.

*　　*　　*

All the women, I assumed, loved Jordan Teller the same way I loved him when we first met, and the same way I continued to love him after we left. There was no reason to think there was something in him other women didn't see. I loved every bit of him. Though I suppose, looking back on it all, one can really love anything.

A watery grave. That's what surrounds me now, since that year of Jordan Teller—a watery grave before my eyes. By the end of it all, I was truly drab at heart. By the end of it all, he was wandering the rocks alone, looking out for something else. He was in his own world, and I had no world. There was no returning from the shore or going down it together. Just a blankness about everything, and no hope in my heart that something good would come for me ever again. I didn't know where it had gone, or why it had all gone from between us.

There would only be boredom in our futures. I saw it before us, and not with each other—boring couplings. We would be thinly dripping faucets after that. It would just be little half-connections, but nobody to lay it all out there with. There would never again be somebody to give all of everything to, only little disconnections, which I would offer up, and which would dwindle away once they were discovered as only half-bits, just the used-up parts of me.

I said goodbye without any sorrow. And my heart evened out like a ship in quiet seas.

BUT DON'T WORRY

by MATTHEW SHARPE

BRIAN LAY HIDDEN IN the tall grass near the Japanese maple at the bottom of his yard at the end of September. He looked up at the sky, which was blue. He looked at the air between himself and the sky, which had no color, unless he looked at it carefully, in which case he saw that it was made of a billion infinitesimal dots of many different colors. These dots were atoms. The whole universe was made of atoms. Brian wondered if he was the only person who could see the atoms with his naked eye. His mother stood a hundred feet away on the porch and called his name for the seventh time. The first six times she'd made his name a question—"Brian? Brian?"—each one slightly higher in pitch than the previous. The seventh calling of his name was not a question but a warning to Brian and the universe—*You'd better come back here!* and *Don't you dare take him away, too!*, respectively. For Brian there was no question of the universe's being able to hear, or willing anything to happen. His mother, on the other hand, believed that the universe had taken her husband. Brian knew her well enough to discern the thoughts that underlay each of her calls of "Brian!" from the porch—nine "Brian!"s now; ten—but what he did not know about his mother was what she knew about his father's disappearance. He knew that her refusal to tell him, as well as her willful substitution of the actual information with her line about the universe, was motivated not only by her hazy spiritualism but also by her decision to protect him from knowledge of things as they truly were, which, if she would only open her eyes, she would see he possessed in greater quantity and quality than she. Had his father run off with another woman? Was he ill? Was he dead? Brian's mother's insistent euphemizing of his father's absence was not merely annoying to him. Had it been merely annoying, he'd have been able to tolerate it along with the other annoyances that came with having this person as his mother, all of which, taken together, were an easily acceptable trade-off for her dark beauty, her kindness, her delight in his grade-school accomplishments, and her keen intelligence about indispensable things like how to make cinnamon buttermilk pancakes. But no, her unintentionally cruel withholding of this crucial information made Brian feel all the atoms that constituted his body straining to fly off in every direction, whereupon he would become the air and the sky, an eventuality he was not yet ready for, and so, to ensure his continuation in his current form as Brian, he kept his lips sealed, the only response he could make to her cries—yes, they were cries now—of "Brian! Brian!" The distance between them had become that of stars in separate galaxies. Autumn arrived. The leaves of the Japanese maple were aflame.

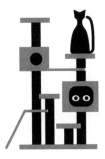

PUPPET MASTER
MADE THE PUPPETS

by VAUHINI VARA

MEE SCRAPES COCONUT OIL from its tub. It melts in her palms like butter. She pretends to eat her hands: "Num, num, num—toast." I sit in Mee's lap. She puts her hands on my head and rubs. I close my eyes. No more room. Only the coconut smell.

I rub her lap with my face: "Mrow."

"No cats tonight, okay?"

"Mrow!"

"Okay, okay—mrow, and goodnight."

Then it's Dee's slippers thumping down the hall and into the room: "Goodnight, little bee."

"Mrow."

I want a cat. I try to wait until Mee falls asleep before I go to sleep again. Car coming down the street and sending a square of light across the carpet.

Dee shouting at Mee. Or sometimes it's quiet except for the crickets and frogs. The morning hurts. Blood on my arms and legs. Brown cream under my fingernails. My blood and skin. Mee rubs coconut oil on my skin. One morning I use my fingernail to scrape the brown from the other nails. I make a little ball with it. Hide it in the bathroom drawer behind the safety pins. The next day I make the ball bigger. I have to roll and roll to make it round. A pearl.

I am going to dive for pearls. I am on a boat. "I am diving for pearls!" Mee's hand on my mouth: "Don't shout—the neighbors!" Then I am in the laundry basket again, and we are in the backyard again, and Mee is hanging up the sheets to dry. We live in a house. In my favorite book, they live on a beach by the ocean. The elephant is in a hammock—

At my grandparents' house, we eat bannock. I say, "More bannock!" Dee tells Mee, "Get her more!" Mee says, "She'll be sick," and I say, "Then I don't want more." Dee suddenly stands and gets close to Mee, and Mee ducks and puts her arm up over her head. Nothing happens. Dee laughs. Mee goes for the bannock. The bannock is on a paper plate and cut in four pieces. I say I don't want any bannock. Dee says, "It's your favorite." I say, "I'm full."

Once my grandparents took us to see dancing dolls. Flinging arms, flinging legs. "Oh-ee-oh-ee-oh-ee-oh!" And people were laughing, even the dolls were laughing, but we weren't laughing. I said, "How do those dolls sing?" Dee said, "They're puppets." I said, "How do the puppets sing?" Nobody said anything. Then Mee said, "There's a puppet master hiding back there to make them sing and dance. Puppet master made the puppets." I said, "Puppet master makes them feel good?"

Mee doesn't like my grandparents; they think we're rich, they fish for money. Mee says, "Easy for people to think others have good lives." Dee says, "But we do have it good—Mee doesn't know anything!" Mee and Dee are opposites. Mee never smiles; Dee smiles all the time. Mee is quiet; Dee is loud. Mee works; Dee stays home. When Mee goes to work, we play Cats. We rub our heads on the couch: "Mrow, mrow!" Dee says, "Okay—you want a cat?" I want a cat. But Mee doesn't want a cat. Dee claps his hands and says, "We'll surprise her! Come on—let's go—"

Prince says let's go crazy. Prince says let's get nuts. Prince says look for the purple banana till they put us in the truck—

Dee peels a banana, and slices fall out—already cut. He gives me a slice. He claps his hands and says, "Magic!" Our cat is hiding under the table. He's afraid of us. Dee laughs: "Wait till Mee sees!" And: "Well? Why did the banana come out in pieces?" And: "What should we name him?"

I have a secret with Magic. In the bathroom I show Magic my ball. He says, "Mrow?" Mee hates the cat. Mee says I didn't listen to the rules. I tell her: "But Dee took me!" Mee tells me to tell Dee to take Magic back to where he came from. Dee says if we take Magic there, they will kill him. They will wait four days to see if someone comes for him, then they will kill him with poison in a needle. My ball is getting bigger and bigger. It will be an egg, an onion, a pumpkin, a beach ball, a snowman's top, a snowman's middle, a snowman's bottom. Wait till my ball is big enough. You wait, Magic. Then I will bring puppet master to life.

I see her at night. She curls on the bottom of the bed at my feet next to Magic. Puppet master lives in the night and wants to come to the day. She makes me scratch. She says, *Only you can bring me into the day—until you bring me I won't leave you alone in the night.* Puppet master wants blood and skin;

she wants me to scratch and give her my blood and skin. In the day, she will make us all sing and dance and laugh. Arms round each other's shoulders, legs flinging. "Ooh-ee-ooh-ee-ooh-ee!" In the night, puppet master says, "In the day, you must sing, 'Ooh-ee-ooh-ee-ooh-ee!' Then I will know you love me, and I will come alive."

In the morning, I am bleeding all over. The brown cream pushes out from my fingernails. In the bathroom I sit on the floor and sing, "Ooh-ee-ooh-ee-ooh-ee!" I come out of the bathroom and sing, "Ooh-ee-ooh-ee-ooh-ee!" I am bleeding all over. Dee brings me all kinds of special medicine. Jars and jars. Mee says, "I'm getting a second opinion. I'm taking her to a real doctor."

At the clinic, the nurses say, "Hi, ladies!" Mee ducks and mumbles. She doesn't want Dee to know we're here. Doctor says to open my mouth. Doctor puts his cold stethoscope on my chest. Doctor holds my elbows in his palms and looks at my arms and says, "And now what do we have here?" Mee says, "It's getting worse—see?" The door opens, and Dee comes in. I go to him: "Dee-ee-ee-ee!" Dee looks at Mee and says, "Thought we decided against this—no offense, Doc." Doctor says to Dee, "Oh, none taken." Mee says, "But I think she's allergic to the cat! Couldn't she be?" Doctor says, "Oh—a cat!" I cry, "It's not his fault—poor Magic!" And I cry. Doctor laughs, "So we're committed to the cat, I see." Dee rubs his head and says, "This little girl has been begging for years—what can I do, Doc?" Doctor says, "Not much you can do."

Doc. In the mornings, when I watch the cartoons with Dee, the bunny says Doc. The bunny says, Promenade across the floor. Sashay right on out the door. Out the door and into the glade and everybody promenade. Step right up you're doing fine. I'll pull your beard you'll pull mine. Yank it again like you did before. Break it up with a tug of war. Now into the brook and fish for the trout. Dive right in and splash about. Trout! Trout! Pretty little trout! One more splash and come right out. Shake like a hound dog. Shake again. Wallow around in the old pigpen. Wallow some more. Y'all know how. Roll around like an old fat sow. Allemande left with your right hand.

Follow through with a great left band. Now lead your partner, the dirty old thing. Follow through with an elbow swing. Grab a fence post. Hold it tight. Whomp your partner with all your might. Hit him in the shin. Hit him in the head. Hit him again. The critter ain't dead. Whomp him low and whomp him high. Stick your finger in his eye. Pretty little ring. Pretty little sound. Bang your heads against the ground. Promenade all around the room. Promenade like a bride and groom. Open up the door and step right in. Close the door and into a spin. Whirl! Whirl! Twist and twirl! Jump all around like a flying squirrel. Now don't you fuss and don't you swear. Just come right out and form a square. Now right hand over and left hand under. Both join hands and run like thunder—

Dee whomps Mee with all his might. Hit her in the shin. Hit her in the head. Hit her again. The critter ain't dead—

Mee gets up. Dee sits down. I sit down. Mee sits down. Now we're sitting very still. Nobody looking at anybody. Mee is mad, because I cried over Magic and made her look bad. Dee is mad, because Mee blamed Magic and made Dee look bad. Puppet master, I am mad, too. You said you would come soon. At night you say, "But how can I come if you don't bring me into the day?" I say, "My ball isn't big enough." You say, "Make it bigger, then—quick. You're the only one who knows how to bring me into the day. If you don't make me, I'll never come." At night, you make me scratch. I wake up. Magic is crying. Oh, poor Magic! Mee wanted him to die!

I scratch. I scratch. I scratch and scratch and scratch and scratch and scratch and scratch and scratch and scratch and scratch and scratch and scratch and scratch. Mee is mad at Dee. She tells him to leave. So he leaves. It is only me and Mee and Magic. Mee says, "Don't you want to stop scratching? Then we need to take the cat back. When he comes home, you tell him,

'Dee, I want to take the cat back.'" I can't tell Mee that Magic isn't making me scratch—it's you, puppet master. I tell her: "But they'll kill him!" Mee says, "My baby, don't cry," and she cries, too. Magic comes around the corner and pushes me with his head. He pushes Mee with his head. "He's saying, 'I love you, Mee. Don't cry, Mee,'" I say. Mee cries and looks at Magic and says, "Is he?" I say, "He's saying, 'I will love you forever—please love me, too.'" And Mee looks at Magic and takes him to her chest and hugs him. Magic pushes his head on her chest, on her arms. I say, "Any time you're sad, Magic wants you to feel better." She says, "It feels good." And she gets the comb, and we go to the balcony, and she puts me in the laundry basket and Magic on her lap and she brushes his hair. Big fluffs of Magic's hair go flying through the air. "Alright," Mee says. "There we go."

Later, Mee cleans the house. She pulls the cat hairs from the couch cushions. She scratches with her thumbnail at the dried onion bits stuck to the floor. "We'll just have to keep it really clean," she says. She goes into the bathroom. She opens the drawer. She sees my ball and says, "Augh," and covers her mouth like she will throw up. I don't know if she knows what it is. I want to speak, but I don't speak. I know something terrible is about to happen. But I don't speak. Mee wraps my ball in a wad of toilet tissue and drops it in the toilet and flushes. I stay in the bathroom and look into the toilet. Where does it all go? Outside, Mee is walking all through the house with an incense stick. The smoke curls then disappears. I say, "Mee—where does the toilet water go?"

Mee says, "To the ocean, I guess—"

Dee doesn't come home. I wait, but he doesn't come. In my favorite book, the old woman is nice but won't let the elephant in her house. She lets in the other animals. "But no elephants!" Mee says. She puts her fingers on the words. I say, "But no elephants!" The house is cold in winter. The old woman and the animals are afraid of the winter. The elephant is afraid, too. He stands outside the window. One night the old woman dances with the animals to stay warm, and the elephant cries outside in the cold with snow piling on his head. Like a mountain. So she lets him in. The other animals dance with him. He eats all the food and crashes through the floor, and the old woman is afraid again. But when he stands, he lifts the house from the ground and starts to walk. He walks and walks and walks and walks. Sometimes I cry at that part. Mee says, "Shush—the happy part is coming—it's almost here." When the elephant stops, they have arrived on a warm beach. There is a sign between the palm trees, WELCOME, ANIMALS. The animals take off their clothes and laugh. The elephant lies on a hammock. Mee says, "Told you, Sheila-love—everyone is happy in the end—"

PLEASE REFILL THE PAPER TRAY

BY DAN KENNEDY

Obviously it gets low. The tray is not so different from you and I, at times full and flush with the abundance of life and its supply, and at other times empty and unable to serve and function. There's a girl in a room over a pub on Barlinger Street who will never understand; I know, it seems like I'm getting off track, but you're standing here reading this, and honestly, what are you in a big hurry to do? Think about being given the choice between the office task you're trying to do and having a moment here with the sign, and maybe choose the latter. It's not like you can get in trouble for this, you're reading a sign so you can see what's up with the machine here, the paper tray or whatever, and then get back to work; nothing wrong with that. The smokers who work here get their little ten-minute breaks, so hey, you're taking a little sign break. If you're a smoker, maybe just skim this quickly, since you already get several breaks that the others don't get. Anyway, the girl on Barlinger street will never understand this thing of life sometimes being full and sometimes being empty, I can tell you that much. A ghost in a stairwell, a bear in the tree line, a man stands crying in the rain... wait, where am I going with this? I want to keep your attention on the fact that the paper gets low, and when it does it needs to be replaced. So many people just walk away from the machine when it gets low. We all think we're pretty terrific people, but fact is, sometimes we walk away from things when they're at their lowest, at their emptiest. That's why we have to make signs for each other. Man, I'm just thinking of it right now: you, standing here, knowing this machine needs something, and choosing to walk away full of secrets. The weight of every time you shortcut something will eat at you gently over years, so really this sign is about helping you more than the machine. I floated in the sea where they found Le Corbusier dead. I stood on the path to Monaco and turned away from it, stared at that crumbling mansion filled with ghosts, there on the cliffs. You could almost hear the voices of every-one, two hundred years gone, there at parties on the Côte d'Azur one night, and the next night probably all torn up over the same things as you and I are on any given day. The point is, sometimes we are full, and sometimes we are empty. And it's been like that through the ages. So, just refill the paper tray if it's empty. You can do that today.

HERO

by JEFF PARKER

THE SERIAL BUTT-SQUEEZER got my mom in the Albertsons cereal aisle.

The local news broadcast the Albertsons CCTV video. The footage showed her reaching for my Golden Grahams while a man backed into the frame. When he was close, too close, his hand fell to her butt.

"What were you thinking at this moment?" the TV journalist asked my mom.

"I thought I'd been bumped," she said. "He said, 'Excuse me.' It took a moment to realize what had happened. He didn't have a cart or a basket. He didn't take any cereal and then he just walked away."

And that's what the CCTV video showed: the man walking away while my mom stood there with my Golden Grahams.

We watched in our living room. Dad held Mom on the couch. I lay on the floor, my chin propped in my palms.

"Why did you decide to come forward?" the journalist asked.

"The detective told me this has happened to others. I thought it might help catch the guy. I wasn't harmed, but I felt violated, and afraid."

"Violated and afraid," the reporter repeated. "Anyone with information on this serial butt-squeezer call the Crimestoppers line, and as long as he's on the loose, watch your backs, and your bottoms."

"You're a hero," Dad said to Mom.

I went to my room to play a new video game in which I'm a kid whose mother thinks God ordered her to kill her son with a kitchen knife. I escape into the basement where I battle, for some reason, piles of shit with eyeballs. My weapons are projectile tears.

In the morning, I passed on my usual Golden Grahams and went to school hungry. The kids were bloodthirsty and waiting.

I had already long been called Blow Job Jr. because on the job my mom went by BJ the Clown. Why BJ? Why not MJ the Clown or JR the Clown or ZZ the Clown or Shirley (her own name) the Clown or anything except BJ? It had no meaning and it stood for nothing. Nada.

"Hey Blow Job Jr., Son of the Squeeze of the Serial Butt-Squeezer," Scott Bevis said. "Do you think that dude would have squeezed your mom's butt if she was wearing her Blow Job the Clown Sr. uniform?"

Mike Reed held a pretend microphone in front of my face and said, "Is your mom's butt squishy or firm? The public has a right to know!"

"No comment," I said. Then I trudged to first period, where I sat next to Jarita, who leaned over and said, "I hope your mom's okay."

"She wasn't harmed," I said.

"Still," Jarita said. "I wouldn't want my butt grabbed by some weird creepo."

It was nice to hear Jarita say *grabbed* instead of *squeezed*. If I heard the word *squeezed* one more time in relation to my mom's butt, I thought I might throw up.

I stood behind Mike Reed in the cafeteria line for the Friday taco bar, and he kept squawking, accusing me of squeezing his butt.

"Let's call the resource officer on him, Mike," Scott Bevis said. "We'll get you on the news. What a scoop: Blow Job Jr., Son of the Squeeze of the Serial Butt-Squeezer, is a homo butt-squeezer his own self!"

I made three soft tacos, then sat by myself and cried at more piles of shit on my phone until I won a dead cat with nine extra lives and graduated to fighting toothy maggots and daddy longlegs.

More than a dozen other victims came forward, all "older" women with stories just like my mom's. In a follow-up, the TV journalist enumerated the locations of the incidents: Costco, Super Walmart, Eckerd's, Family Dollar, Mail Boxes Etc.

"It turns out," he quipped, "the serial butt-squeezer has quite a reach."

"Older," my mother said to my father. "Older?"

BJ's Parties Inc. saw an uptick in business, which was good for Mom and bad for me but Mom said everything that was for the good of BJ's Parties Inc. was for the good of the family. This was her favorite phrase for guilting me into whatever.

Mom had started turning me out as a superhero for BJ's Parties Inc. children's parties when I was twelve. She didn't pay me directly but she used the money to buy my school clothes and supplies and supplement my allowance for the occasional video game.

The problem was that I was short for my age, chicken-legged, and boney. The homemade getups sagged across my concave chest and bunched at my narrow ankles. Birthday boys ogled me with disappointment.

Over dinner Mom said that she needed a Superman for a Portuguese kid's birthday Sunday. I shouldn't have felt like telling her she embarrassed me enough by being a clown and having a profane clown name and getting her butt squeezed and going on the TV news about it, but I did feel like telling her that.

Instead I said, "All right, Mom."

The Superman getup was blue pajamas with an *S* silkscreened across the chest, a red nylon cape, and shiny black sock-boots. Over that went a Clark Kent ensemble made from a Goodwill suit, the slacks rigged with Velcro seams running down the legs for more dramatic tearing off. A white polyester button-up, glasses with clear lenses, and gelled hair.

The whole Portuguese family came out to greet us, and I was mortified to see Jarita standing next to the birthday boy, her little brother, Joachim. My mom ran down the driveway to wish Joachim happy birthday in her squeaky, high-pitched BJ the Clown voice. What color and animal were his faves? "Green and slow loris," he said. She fished a long green balloon from her back pocket, blew it up, and twisted it into the shape that she made for any favorite animal from approximately otter to bear.

"That's no slow loris," he said.

"Right you are, birthday boy. That is no slow loris!" BJ the Clown said. "It is a near cousin of the slow loris, however. The slow lorisoverine."

Joachim took the green balloon animal. "A slow lorisoverine?"

BJ the Clown winked at Joachim and he darted around back, growling and shouting, "Slow lorisoverine, slow lorisoverine!"

Me and Siel the mime and Willy, an insurance agent who likes wearing a giant party rat costume on the weekends, unloaded the parachute and milk crates of party supplies.

"Hey," Jarita said. "You clean up all right."

"Yeah," I said. "Hey."

I opened the top buttons on my shirt so that she could see the *S*.

"No way!" she said. "You're my brother's man of steel? You going to leap our house in a single bound?"

"I was thinking to, yeah, also maybe bend a few steel bars, save the day, reverse the earth's rotation... You know, the *yuzh*."

Jarita laughed. "Very cool, man. Come on, I'll show you where the action is, and by action I mean twenty sugar-stoned nutballs."

I followed her inside, where we found Jarita's mom and BJ hugging in the kitchen. BJ looked at us, the black pyramids under her eyes smeared. BJ never broke character. BJ did not cry.

Jarita whispered, "The butt-squeezer got my mom, too. She didn't report it."

"Girl talk," Jarita's mom said. The side of her face had a ghost image of BJ's cheek, white with a red dimple.

"Bathroom?" Mom said. "Bud, get Siel and Willy spreading out the parachute would you?"

"Yeah, Mom," I said.

"Yeah, *BJ*," she said.

While BJ and co. did their parachute thing, I sized up the trampoline. Jarita had given me an idea. I dragged the trampoline closer to the house, then went around and climbed onto the roof from the front-porch railing.

At the top, I posed. BJ noticed and got the picture. "Say, Joachim," she said. "Do you hear something?" BJ pointed at me. "Is it a bird? A plane?"

The kids looked. I took the glasses off and unbuttoned my shirt. They cheered when they saw the *S*. I let the sport coat and shirt fall. I yanked the pants, but the Velcro held. I yanked again and whoosh. I stood with my hands on my hips and stared heroically at a cloud.

The rest of the family came into the yard to see. Jarita's mom and dad and Jarita and an older boy. He was holding hands with Jarita. Scott Bevis. He smiled like he couldn't believe his luck.

I peered over the edge of the roof. My sock-boot slipped on a loose shingle and BJ's hand shot to her mouth. It looked a lot higher than it had from the ground, and I was wobbly, but I jumped anyway. I hit the trampoline right where I aimed and it shot me high and far. Superman flew.

It would have been perfect had I got my feet under me, but my shoulder hit the ground first and I buckled. I wheezed. I heard Joachim say, "Is Superman dead?" and I looked up into BJ's clown face. "Breathe, bud," she said. "Breathe."

"Someone must have slipped kryptonite into his pajammies," Scott Bevis said, and Jarita said, "Shut it, Scott."

Siel and the party rat led me to the car while BJ closed things out. I was fine except my shoulder had turned the color of a turnip. I tried to avoid thinking about the torture material Scott Bevis was dreaming up by making it to the last level and going mano a mano against the God-crazed mom, who stomped me with her big red heels, sending me back to the beginning.

*   *   *

We stopped by Albertsons to pick up a few things. BJ leapt around, hamming it up for everyone in the store. She gave me the grocery list and disappeared into the bathroom to change and take off her makeup.

Over the Superman pajamas, I wore the white Clark Kent button-up untucked and the thrift store blazer and Velcro pants. I didn't even pick up my feet, preferring the sound the sock-boots made sliding over the polished linoleum. I found everything except pomegranates. I knew that my mom made a dish with pomegranate seeds, but I had no idea what a pomegranate looked like.

Finally I asked a stock boy a little older than me. I envied him his non-humiliating job. He pointed to a bin of hard-skinned ovals, which I was picking through when I noticed a woman bent over in the meats section. She wasn't decrepit old, but she was older-than-my-mom old. You could tell she had trouble bending over. A man facing me backed toward her. I instantly knew him from the CCTV footage. An instrumental, classical version of "Don't Stop Believin'" played. The stock boy was gone.

When the man's hand fell to her butt, she jumped. He said something to her, snatched a package of meat, and walked away. She stared after him and then her glance met mine. I looked down at the pomegranates.

My mom appeared. She had splotches of white makeup on her neck and her face was shiny. The wig and hat and the baggy bright clothes that made her BJ were stuffed in a beat-up plastic Dillard's bag and she was just my regular embarrassing mom again.

"Did you get everything, bud?" she said.

"Everything except pomegranates," I said.

She picked some up. "You want one that feels heavy for its size. And the skin should be bright red or yellow."

We checked out. I carried the grocery bags, and she looped her arm around my arm. On the elbow tray of the blood pressure machine, just before the exit, lay a package of pork chops—a four-pack of pork chops—the cellophane wet with condensation.

"It was brave, that stunt you pulled today," my mom said.

SELF-PORTRAIT IN AN OPEN MEDICINE CABINET

HOW GOING BLIND IS LIKE LOOKING AT GOOD ART

by ANDREW LELAND

WHEN I WAS A TEENAGER, as I was first realizing that the pleasures I got from art and literature might be deep enough to justify devoting my life to them, I was reading a lot but also spending a shameful amount of time in the basement of Borders Books & Music, trying to determine what else I should be reading by looking at back-cover blurbs and promotional copy.

I remember noticing a theme emerge: a lot of the books I was reading had some version of this back-cover blurb: X's writing *makes the everyday strange*. It's a little embarrassing to admit that the origin, for me, of the idea that art can transform everyday life into something unfamiliar started with promotional copy. But it did.

Twenty years later, this is still something I want from art: a pleasurable deranging of the familiar. For the world, through some magic of the artist's perception, to be made weird—or for the sometimes hidden weirdness of the everyday world to be made clear.

There are a bunch of writers who made this happen for me. Chief among them is Lydia Davis. Here's a story of hers called "Birthday," in its entirety:

105 years old: she wouldn't be alive today even if she hadn't died.

On the one hand, the narrator is making an ordinary, even obvious, observation: very few people live to be 105, so this woman would most likely be dead by now even if she hadn't died when she did, which was presumably years ago. On the other hand, something about the way the line is built makes its statement of the obvious feel more complicated. It reads to me almost like a formal proposition or a paradox: if she hadn't died, how could she not still be alive? The anniversary of her birth becomes a sort of fictional second death. Which is, again, totally ordinary—happens to everybody—but also somehow paradoxical and philosophical and strange.

Here's another one, called "They Take Turns Using a Word They Like":

"It's extraordinary," says one woman.
"It is extraordinary," says the other.

Banal conversation like this lines the periphery of our ears. But by calling this snippet of it a story, and putting it alone on a page surrounded by blank space, Davis has pulled a microscopic detail out of whatever larger narrative might otherwise contain it. She puts great pressure on these two sentences, forcing our attention down into the fissures that grow along the edges of speech.

The title tells us that *extraordinary* is a word these women like, which probably means they use it a lot, which probably means they use it to describe things that, if you seriously consider them, aren't extraordinary at all: social facts, perceived slights, turns of events that happen all the time. But when Davis takes the word and isolates and illuminates it like this, she restores some of the genuine extraordinary to it—even as she points out its misuse.

Work like this sharpens my own awareness of the ways language empties itself of meaning and then refills itself, all day long, on the edges of perception.

Visual art does this, too. The artist Tom Friedman, a master of making the ordinary appear miraculous, took a piece of paper and stared at it for a thousand hours over the course of five years. The empty page becomes supercharged with meaning: the knowledge that Friedman looked at the sheet so intensely changes the way we see it.

Tom Friedman's untitled cereal-box sculpture, created by cutting up nine Total cereal boxes and assembling them into one giant, pixelated box.

In another piece, Friedman took nine boxes of Total cereal, cut them up, and combined them to make one large box. Looking at the sculpture, I see the cereal box and, at the same time, an argument about *how* I see a cereal box. Friedman's choice of the brand of cereal—Total—is part of this idea: when we look at something, what we perceive as a totality is actually built up out of hundreds of little sub-totals, tiny micro-gazes.

This is what my favorite art does: it refines or maybe expands my perception, allowing me to see the world—the everyday world of overheard conversations and cereal boxes and birthdays of dead loved ones—through fresh eyes.

And I think steeping myself in work like this has had an effect on the way I live: I savor these derangements of the banal so much that I encourage

TOM FRIEDMAN, UNTITLED, 1999 © TOM FRIEDMAN; COURTESY OF THE ARTIST AND LUHRING AUGUSTINE, NEW YORK.

them in my everyday life. Driving home from that Borders Books & Music as a teenager, I'd always pass a billboard that, as I glanced at it, appeared to say something incredible:

POISON IS THE FUCK-TEETH OF DESIRE:
ASSOCIATE @ YOUR SEXUAL VILLAGE

I'd be driving, my eyes back on the road, and asking myself: Could there really be a billboard in downtown Santa Barbara that says this?

And I'd really, deeply savor this what-the-fuck moment, luxuriating in it before I glanced up again to reread it, knowing—but consciously pushing away the knowledge—that it didn't, *couldn't*, actually say that. At the last possible moment before driving out of view, I'd look at the sign again and see that, of course, it said something totally ordinary:

POISNER FOR YOUR FAMILY'S TEETH:
DENTAL ASSOCIATES @ SUSSEX VILLAGE

That moment before my perception resolves itself into something ordinary is deeply valuable to me. It's why I go to museums and read literature. It may even be one of the reasons I get out of bed in the morning. It's a sort of living fiction—a semi-willful misinterpretation of my surroundings that might actually tell me something about the world.

Around the time I was driving around Southern California half-intentionally misreading billboards, I noticed that I was becoming much worse than my friends at running through the woods at night on the weekends. After I turned sixteen, I began to have a much tougher time finding my way around at night in general. Eventually, using some pre-Google search engines, I determined that I probably had Retinitis Pigmentosa, or RP, an inherited degenerative retinal condition. I was diagnosed with it when I was nineteen.

RP works like this: in the back of your eye is a bunch of light-sensitive tissue called the retina. The retina is made up primarily of two kinds of photoreceptor cells: cones and rods. Cones handle bright-light and color vision; rods are responsible for peripheral and low-light vision. The main thing RP does is gradually kill off your rods. At first, after a small number of rods die, it manifests only as night blindness. Then, when more die, it becomes tunnel vision, impairing sight during the daytime. Eventually, after enough rods die, RP begins to affect central vision, which can eventually lead to total blindness.

When I was diagnosed, the doctor told me I would experience a gradual decline through my twenties; then, beginning in middle age, the degeneration would become more precipitous. This has pretty much been my experience: at first I stopped driving at night; then, about six years ago, I stopped driving during the day. When I moved to New England last year, I decided to start using a cane full-time in public. This is more to signal to other people that I won't see them when they cross in front of me than it is to actually tap my way around my environment, since I still maintain some central vision—I can still read print, and I can still tell when I have a bad haircut (as I presently do).

Various science and medical websites have posted images to help demonstrate what the world looks to a person with advancing RP. These usually present a picture of something benign—multiethnic kids holding soccer balls, say—tightly cropped so that only the center of the image is visible through a circular frame, everything else blotted out by a field of black. When people ask me what I can see, "I see the world as though I'm looking through a toilet-paper tube" is effective shorthand.

The problem with these images, though, is that they represent what I don't see as a black field. That's really not how it works. I don't feel like I'm walking around with my head covered by a black veil with a small peephole cut out of it. When you look at the world, O sighted readers of McSweeney's, the stuff that you can't see, that lives beyond your periphery—it doesn't register as black, does it? It just doesn't register.

So even if the vision of someone with advancing RP is like a redacted document, with crucial passages blacked out using government-issued Sharpies, the experience of seeing is actually more like the document *after* it's been reformatted and republished with the redactions already elided: you're aware there's information missing, and you might be able to guess what sort of information has been censored, but you can't see which sentences have been blacked out: they're just gone. My brain reformats what I see so that I think I'm seeing a whole image—and I am, even though it's a fraction of what you would see, what I used to be able to.

There are exceptions to this experience of invisible invisibility, cases where I feel I actually can see evidence of my RP. It's in these moments that my experience of vision loss takes on a strange resemblance to the experience of looking at art. In these cases the world doesn't quite look like the world, much the same feeling as I get when I'm looking at that giant meta–cereal box or reading Lydia Davis's microfiction. As with those examples, I experience these derangements of the everyday world in a sort of perceptual twilight, oscillating between the ordinary and the extraordinary, in that dilated moment between my misreading of the billboard and seeing it as it actually reads.

I'm very lucky that I can still read print, even as I brace myself for the coming years when I will likely have to switch to screen readers, audiobooks, and maybe Braille. In the meantime, RP has made me into a new kind of reader: even while I can still read coherently, the chance of a pleasurable billboard-style misreading has increased exponentially. Unlike moviegoers, readers tend to know when the passage they're reading will end—they reflexively glance ahead to see when the sentence, paragraph, or chapter stops. But these days I've been having an almost cinematic experience of reading: chapters end suddenly, without warning. It can have all the shock of a sudden cut to black.

Images have lately been taking longer than usual to resolve themselves in my field of vision. Say I'm on an airplane and there's a person across the aisle and up a row from me: she's wearing a neck pillow that's covered with her overflowing hair, as well as an oversized hoodie with cartoon characters dancing across the front. The first time I see her, there might be several long and wonderful moments where she looks for all the world like a Rachel

Harrison sculpture—the arrangement is wrong, she has no neck, and she seems to be made from bright, injection-molded plastic. Finally my eyes begin to make sense of the image and, like a ghostly Rubik's Cube, she resolves herself until nothing is out of the ordinary.

I've been spending longer and longer stretches in this twilight, where I almost know what I'm looking at, where I'm working hard to correct the mistake but, at the same time, fighting to extend the weird pleasure of the error as long as I can.

The other day I happened to glance at myself in a bathroom mirror, looking for that moment of auto-commiseration I sometimes indulge in as I wash my hands: a quick self-regard before heading back out to bear the gaze of others.

But this time my eyes bounced all over the mirror. Glance after glance, I failed to find anything I might sanely describe as *me*. As I kept searching, I remained unrecognizable to myself, even as I rationally knew that I really was—and had to be—looking at myself in the mirror.

Then, in a beautifully slow dawning, I came to realize that the door to the medicine cabinet was hanging open. What I was seeing wasn't a mirror, wasn't my reflection at all. I realized it was the interior of the cabinet, and that I was looking at shelves of vitamins and medicine bottles.

And I was delighted.

CARAVAGGIO APOLOGIZES FOR THE LOW LIGHTING

by JAMES FOLTA

MAY 12, 1595

Starting a new painting today! Got a bunch of live models (Mario, Francesco, and the Eastside Studio Bambinos) to pose. But I totally forgot to buy candles and my studio was really, really dark. I kept apologizing over and over and I think it made the models uncomfortable, especially Francesco. I had him in this voluminous red shawl and holding sheet music, but no matter how he posed, he cast a huge shadow across Simone. I mean, I could barely see the end of my paintbrush! Hopefully tomorrow's better and brighter...

MAY 13, 1595

Another day of dark painting. Tried having everyone pose one by one near my only window, but it took forever and was useless after noon. Mario, posing as an aghast Roman soldier, kept saying, "Hey, maybe dark paintings can be your thing." I think he was trying to be nice but I turned so red that I was almost glad to be in complete darkness.

MAY 15, 1595

Made a little pyre out of old paintings, brushes, and a dresser I found out back. Gave me only a half hour of workable light but then my neighbor smelled the smoke and burst in. Long story short, it was his dresser and I barely escaped having to duel him.

MAY 18, 1595

Took a few days off to scrounge up some Florins for candles or a big mirror to reflect the light from my window. But of course that same day I got an invite to Salvatore's wine thing and had to spend what little I had on a new and comely tunic. Those parties are a can't-miss opportunity to network with rich Venetian traders with their fancy doublets and ornate codpieces. Maybe with some more patrons, I can finally afford candles. So many candles! Enough candles that everyone will know once and for all that I, Caravaggio, hate darkness and shading!

MAY 19, 1595

I can tell the models hate how dark it is. And now I'm working double time because I have a new commission: a well-connected jurist wants something for his personal chapel. So I needed new canvas and paints and once again had no coin left for candles or brazier fuel. Mamma mia, it's so dark. Prospero almost walked out on me while he was posing as a fiendish rogue. I asked him to lift up his rapier and he snapped back, "It's already up, you just can't see." And he was right. Ugh diary, if I had been able to see his rapier, I would have thrown myself on it right then and there.

MAY 20, 1595

Tried painting outside in the sunlight

and one of the models got hit by a deranged mule. It was a mess. Made it up to them by buying everyone lunch out of my dwindling candle fund.

MARCH 21, 1595
Couldn't sleep last night. I lay awake imagining people in the future saying, "Oh yeah, Caravaggio, he's the one whose paintings are so dark because he couldn't get enough candles. What an idiot!"

MAY 22, 1595
Finally got some candles!! Glory, glory! Just gonna take a quick nap and… Fell asleep with the candles still lit! What is *wrong* with me?!

MAY 27, 1595
Set up an easel outside the studio to draw portraits of couples and raise some quick coin. Of course, who should walk by but the well-connected jurist! He wanted to come up and see the painting he had commissioned. I was beside myself—the piece looks completely insane, it's half in darkness, half in brilliant lighting. The jurist said he loved it, that it was dramatic and drew attention to internal drama, but that means he's either being very nice to me or has no idea how art works. I mean, you can't see the swords! What's the point of painting if you can't see the swords?! I begged him to hang the piece at his out-of-town Umbrian villa instead of in his estate in Rome.

Hopefully in Umbria it'll be out of sight of the big papal movers and shakers. I can just imagine them laughing at my painting, saying, "I can't tell, is this the crucifixion of St. Peter or of St. Paul?"

JUNE 15, 1595
I'm dead, diary. Guess which Pope decided to drop in on his friend's out-of-the-way Umbrian villa?! That's right, *The* Pope! And he said he loved my painting!? Even though I think it looks like it was painted from the inside of Jesus' tomb before He rolled back the rock! *Ugh!* I should just go back to grinding out hacky baskets of fruit and fat cherubim until I die.

JUNE 16, 1595
Now that word's gotten around that The Pope loves the paintings by the guy who doesn't know how candles work, I really have to own this reputation. So from now on, my paintings are going to have the most insane lighting that anyone has ever seen. Let them talk! Now that I don't need it, I used my candle fund to get drunk.

JUNE 23, 1595
Of course, as soon as the darkness-and-shadows thing settled down, word got out that I did a painting of my pals playing cards and lutes. Now everyone's talking about that. If I have to keep painting stuff like this, I'll scream. Why did I ever become a dang painter in the first place?!

THERE ISN'T INGRATITUDE, THERE'S JUST "GHOST GRATITUDE"...

by DORIAN GEISLER

'There isn't ingratitude, there's just "ghost gratitude"—like for the curing of polio. It's not that we're ungrateful. It's that you have to catch the "ghost gratitude," and for this you need a certain kind of net.'

Daniel would say anything to sleep with a woman. He liked sex like a puppy likes bacon.

He was once in this situation: holding a paper cup of coffee (already cold), on crutches, in front a bathroom door outside a Chevron somewhere in Wyoming.

It was with difficulty that he opened the bathroom door. As he was peeing in the urinal, he thought about Becky. Where was she now?

Twenty years later, his leg was healed—and he was married to Sandra. Sandra of the photographic memory.

Sandra of the photographic memory, impeccable integrity, and extreme forthrightness. He knew then that the photographic memory of a spouse is the closest thing to an avenging angel—at least in marriages that might be called 'imperfect.'

Of course, Sandra didn't believe in angels.

ON SCREEN

by KEVIN MOFFETT

HAVE THE SADDEST SUPERPOWERS: an allegiance to birds, a marathon threshold for boredom. I can make a body part ache just by thinking about it. There is squealing in my ears and I'm afraid to ask my wife if she hears it, too. My wife, her name is Corinna, she's a much more natural person than I am. She smiles when she's happy, cries when she's sad. Or when she's frustrated, or nostalgic. Or really happy. I never cry. It's become a problem. My son listens to a song by a retired football player that goes *it's all right to cry, crying gets the sad out* and he's decided that if it's all right to cry, then it is not all right to not cry. Why don't I ever cry? I tell him I cry all the time, just not out loud. In fact, I say, I'm crying right now. This doesn't satisfy him. No matter how much I explain that crying isn't like a train with a set schedule, something you can predict, he wants to know when I plan to cry next. Would you cry if Otis died? he asks. (Otis is our dog.) Of course, I say. Would you cry if you woke up with feet for hands? Without a doubt, I say. Would you cry if you found out you were just a pretend person who disappears when people stop believing in you?

One night, tired of his badgering, I tell him that I will cry on the afternoon of October 18. After school I'll be waiting and while he's eating his snack I will cry like he's never seen me cry before. Sobbing, shoulder-heaving, the whole stinking opera. You'll probably have to call the fire department to stop me, I say. He runs downstairs to tell his mom. He runs back upstairs and circles October 18 on his wall calendar, draws a neat little teardrop inside the circle. Is it okay if we film it? he asks.

Corinna thinks my plan is ill-conceived. She says I'm just burying another time capsule of disappointment for him. Like when I told him the game Candyland was based on a true story. But October 18 is four months away—plenty of time for him to forget about our deal. I say, You know how kids are, one minute they're obsessed with spiders and tractors and the next they're onto pirates and ancient weaponry. Remember that phase he went through where he always wanted to pray to our ancestors before dinner?

It lasted over a year, she says.

I can't even remember the last time I cried, I say. I used to cry all the time. Fireworks, Christmas music, mirrors. Everything used to make me cry. Cats, harps, swastikas, the way Burger King smelled, rain, watching my father shave, puppets, oil stains, Tip O'Neill, clocks.

Start practicing, Corinna says. It'll come back to you.

The morning of the eighteenth my son wakes me up before dawn and says, Today's the day. He crawls atop me and lies with his back flat to my chest. He is impossibly warm. Ever since he was an infant he's loved lying on me and ever since he was an infant I've thought the same thing when he does it: I am the grave and he is the marker. And then: If I don't die before him I'll die very soon after him. He sings, *I know some big boys who cry too.*

While he's at school, I watch old movies. Suffering detectives, cowboys riding slow horses, secretaries gently performing on typewriters, dogs. I start noticing the dogs. All long dead and their puppies and grandpuppies, dead. Otis lies ghost-faced and asleep on his mat, his name monogrammed on it in cursive, even though he can't read, plus he's the only dog in the house. The bony terrier on screen scampers his way through a movie with no idea. He hops on his hind legs, following a hapless prospector around, wanting to be fed. The actor acting and the dog blithely being a dog. My chest tightens. The dog never breaks character. He isn't aware of an audience beyond the man in front of him. The man, finally, offers a steaming turnip, which the dog sniffs at and refuses. It's perfect. Award-worthy. Tears form and fall and I let them. The prospector tries to reason with him but the dog won't be reasoned with, so he feeds the dog his own dinner and eats the turnip himself. I cry and cry, wiping away tears with the sleeve of my T-shirt. I feel agreeably pathetic until I peek at the clock and realize my son won't be home for two hours. I try to ration the sadness, keep it cupped and lit like a flame, but it's brittle, half an inch long. The second the dog is off screen, it's gone.

I spend the rest of the afternoon doing research. I google "how to cry on command" and find lots of websites written by and for amateur actors. Smear some mentholated rub under your eyes, dab some onion juice on your fingers. They all agree that you have to think of something sad, people you love being dragged to their deaths. People you love crying for help in a faraway land and you not hearing them. A bad actor, one site says, cries with every part of his body. A good actor can cry with none at all.

When he gets home, I hand my son a plate of sliced mango and say I will now commence to cry. I lean on the counter, clear my throat, and swallow a few times. I imagine an impatient conductor holding his baton in the air. My son positions his stool right in front of me. He chews and chews and for some reason, my thoughts don't latch onto someone I love, or even the dog in the movie, but a bird. A tiny bird I saw, on a nature show about endurance, that absorbs its own guts to make room for fat and then flies west across the Atlantic without stopping, regrowing its insides along the way. Which is vaguely sad but mostly, I don't know, inspirational. My son waits. I imagine the bird getting tired as it reaches the shoreline and I kind of rhythmically hunch my shoulders, priming the pump. The bird sees the Statue of Liberty—it's a tiny bird with brand-new insides but it knows what the statue means, it can feel liberty weighing down its wings, because liberty is heavy, and it begins to lose altitude. I squint and make pitiful noises. The bird collides with the concrete retaining wall, sinks into the grimy water, and falls slowly to the seafloor. I rub my eyes in hopes of squeezing out some tears. It works. I am crying again, sort of. It feels slightly pornographic: not quite fake and not quite real. My son comes to console me. Rests his hand on my waist. Tells me I'll feel better when I'm done, because he always does.

I used to watch him sleep sometimes. I'd stand over his bed like some ghost haunting the remains of my old life, too stubborn and attached to pass into the next world. I would watch until it felt like I'd disappeared. One time, he started laughing in his sleep, laughing so hard he woke himself up. Imagine. When he opened his eyes he saw me standing there. He didn't ask what I was doing. He just closed his eyes on me. And I was gone.

FORTY-TWO REASONS YOUR GIRLFRIEND WORKS FOR THE FBI, CIA, NSA, ICE, S.H.I.E.L.D., FRINGE DIVISION, MEN IN BLACK, OR CYLON OVERLORDS

by HARIS A. DURRANI

ISTEN CAREFULLY. I got forty-two reasons your girlfriend works for the FBI, CIA, NSA, ICE, S.H.I.E.L.D., Fringe Division, Men in Black, or Cylon Overlords, so drop this tapped line, find the nearest payphone, and take notes.

REASON #1

She won't call you Jihad.

No matter how many times you tell her, she can't get it into her head that it doesn't mean you're going to strap dynamite to your balls, walk into

Penn Station, and blow yourself so bad your head pops off your shoulders.

Truth is she doesn't actually believe that bullshit, but the name does bother her. So she calls you Joe.

You don't complain because everyone calls you Joe, including you. You don't want to admit you're experiencing a black-skin-white-mask cultural inferiority complex, so you assume you're also a spy sent to rat on your own self. You don't know all the details yet. You're like a character in a Philip K. Dick novel. You have no idea which you is the real you. You're waiting for someone from the Impossible Mission Force to arrive with a secret task delivered in a knickknack that'll self-destruct in five, four, three, two, one—*bam!*—because, deep down, you really want to rock hot shades and ride fast cars and scale Burj Khalifas like Tom Cruise.

Jihad means struggle, but you've forgotten that.

REASON #2

She likes you.

For most people this is a good thing. For someone like you, it's too good to be true. She's out of your league. You suspect she's dating you because you're three birds with one stone. Three more notches on her belt. You're her first Pakistani, her first Dominican, and her first Muslim boyfriend wrapped in one. You know that.

You know you're her exotic boy toy.

Even that's too good to be true. Before her, you hardly knew how to talk to a girl. You hardly knew how to look at a girl. And suddenly in comes Glory Drayer with her freckles and her short-short jeans. She's crazy about you. Once you hadn't seen each other for twenty-four hours, and when she caught sight of you from across the school corridor, she ran through the crowd and jumped you like Scooby-Doo.

Too good to be true. You're a nerd, not a player.

The exotic boy toy thing must be an idea she planted in your head. You know the truth. She's here to keep tabs on you, make sure you don't sneak anthrax into school or plot a revolution or pray too many times a day.

The other girls in your calculus class hit on you, too. You suspect they're all in cahoots. Maybe competing agencies. Departmental rivalry is the bane of American national security. You know that for sure.

REASON #3

After you make out on your first date, she puts her ear against your chest and listens. "You're going wild," she murmurs. You blush. She grins and says, "You're gonna get in a whole lot of trouble with me."

Bad girls don't exist. There are only girls pretending to be bad girls. These girls pretending to be bad girls are usually secret agents. QED.

REASON #4

She builds an army of paper robots.

It's taken three months for her to get this far with you because you're not very good at identifying that social convention called flirting. Now that you know she's an agent, you realize why she made those origami animals for you in calculus. You fear they are tiny paper Transformers that will come alive and slit your throat in your sleep. They sit there, red and pink, like a collection of evil dolls from something out of Stephen King.

Foolishly, you keep them by your nightstand.

REASON #5

She thinks you're paranoid.

It's a smart move, getting you to question the depth of your insanity.

You're not actually insane. She's in your head. You need to shut her out.

REASON #6

She asks why you believe in God.

It's an old informant's trick. Goad people to say crazy shit.

You think about it for a while and you don't really have an answer, not then, so you tell her something about the Qur'an being historical, that it's lessons from history, history repeating itself.

"But do you believe it?" she repeats.

You'll realize, later, that you can't rationalize the conviction of your faith. At this point in time, you don't have much conviction because you don't know right from wrong. This is because you're dating Glory. She's good at her job.

REASON #7

She tells you she's okay not having sex.

This is bullshit. Of course she isn't. Or she wouldn't be, if she were for real.

After she helps you remove her bra for the first time—yes, she actually helps you—you tell her you don't know how far this is going, but you're not comfortable *going all the way*. She asks you if it's a personal or a religious decision, and you tell her it's both. She says something about planning to lose her virginity the summer before college, which is now, but she's cool with your request. She smiles and squeezes your hand. You want to tell her you love her.

You've got no idea she's playing you, do you?

REASON #8

You realize she's been pursuing you since seventh grade.

About a month and a half into the relationship, you recall her Save the Tigers project in middle school. You forgot you were in the same class. You remember her years later, asking you questions about your stories in sophomore honors English.

This is when you truly come to terms with that word. *Surveillance*. It freaks you out and you spend a day locked in your room. She bikes to your place, tackles you, and drowns you with kisses. You can't help but feel light. You can't help but reinterpret what you've remembered. She's liked you all along, you tell yourself.

REASON #9

In eighth grade, she traveled the world with her mom and dad.

This is a lie. She was training in Nicaragua. The family pictures are Photoshopped.

By now, at the tender age of eighteen, Glory must be a pro.

REASON #10

She calls herself a nerd.

Pay no heed to this ploy. She clearly has no idea what it means to be a nerd. It's like she's reading from a script written by a washed-up Pentagon bureaucrat whose sole research consisted of a *Lord of the Rings* marathon. For her, *nerd* translates to novice coding, an obsession with indie films, and enrolling in all the honors and AP science classes—which basically every self-respecting stuck-up does in your town, including you—even if she only gets Bs. She's never read Isaac Asimov and the only Arthur C. Clarke novel she can name is *Childhood's End*, not even *2001*, because she had to read it for school. She doesn't understand basic astrophysics, and quantum mechanics only gets her to tease you about being so smart, which you aren't really. When you talk to her about black holes and parallel universes, she tunes out, waits for you to finish, says it's cute, and smothers your lips with hers.

You find this endearing and sincere, but really? She calls herself a nerd? Definitely a spy.

REASON #11

She googles Muslim dating rules and asks, "So if you date me, what am I, a whore?"

This is another attempt to trigger a reaction. Ignore it. She probably wants you to try an honor killing, after which she'll knock you out cold and violate you in a cell in a shithole like Gitmo or Abu Ghraib.

In fact, this is a clear violation of character. She complains to you constantly about red tape at her YMCA job, and always questions the validity of your leftist media sources, yet somehow she'll believe the first result Google spits at her.

You don't tell her any of this. You say, "Don't believe everything you read online," and lay your head against the cafeteria table. She rubs your back and asks you what's wrong.

REASON #12

She tells you not to mumble.

"Say your mind," she says. "Speak like you mean it."

Is she trying to make you incriminate yourself? What crime have you committed? How do you stop yourself from saying the wrong thing?

Before you realize it, you've assumed your criminality.

You don't notice this. You like what she's told you. You like that she wants you to be you.

REASON #13

She doesn't think Apartheid is that bad.

You go to the MoMA and there's an exhibit of Apartheid-era protest art. You find out her African Studies class didn't cover Apartheid. You think this is ridiculous, and you tell her so, and she looks away, mumbling quiet apologetics.

On other occasions, she's been an apologist for everyone from Christopher Columbus to George Bush the Second to your high school's western-centric curriculum. She thinks affirmative action is racist and *Othello* isn't.

She probably brings up *Othello* to fuck with you, see if you go into a breakdown and smother her with a pillow or some shit like that, but you don't, because you assume she's stupid.

Of course, no one is actually this stupid. You're the idiot. Clearly, the only possible explanation is that she's a spy.

On the train home from the MoMA, you calm down. You lay your head on her lap and she strokes the hair from your eyes. You keep looking at her. Her eyes are gray and translucent, reminding you somehow of baby spittle. You have no other way to describe it, that look. It's like a sedative. It's probably hypnosis. She brushes her fingers over your eyelids and tells you, "Rest."

REASON #14

She asks if you think she's dumb and racist.

You don't have a choice. You have to reassess yourself. You have to become understanding. You have to tell her that no, it's cool, she just *doesn't know*.

You know that's bullshit. You know that *doesn't know* is no excuse, especially for a kid who grows up in a ranked school system like yours. Then again all the kids at school think like Glory.

Maybe you can't blame her. Maybe she's indoctrinated. Maybe she's not a spy.

Although you suppose spies get brainwashed, too.

REASON #15

She has a dream your mom won't let the two of you get married because she's not Muslim.

It gets you riled up, but you bite your tongue. You know she's trying to incite you to violence, entrap you for intent to murder. You're not a killer.

REASON #16

You keep dating her.

This is because you are delusional and you think you love her, which is because, again, she's a damn good agent. She's got tomboy charm. She's got long, Celtic hair. She may not be your type, but she's made you redefine what you think your type is.

REASON #17

She says she loves you. You've told her the same thing about five times already.

You're making out half-naked in the back of her car, parked on the hiking trail behind the high school, when a cop pulls up behind Glory's Jeep and scares the shit out of you. You sit straight like a meerkat out of its hole. She takes you by the shoulders and draws you down.

"It's nothing," she says, pressing her hot skin against yours.

You hear a car door shut. The cop's flashlight beam fills the space above you, thick and blue on the roof of her car like the surface of a pool seen from below. The cop screams at the two of you to open the door. He points his flashlight like a scientist peering down his microscope.

"Get out of the car!"

You both duck onto the floor. Glory covers herself.

"Fuck." She fumbles in the dark. "My bra. My fucking bra."

You hand it over.

"Fuck fuck fuck."

"What do we do?" you whisper. "What do we do?"

"I don't know." She wraps her bra around her breasts. "Do something. Fucking do something. Do anything."

She's shaking. You try to rationalize her fear. You tell yourself this guy must come from a competing agency. You've never seen her tremble, never heard her voice falter. She's no longer the tough girlfriend. Not the tomboy. Not the self-declared nerd in ripped short-short jeans. Not the jaded white girl. No longer wears the pants in the family. Not wearing her pants, either.

"Get outta the fucking car!"

You're both yanking your clothes on.

"Whadoido?" It rolls out as one word.

The flashlight beam is on top of you, eddies of light whirling across the dank upholstery.

"Do something, dammit!"

You reach around the front seat, grab your windbreaker, swing it around your bare torso, and launch out the door, jaw clenched. You tighten every muscle in your body, like a Jedi Knight rushing consciously into an ambush. Like Wolverine tensing, bracing himself for the pain of releasing his claws.

"Can I help you, Officer?" you ask, looking him in the eye. "Is there something wrong?"

"Park's closed. What're you doing here?"

"Sorry, Officer. We didn't know."

He takes you aside and questions you. Name, age, address, school. He flashes a light in your eyes to check if you're tripping. Your bravery dissipates. You stutter and shiver, asking if this is going on your permanent record. The repeated answer is "No," but you know what he really means: *Shut it, pretty boy.*

He sends you back and calls for Glory.

She returns ten minutes later and drives the two of you off the dirt path. The cop waits behind the wheel of his car, headlights filling the Jeep. He's watching you.

You want to know what he asked her.

"He wanted to make sure you weren't raping me," she says.

You listen to the crickets and the wind in the trees.

You find another secluded spot in town, where she parks her car and climbs into the back with you. She slips your finger between her legs and asks you to pleasure her. She makes sounds as if she likes it and she gives you instructions so you don't bruise her, which you'll do anyway. It is your first time trying anything like this. She claims it's hers, too. It isn't sex, not strictly, but it's close.

When you're done, she asks you to do it again.

"Do you know why?"

"Why?" you say, looking up.

"Because I love you, Joe. I love you."

"I love you, too," you say, believing it in the moment.

Obviously, the run-in with the cop is a setup leading to her reveal. That way you'll believe her. Of course, you don't believe it's a setup. You believe you're in love.

REASON #18

Your English teacher hates her.

He says she has a problem with authority. Secret agents planted in high schools always have problems with authority. They know they're better than this. She must have failed her last mission. You're her punishment.

She is good at hiding it. If you truly knew what was going down—which you don't—you'd decide to believe ignorance is bliss. That's where you are now. Bliss.

REASON #19

On her nineteenth birthday she sidles up to you, dancing to the radio. She crosses her wrists behind your neck and asks you to promise to love her forever.

This is an impossible request. It only happens in movies. It's not genuine. It can't be.

You find yourself compelled to say yes.

REASON #20

There's a raccoon on the fence outside her car, watching the two of you make out.

You know it's not a raccoon. It might be an alien. The interstellar community has some vested interest in you, and they're competing with the government to farm your brain.

Or else it's a mechanized drone. You can tell by the impossibly white eyes and the perfect strips of gray and black fuzz, barely distinguishable in the haze bleeding from the dim streetlamp across the road. Glory is as shocked as you are. Her eyes are large and wet. She has yet to dig up any militant dirt on you, and you bet her boss in D.C. thinks she's doing a shitty job. He's probably set aside a small budget so his department can send animatronic drones to keep an extra eye on Glory. Make sure she isn't doing her job wrong.

To you, at that moment, it's just a pervy raccoon. As far as you're concerned, she's doing everything right.

REASON #21

You love her. Again.

You'd fallen out of love for a while. Or maybe it wasn't real until now.

You need to go to a robotics team meeting. The freshmen under your mentorship have no idea what they're doing. You have a competition in a few weeks, and you have to be there tonight. But Glory and your friends are going bowling. Glory begs you to come. Her friend Carrey tries to guilt you into it. Carrey's your how-to-date-Glory manual, your human Siri for the labyrinth of young love. She got you to ask Glory out for the first time, after you were holding hands for a week without any real action. You suspect she's in league with Glory's agency.

"Joe," Carrey says, "you need to spend time with your girlfriend. She's my best friend. She really likes you. Forget this robotics stuff this one time. Pete's coming with Moira. He's not going to your robot stuff, and he's on the team."

Glory's in the bathroom. You've just seen a movie at her place.

"I dunno," you say, placid, "I need to make sure these kids get their act together."

"Suit yourself."

You decide on bowling. What choice do you have?

Glory doesn't know Carrey has had a talk with you. She stopped begging before you even told her you'd decided to join their night out, and you're in her car on the way there. You've done that thing you do, where you put your hand on the shift and she puts hers on top, guiding the Jeep in and out of gear, left hand on the wheel. She drives stick.

"If you really need to go to your robot thing, you should go," she says.

Your eyes meander from the road to her. She glances at you and smiles.

"Really?"

"Really. I won't mind. Do what you got to do. I'll drop you off."

You grin and rest your head against the window. "Thanks, Glory." You exhale slowly.

On the shift, she massages the back of your hand with her thumb.

"No need to thank me."

It's as if she's read you. She probably has read you. She's a secret agent. They read people for a living. Except in your head you believe she understands that this small decision means something to you. That she cares.

She dials up the volume on her CD player. A song is playing. It's cacophonous with words you can't hear but have to pretend to understand. The kind of song YouTubers spoof with weird lip-syncs.

"'Fake Palindromes,'" she says.

You catch a piece of the lyrics. It's as if you've popped up briefly from beneath turbulent waters and caught the interrupted shriek of an onlooker before the waves take you back into muffled, fluid chaos.

... Monsters...

"What's that supposed to mean, 'Fake Palindromes'?"

... Jesus, don't you know that you coulda died, you shoulda died
with the monsters that talk, monsters that walk the earth...

"It's a song, silly." She squeezes your hand on the shift. "Listen. This part, here—"

All you hear is something close to white noise.

"I don't get it. Sorry, my taste in music sucks—"

"Oh, Joe." She dials it back. "Right... here!"

You hear it then. The words emerge from the noise almost melodic, not beautiful but with rhythm. Like a mundane conversation, overheard, echoing down an air duct and imbued gradually with a song not its own.

... and she says, "I like long walks and sci-fi movies"
if you're six foot tall and East Coast–bred...

Glory yelps. "Just like you, Joe! Just like you."

The song finales in a riot of disjointed sound, somehow mellow.

You think the song is silly, the science fiction reference included. It's another thing Glory thinks will tap into your inner nerd. This time you don't mind. She doesn't get you, not totally, but she's trying. She's tried harder than anyone else you know. She gets you better than anyone else you know. No one really does understand you, including yourself, but she almost does. You hold no suspicions. No conspiracies, no qualms about aliens in your midst, no multiverse theory. None of that. If any of it is true, it's irrelevant.

Her eyes are gray and sparkling. Headlights from the opposite side of the road circle her pupils like neon bytes of data speeding along a racetrack in Tron cyberspace.

This is when you know with conviction that you love her. You say the words in your head.

I love you. I love you. I love you. I love you Glory Abigail Drayer.

REASON #22

You don't know how to make the secret agent argument anymore.

You're tired of it. You really like this girl. She's the best thing that has ever happened to you. For the first time, you question your doubt. Maybe she is who she says she is.

REASON #23

She asks if you pray five times a day.

"Yeah," you say, as if apologizing for something.

You're not sure if this counts as a good reason to say she's covert ops. But it bothers you.

REASON #24

You have another fight, this time over what you'll watch at your house for movie night with her friends.

Your fights are always over mindless crap like this. You know it's deeper. You know it's about being flexible and supportive in the little things and that guidance-counselor bullshit. She admires your confidence, your adamancy. In fact, this is why she likes you. But sometimes it's too much, she says.

You make up and make out. It seems too easy. You suspect you may have slipped from this universe into an overlapping one, where the rules of physics are subtly off-kilter. Glory could be a Fringe agent sent to retrieve you, occupying a doppelgänger as part of the extraction mission. But you can't seem to read her signals.

REASON #25

She's not convinced by socialism.

You try to convince her but it's not her cup of tea. You don't know if it's yours anymore, either, but you persist because it's all you believe anymore. Railing against the system. You hate living in a town that's ninety-six–percent white. It bothers you in a way you won't admit that your girlfriend is a stereotypical rich white chick who doesn't think she's a stereotypical rich white chick even though she is.

It bothers you that you're another rich white kid like her, no matter the color of your skin. Snobby and dog-eat-dog and well-meaning and liberal and subconsciously racist.

REASON #26

One night when the two of you lie scrunched side by side in the backseat of her Jeep, she looks deep into your soul and asks, "Joe, what are you most afraid of?"

"I dunno," you say.

She locks the fingers of one hand with yours.

"C'mon, Joe."

"War? Injustice?"

"Really?" She laughs.

"Yeah," you say.

But that's a lie.

What do you really fear? Spiders? The dark? You're kind of afraid of the dark. But no. You're afraid you don't know yourself. Are you your DNA, the color of your skin? Are you nurture, this hellish verisimilar utopia called the modern state and its mass production of objects and people like you? Are you history, the Dominican Republic, Hispaniola, Italy, Germany,

Corsica—Pakistan, India, the King of the Pashtuns, a nomadic Jewish tribe crossing pre-modern Afghanistan? Do you belong to any of these? And if you belong to no civilization, do you belong at all?

You remember playing on the beach as a kid. Mom asked if you wanted to play with your friend Andrew Chen. You said no. You wanted to play with Jon Wyce.

"He's vanilla," you told her.

That is what you fear most, that that kid is lurking around inside of you, whispering in your ear like a symbiotic parasite, latched to your consciousness like a leech, incapable of eradication without obliterating a part of who you are.

REASON #27

You give her a box of chocolates and she tells you her family calls you "a keeper." She says you're the best boyfriend she's ever had.

You believe her because you still love her.

REASON #28

You think you're unappreciative of her because you still harbor these feelings about her being in the CIA or NSA or FBI or ICE or S.H.I.E.L.D. or Fringe Division or Men in Black or Cylon Overlords.

They bother you, these thoughts. They are very dark and wrought with conviction. Conspiracy theorists bear no dearth of conviction.

You are deeply troubled. You suspect this is evidence that Glory has tampered with your brain.

REASON #29

She calls you baby the morning after prom, when you wake up next to her.

You rub noses and sniff each other's halitosis. Neither of you minds. You like it like this, without ornament. She's not the kind of girl who's into lipstick or nail polish. You dig that. You tell her so, and she appreciates this.

In the morning sun, her dirty-blond hair is gold and her light freckles disappear.

"Do you think the freckles make me less than pretty?" she asks.

"No," you say. "You're perfect the way you are."

She puts her ear against your chest and listens. She's as quiet as your heart.

REASON #30

She stops calling you baby.

REASON #31

When you tell her you love her, she says, "Yeah."

REASON #32

You start praying that God will end it for you.

You wonder whether you can't end the relationship yourself because you still love her or because you simply lack the balls.

Either way, if you were going to become a terrorist or a revolutionary or an enemy of the state or a telekinetic mutant emissary for Earth's evil alien invaders or the Avengers' next villain or whatever the Feds suspected you'd become, you won't become that thing. You've lost your edge.

She wins. The system wins.

REASON #33

She returns from a weeklong trip with Carrey and the two of you are in the back of her Jeep within the hour.

You're making out topless when you separate your lips from hers and press your bodies together, tucking your chin over her shoulder and tracing your fingers along the chilled, bare ridge of her spine. You've missed her.

"Thank you," she says.

You keep holding her. "What do you mean?"

She pulls away gently and points at the road, where two cars just sped by.

"For covering me." She smiles.

You stare at the headlights across the trees as they decelerate near the opposite intersection.

"Oh," you say.

You had no idea.

You suggest going one step further that night, doing something she's wanted to do for a while. She hesitates. She knows you had no idea about the cars. It's not like she's an agent. It's like she's actually hurt. This boggles you. She's gone so undercover that she's gone native. She's apparently forgotten her mission, as you never had yours. There's a kinship in this, that you are both lost.

REASON #34

You're still waiting for your assignment-declaring knickknack from the Impossible Mission Force that will self-destruct after five, four, three, two, one—*bam!*

You're hoping it will tell you who the hell you are and what your mission is, because you have no idea what you're doing. Not that you've ever had any idea what you were doing. You're spiritually dead, in a no-man's-land of the soul.

She's got to be a Cylon, a sexy cybernetic thing from deep space sent to unravel humanity's darkest secrets from your mind. Nothing else could do this to you, take you apart not to question who you are but to make you realize you never knew who you were. Interrogation at its finest: subtle, alluring, hollow. You're near the end. You're a shell, a carcass, a desiccated thing.

REASON #35

She dumps you.

You see the signs. She doesn't want to meet at night. When she picks you up, wearing her dark red tank top and short-short jeans, she makes sure to say hi to Mom and Dad, like she knows it's the last time she'll see them. You go to Subway. She doesn't let you pay for the two of you. She mentions her first kiss on the ride to the beach. It was during *Iron Man*; this makes you jealous. You eat in silence beside the shore and stare into the gray clouds.

"Joe," she says. "We need to talk."

You two are incompatible, she explains. You have different interests. You're heading to college. Long-distance never works.

You nod, remembering your debates over Shakespeare, Conrad, Mandela, and Marx.

"I've been a jerk to you," you admit, not sure if it's true. "I've been meaning to say sorry."

"No, it's not that."

You breathe. "I've been meaning to end it myself. I didn't know how."

She doesn't have anything to say. It's like HQ put her on pause, afraid her cover's blown. *Why would he consider the idea?* HQ is probably thinking. She did such a great job wooing you, understanding you, that it's hard to comprehend. How you could you have fathomed breaking up with her yourself unless you knew she was an agent?

The reality is you've forgotten your paranoia. You no longer think of her that way. You no longer think of her in any way.

REASON #36

Before she drives you home—yes, that happens after all this—you embrace one last time.

"I think I loved you," you say.

"If you loved me, you'd know."

REASON #37

She wants to meet after the breakup. Over pizza, you are telling her something about Congress and the left and the right when she stops you to ask, "Wait, which one's Republican, left-wing or right?"

It's not possible to be that dumb, is it? She's playing you. She's got to be. You're not crazy. You know you're not crazy. She's got to be a secret agent or an informant or something. This can't be real.

REASON #38

She shoots you in the face.

It's a dream but you're certain it's real. It's a vivid dream, the kind you won't forget for years. You're running through a glass tunnel that winds its way through the canopies of some forest. The town is chasing you, including the principal. The principal is a sleazeball, lets the rich white kids do whatever they want and lets their parents pester and sue the teachers dry and rolls around in his open-topped blue Corvette like some kind of hotshot, which he is, because your high school is ranked first in the state.

You open a door and your best friends are waiting for you. Glory is standing there in front of a big white van under a vast gray dome, like a spaceship hangar in *Star Trek*. She's a surprise for some reason. Dream logic indicates she's not supposed to be there, in your head, but she is.

She brings a hot, black thing between the two of you and clicks.

You wake up terrified. If you ever had thoughts about overturning this racist piece of shit town, you forget them. You believe this is proof that inception is real.

REASON #39

She gives you a call from college and says she's changed. She thinks about life differently. You're not sure what that means. You think she's defected.

REASON #40

She is a spy.

It's obvious now. It's empirical. She got in your head and shot you in the face and now she's fallen off the grid. No one knows where she is.

This surprises you. You never believed it was true. You thought it was an elaborate game you'd played in your own head, a fancy of your imagination. You're bitter. You liked her. You never saw it ending.

What is it you miss? Do you miss being in love? Do you miss her?

She's a part of you now. She's left a piece of herself inside of you, in your convictions, your fears, your desires.

You wonder how the Pentagon decided you were such a massive security risk that they were willing to commission someone for six years to keep tabs on you. The national security budget dwarfs any other. You always wondered where all that money goes.

It freaks you out. You don't trust anyone again.

REASON #41

You look up "Fake Palindromes" and play it on loop for hours.

You believe that Glory programmed your attachment to her, a hypnosis, and that there's a sensory trigger that will release you from the neural bond. A sensation that'll set you free from whatever it is that makes you miss her. You're pretty sure this trigger is somewhere in "Fake Palindromes."

If it is, you can't find it.

REASON #42

You're afraid you've never loved and that you never will.

At least you got to date a secret agent. Maybe that will land you a few numbers down the line. It's like a scar. Chicks dig scars, don't they? Or is that just a thing people say?

Don't let the next one pretend to understand your nerdgasms or your racial confusion. Tell her you believe every word of the Qur'an and that you pray five times a day and that Apartheid is real and Shakespeare is a racist pig. Tell her your name is Jihad and it means struggle and that's what people call you, and if she doesn't call you that too then she can go to hell. Most importantly, make sure she doesn't work for the government.

EM JAY

by LUCY CORIN

THE MAILBOX WAS SHAPED like a tunnel, so M. (for short) looked into it when she got to it across her yard. On the science-fiction channel, it would morph into a tubular wormhole. On the channel with kids' shows, a kid would sit up in a sun-drenched bed. Similar graphics would mean *dream*. Kid shakes his head to get rid of the dream like water, like bugs. Kids rarely have lunch boxes that look like mailboxes anymore. When you mail something you are going for that folded space of reach-out-and-touch, trading similar sandwiches that still matter. As an evolution, M. knew, email was the brushed-off dream of infinite contact, an all-meta-all-the-time strip show of communication. She looked into the mailbox knowing it would contain messages from *entities* if anything. But looking in is a physical expression of desire and desire is the tunnel vision of sentience. It's all a little automatic.

When they were teens, M.'s sister, J. (for short), had realized a brain disorder, and now, many years later, M. had begun to read her own experiences via imagining it. Not all the time, but definitely when she felt acute desire for contact, for the childhood sister feeling of being effortlessly on the same page that had been severed by the disorder. Among other things, the disorder often collapsed the literal and the figurative, and this became, for M., emblematic of other desires. She sometimes went to the mailbox out of habit and stared in, thinking of J. on the other side of the country, and sometimes the other side of the world, sometimes literally *and* figuratively, as if something might come in the mailbox from her or someone like her, rather than the entities that sent mail these days that you never met, heard of, or signed up for. Looked into that mouth. Imagined a letter she could write that would mean something.

M., as a child, made a dollhouse baby's bed from matchsticks. She'd used an X-Acto for the first time, painted it with acrylic paints, and, only once it was dry and cute, saw that it was out of scale, just too-big enough that what were those dolls doing with that baby, how would it ever have come out of them. The girls shared the dollhouse, and in its bathroom, a narrow space between two larger rooms, their mother had painted a window and a tree outside, explaining about ventilation, fire codes, and claustrophobia. It was unclear whether, when the dolls were looking at the little painting, they were meant to be looking out a window or looking at a painting of a window. Also, the dolls were little dressed mice the size of real mice, made of real fur that might have been actual mouse fur. M. was the child who could not put a bed in the dollhouse unless the bed fit the house and the doll-mice fit in it. J. was the child who put the bathtub on the porch and paper flowers in the chimney. A little friend who came over took her socks off and put them in the bedroom and M. and J. both said "*No!*" and yanked them out like you put out a fire. When M. came home to visit from college, a new kitten had eaten most of the mice. When she came home again, the kitten, grown, slept curled in the mice's master bedroom. When J. went home to their mother for one of her recoveries, she wrote a letter to M.

"You know what she put in the room with me?" she asked in the letter, as if they were face to face. "That old dollhouse. Like I'm a child. She wants me trapped in this house forever. She likes me here, on drugs. You know they do that to prisoners." It's true that their mother was multifaceted.

On television, in 1992, aliens captured Captain Picard of the Starship Enterprise, put him in a void-like chamber, stripped him, surgically embedded an electric shocker near his heart, and pronounced him without rank or privileges of person, with no identity other than human. In a room like a black box theater, his torturer shined four lights on him and told him to say he saw five. The war between the species and the specifics of the incident leading up to this disappeared. "Say you see five." In the climax we know that Captain Picard does see five lights, though we see only his head in darkness, and then he lies to his torturer and says *four*. It's all an ode to some other classic sci-fi moment you can look up. In their twenties, M. gave J. a bright red lipstick that took guts to wear, and J. wore it a lot—it was a successful communication between sisters. But once the brain disorder picked up, J. said, "You know red is blood. You know it's vagina, word-hole, fuck-hole." What if you are the child whose hands approach the rooms and stop at the threshold because you are about to feel your hands touch your brain?

"But J! There's nothing wrong with your vagina!"

That'll make you shut your mailbox.

By then, M. was back inside on the couch where she belonged, dozing with the TV on mute for commercials. Her enormous hand put the bathtub in the toilet, and then put the bathtub in the bathtub down the toilet and so on.

SOME DRAWINGS IN JAPAN

story and illustrations by JASON POLAN

mARVEL
COMICS
1

ROPPONGI HILLS
TOKYO CITY VIEW
4·23·2017

SUMO

I was in Japan earlier this year for a project and had the chance to meander around a little. I had mentioned to my friend Risa that I was interested in seeing sumo. I wanted to draw the wrestlers if I could. She said it wasn't really the season but maybe we could see them training somewhere. She called around and I think it was a bit of a stretch but one of the trainers at one of the places said we could come there one morning to see them working out.

I got to the train stop where we were meeting early so I went to a convenience store called Family Mart. I got this really good melon bread (that I want again right now).

We met on the corner and walked over. The place was little and nothing special from the outside but really impressive inside. We took off our shoes and there were four pillows on the ground for us

HARUKI MURAKAMI'S OLD POST OFFICE

POST OFFICE 4.24.2017

to sit on (there were two strangers there doing the same thing we were doing). About eight large guys were on the dirt floor that was a step down from where we were sitting. They were taking turns wrestling each other or doing exercises or drinking water or sweeping the dirt. There was one guy that was a little smaller (maybe he was younger?) and he was really being pushed physically by the other wrestlers.

He was making this really intense guttural noise and at one point I moved my sketchpad from my lap to behind me because I thought he was going to puke on us.

The coach yelled out loud orders. (I didn't know what he was saying; he just sounded like any coach.) He was sitting next to us. I was beginning to get a little uncomfortable on the floor (because I am so out of shape—this seemed like a metaphor

HEDGEHOG
IN HARRY
HEDGEHOG
CAFE
HARAJUKU
4.24.2017

~$86
MANGO

At
KYOBASHI
SEMBIKIYA

DUCK
IN YOYOGI
PARK
4.24.2017

THERE
IS A MAN
HOLDING A
HAWK.

for something at the time, getting uncomfortable as I watched strangely strong men exert this amount of energy) so I rearranged a little. After a couple minutes, my feet started to fall asleep so I turned a little again. I was kind of embarrassed because there were only four of us and I was the only one squirming all over every couple of minutes. I could hold a position for a bit and then I would need to rearrange my legs.

The coach continued to yell at the wrestlers as they took turns plowing into each other. It sounded like a strong clap when they would embrace in the middle. I drew several pictures that all mostly ended up looking the same because they were all large men pushing against each other.

An even bigger clothed wrestler man walked in. Risa nudged me to make sure I realized he was there. I got the idea that the enormous

NEWSSTAND IN FRONT OF SHIBUYA MARK CITY 4·28·2017

guys we were watching were younger wrestlers that were training and were not even as enormous as the older, more experienced professionals. After a couple more minutes I rearranged again.

Just then, the coach stood up, walked behind a sliding door, grabbed a little folding chair, and handed it to me. It was about 130 percent embarrassing but I thanked him a lot, unfolded it, and sat on it.

I couldn't figure out if it was because I was driving him crazy, or if he actually just wanted me to feel better (I assume about fifty-fifty).

We left a few minutes later, after thanking the coach and another trainer (that I think may have been the one Risa talked to on the phone). It felt weird to be outside. We could hear them through the window as we tied our shoes. We got coffee and went to a park.

PLEASE RESERVE CONFERENCE ROOM AHEAD OF TIME

BY DAN KENNEDY

That's all, really, just reserve it ahead of time. And don't draw stick figures with dicks on the dry-erase board. Someone did that last time and Samantha was distressed by the whole situation and she was yelling about stick men with huge dicks, and some of you (like Kelly) made the mistake of laughing. Anyway, nobody has yelled about men with big genitals since Janice dumped Craig from Sales. And she was yelling that in the parking lot, so...

SIGNS IN YOUR WORKPLACE ✂ PLEASE FEEL FREE TO POST THESE OFFICE SIGNS IN YOUR WORKPLACE ✂ PLEASE FEEL FREE TO POST THESE OFFICE SIGNS IN YOUR W

ORANGE JULIUS

by KRISTEN ISKANDRIAN

OKAY, DOROTHY THOUGHT. So they'll have a memory of being locked in a shower. One day it will probably seem funny. And it's good for them to know, she reasoned, that parents are human beings. That they, too, get angry. Dorothy had a vision of telling a friend—she wasn't sure which one, she'd have to choose carefully—about this day, this moment, and the friend saying, Oh Dorothy, don't be so hard on yourself.

All her life, people had been telling her to stop being so hard on herself. Which was confusing, since it seemed clear that the person she was generally the hardest on was actually two people, two small people she'd admitted into this world through her own fallible flesh. Is a criminal who feels guilt—is a murderer who feels guilt—hard on themselves? At what point was it necessary to be harder on oneself and softer on others?

Everyone was in a frenzy to be forgiven.

She was mid-thought when she heard the key in the lock. Lewis appeared next to her, knew. "It's okay," he said. He put an arm around her.

"Is it?" she asked. She wished he would be mad at her.

"Where are they now?"

"I put them in the shower and told them not to come out."

Lewis paused. "Is the shower on?"

"No!" she said. "God, no. I'm not a monster."

"Let me take over," he said. "Why don't you take a walk or something."

Dorothy looked out the window. The early spring sun was so pretty, now starting its slow descent. She really had wanted to play with the girls, swing on the swing set, do some chalk in the driveway. Sometimes, in those contained, controlled activities, she could feel like other mothers, the ones whose enjoyment of their kids seemed pure and instinctual.

"Okay," she said. "I guess I'll do that." As she was putting her sneakers on by the front door, Dorothy heard Lewis head downstairs toward the bathroom. A moment later, she heard shrieks of joy.

"Daddy Daddy Daddy!"

Dorothy left, but not before she heard Lewis ask, "Was Mommy being silly? Was she playing a silly game with you?"

More than once, Lewis had told Dorothy how his coworker dosed her eighteen-month-old with Benadryl when she went to the beauty salon for her two-hour wash and set.

"Benadryl!" he said.

Dorothy would give a gentle murmur of shared horror, but really, it sounded nice, a good scrub with a baby sleeping soundly in her arms, the heat from the dryer and the heat in her lap anchoring her like some elemental, blameless thing.

Mornings, Dorothy would wake up with an with an asphyxiating combination of dread and hope. She would fight the urge to hit the snooze button and force herself into the shower, where she would resolve under the pelting hot water to have a good day, a patient day, a no-yelling day, where she would remind herself that these were *children*. Each night, flossing her teeth next to Lewis at the sink, she would know that she had failed—failed to have not-yelled, because the nature of rage is that it has no memory, no safety switch—and, over time, it became harder to share her sense of failure with him, to ask to be absolved.

There was that time when, on the way to the depressing Air and Space Museum, Dorothy reached behind her *while driving* and snatched the doll the girls had been arguing about and threw it out her window. A long honk blasted from the conversion van whose windshield it bounced off.

Objectively speaking: her children were not great children. They seemed to do best—putting on shoes, cleaning up the playroom—under duress. Kindness and gentleness enacted upon them did not succeed in making them kind and gentle.

One ordinary Saturday, after ballet, while the girls were cashing in their hour's worth of TV time and Lewis was working at his computer, Dorothy reheated a cup of coffee from the morning and read a news story on her phone about a homeless woman in California who birthed her baby in the toilet of a sandwich shop, left him there, and staggered back out into the street, bleeding heavily. The story had just broken earlier that day, and although Dorothy forced herself to put down her phone a few times to wash dishes and fold laundry, she kept checking in, refreshing the site to see if new details had been released. The baby was found alive, upright in the shallow water, and rushed to the hospital. The mother was located a block or so away at an auto mechanic's, dazed and disheveled, and taken to the same hospital.

The story brought Dorothy an overwhelming sense of calm. Toilet Baby, she was convinced, was destined for incalculable greatness. Her own daughters were going to muddle around in mediocrity, she thought wincingly, interning into their thirties and wheedling her and Lewis for rent money.

In Switzerland—and Dorothy knew this because she'd read an article entitled "15 Fascinating Facts About Parenting in Europe"—parents let kids as young as three and four walk to the playground alone. In Sweden (same article), babies were bundled into strollers and placed outside for naps, even in subzero temperatures. Brisk air was thought to be a cure-all. Depression rates in both countries—for children and their parents—were up to 75 percent lower than in the United States.

Dorothy heard, for the fourth time that morning, the opening bars of the *My Little Pony* theme song. It was time to turn off the TV. But it was also peaceful, and what was she always saying to Lewis? She needed more peace. She stood at the counter, the loose threads of an appalling idea tickling her brain. She considered Toilet Baby. She considered Sweden. What if she could reprogram the kids to be better? What if she could reprogram herself to be better? Absently, she opened a tub of cream cheese but couldn't decide what to put it on. She stood licking it off a knife, her pensiveness feeling like the plush bathrobe she never had time to wear. She tried to remember what it was like to be fully dry before pulling on her clothes. The servility, she thought, has got to stop. Who was it helping? All along she'd believed that *spare the rod and spoil the child* was two directives: first, spare the rod, and after you've done that, spoil the child. This was how she herself had been raised. Nobody hit her. Nobody hollered. She wasn't rich-kid-on-a-sitcom spoiled, but when she really thought about it, she couldn't think of a thing she had really wanted—besides a trip to Mexico her senior year of high school—and not gotten. Now she knew that the maxim was meant to be causal: by sparing the rod, it warned, you will undoubtedly spoil the child.

Lewis had been raised by his stepmom, who beat him with a shoe at least once a month.

Consider this man, Dorothy said to the invisible jury, who was raised in terror and now barely even yells at his kids. Who can predict what will lead to what? And it's not as though—here she paused to take in the entire courtroom, the press, the judges, all of whom had her face—I *hit* my children.

She put the knife in the sink, feeling satisfied.

There is a certain giddy, if cautious, relief that comes with realizing that every nature/nurture theory in the book is utter bullshit. The only bottom-line, sure-fire certainty is: Nobody Fucking Knows. There's no evidence to suggest that the boy who cried wolf didn't cry wolf the next time he had the blessed chance. We are supposed to take on faith that he had the wickedness scared out of him, but we don't know for sure.

Later that Saturday afternoon, Dorothy didn't want to admit her excitement. That seemed like taking it a step too far. But it had been so long since she'd had a plan, and this felt like a really good one. Everyone just needed to *relax*. Wasn't Montessori once considered controversial, too? The kids and Lewis thought they were going to the mall for dinner and a carousel ride and Orange Julius and maybe, depending on behavior, a stop into the toy store.

They pulled up to the mall entrance and Dorothy instructed Lewis to stop. "Why here?" he said.

"Just do it," Dorothy said, keeping her voice breezy. She hopped out and opened the back passenger door. She felt light as air.

"Go ahead and unbuckle, Delphine," she said, as she released Iris from her car seat. She faced the two girls on the sidewalk. People, families, streamed past them.

Dorothy unfolded a twenty-dollar bill in front of Delphine's face. "Do you know what this is?"

"A dollar? Gimme!" Delphine said, grabbing for it.

"Twenty dollars, actually. That's enough for you and your sister to get dinner, dessert, and a ride on the merry-go-round."

"What about a toy?" Delphine asked. Iris was kneeling, picking up a small pebble. She collected them.

"You have to pass the test to get a toy. You're going to take your sister inside, all by yourselves, and buy some food, and eat nicely at a table, and throw away your trash, and then get tickets for the merry-go-round. I trust you to take care of your sister. I know you can do it." Dorothy folded the bill and put it in the pocket of Delphine's little jeans.

Delphine's eyes were huge, though not fearful, exactly. "Is this a—adventure?"

Dorothy nodded solemnly. By this point Lewis had put the hazards on and come around the front.

"What's going on?" he asked, looking at Dorothy.

"We're having a adventure, Daddy! Me and Iris are going to buy things all by ourselves!"

Lewis squeezed Dorothy's arm, hard.

"Get back in the car, Daddy," she said, her voice even.

For whatever reason, he did.

"We'll be back very soon! Take care of each other and have fun!" Dorothy gave them each hurried kisses and turned them around so their backs were to her. "Go, march. The adventure begins now!"

Lewis's mouth was hanging open. He was trying to remember whether this was something they'd discussed, perhaps late at night in front of the TV, where his eyes always glazed over and Dorothy always became her most talkative self. Had he dozed off?

The girls hesitated for a moment, then ran toward the entrance, holding hands and giggling.

"Dorothy," Lewis said as she got into the driver's seat, his voice reedy, "what in God's name is happening?"

Dorothy pressed down on the gas pedal. She opened up the sunroof. The sky was streaked pink and orange and blue, a gorgeous sunset. "It's good for them," she said, and joined the line of cars in the right-turn lane.

"What's good for them?" Lewis was coming to life, finding his anger, still not yelling. "Abandoning them at a busy mall to be kidnapped or—?"

"Nobody's kidnapping them. Do you know how many things we do on a daily basis to avoid worst possible scenarios, the rarest scenarios? That's not living, Lewis! They're going to have fun. It's a good exercise for them. Even if they're a little afraid—it's not going to kill them." Dorothy put her signal on, adjusted her mirror, merged onto the busy road.

Lewis looked helplessly out the window. "Do they even know our cell numbers?"

"They won't need them. We'll be back before they're even on the carousel."

Lewis looked sick. "You know what, hon," he said, "just U-turn up here and take me back. I'll stay with them. You take the night off. Go and do whatever you need to do, and come get us when you're ready." Lewis sounded near tears. "Let's just do that, okay?"

Dorothy couldn't tell whether her exhilaration was from feeling a total sense of control, or the complete opposite. At the next light, she made a right, then two lefts, pulling into the back parking lot of the apartment complex they'd lived in years ago, before Lewis's big promotion. Delphine had been conceived in that crappy two-bedroom, where the toilet always ran and pieces of plaster flaked from the ceiling into their eggs.

"Now what, Dorothy? What are you doing?"

She parked and got out of the car. Lewis had no choice but to follow her, follow her the way the puppy she wanted instead of a second baby would have. Dusk had peaked and the night was chilly. Dorothy led Lewis into the wretched playground lot where they'd imagined Delphine would have to play, where she would have had to learn which swings to avoid, which monkey-bar rungs were too loose. Dorothy sat on the one good swing. She pushed off and gently pumped her legs, enjoying the flutter in her stomach, marveling that it could still be there after all these years. She wondered if it was the body that let go of childhood first, or the mind.

Lewis sat on the ground, put his head between his knees. Dorothy pumped harder, went higher. She was almost level with the top bar.

"Dorothy."

She tried to answer him but her throat just filled with air.

Lewis stood up, took his phone from his pocket, looked at it for a second, then put it back.

Dorothy closed her eyes and felt an impressive vertigo. She was pretty sure she was higher than she'd ever been, teeming with a bravery she'd never known, her legs almost flailing, true fear drilling her insides. What an insane contraption this is, she thought, just before counting—*one, two, three*—and jumping at the top of her arc. She came down hard on her right ankle and crumpled.

"Jesus Christ," Lewis said. "What's the matter with you?"

The pain was intense. She fought back tears. "I need help getting up."

Lewis sighed and kneeled down, offered his shoulder. She stood up gingerly, balancing on one foot. "I hope I didn't break anything."

"It would serve you right, honestly," he said. His anger made his face look weird. It moved Dorothy, in that moment, to realize how hard it was for him to be mad.

Silently, Lewis drove them back to the mall. When they pulled in, the parking lot was much emptier, and only a few people straggled in and out of the doors. Lewis screeched up to the curb, exactly where they had been less than thirty minutes before, parked the car, and got out with it still running.

Dorothy stared at the mall entrance.

Lewis hesitated and then ducked back into the car, turning the ignition off and taking the keys with him. "Turn the hazards on," he said, before slamming the door and running—when was the last time he'd run?—through the automatic doors.

Dorothy's ankle throbbed and she suddenly felt cold all over. She zipped her jacket all the way up. She closed her eyes and counted to twenty, and then opened them and looked at the doors. No one. She did it again, this time counting to sixty. A few people trickled out eating ice cream cones. She started counting to a hundred but only got to seventy before opening her eyes. She saw the security guard first, standing just outside the doors. Next to him was Lewis, holding Iris in his arms, Delphine leaning casually against him. The two men were talking animatedly. Lollipop sticks stuck out from the mouths of both girls, and when they registered the car under the parking-lot lights, the shape of their mother in the window, they broke into grins and started waving frantically. Dorothy waved back as her face went wet. They looked so happy.

THE LOVE SONG OF J. ALFRED TRUMP

by WENDY MOLYNEUX

Let us go then, you and I,
Because I am the best at going, I am great at it—okay?

When the evening is spread out against the sky
Like a patient etherized upon a table;

Melania picked out this table, and we etherize the best patients on it.
Some of the most amazing patients, you know? Top guys.

Let us go, through certain half-deserted streets,
Where the people love me, everyone, all the—
The street people. Hispanics, Jewish persons, they all love me, they say, Donald—

The muttering retreats
Of restless nights in one-night cheap hotels
Which are not like my hotels,
My hotels,
Kings, Princes, I had the—do you know this guy who owns
All the—all the guests—top guests

And sawdust restaurants with oyster-shells:

Streets that follow like a tedious argument
Of insidious intent
To lead you to an overwhelming question…
Oh, do not ask, "What is it?"
Because I'll tell you what it is
It's me, and I'm great, some people say I might be the best President ever
And then later they don't say that and whatever
And my hands are fine.

Let us go and make our visit.

In the room the women come and go
Talking of Michelangelo.
One of these women is my daughter
She is good at going

And when she goes, you hate to see her leave
But you love to watch her go, you know? You know!
But not Tiffany.

The yellow fog that rubs its back upon the window-panes,
Tremendous fog.
The yellow smoke that rubs its muzzle on the window-panes,
The best smoke, the best window-panes.
Licked its tongue into the corners of the evening,
I have—my tongue is normal—you can ask—
Everything is fine in there!

Lingered upon the pools that stand in drains,
Beautiful pools, amazing drains
Let fall upon its back the soot that falls from chimneys,
Slipped by the terrace, made a sudden leap,
I can jump higher than anyone, especially Hillary Clinton who I think is in very bad health and
    probably died
And seeing that it was a soft October night,
Curled once about the house, and fell asleep.
I'm very good at sleeping. My dreams are—have you seen them?

And indeed there will be time
For the yellow smoke that slides along the street,
Rubbing its back upon the window-panes;
There will be time, there will be time
To prepare a face to meet the faces that you meet;
There will be time to murder and create,
You bet!
And time for all the works and days of hands
Of which mine are very normal, large even, some people say
That lift and drop a question on your plate;
Time for you and time for me,
But mostly me
And time yet for a hundred indecisions,
And for a hundred visions and revisions,
Before the taking of a toast and tea.
One thing I like to do with my free time is make Don Jr. and Eric fistfight,
And then I tell them both they were bad at it
And that I made love to their wives

In the room the women come and go
Talking of Michelangelo.
I don't know who that is?
Is he the—is it the Turkey guy? Is it the internet?

And indeed there will be time
To wonder, "Do I dare?" and, "Do I dare?"
Time to turn back and descend the stair,
With a bald spot in the middle of my hair—
(They will say: "How his hair is growing thin!")
They never said that.
My morning coat, my collar mounting firmly to the chin,
My necktie rich and modest, but asserted by a simple pin—
(They will say: "But how his arms and legs are thin!")
That's correct.
Do I dare
Disturb the universe?
In a minute there is time
For decisions and revisions which a minute will reverse.

For I have known them all already, known them all:
I know all the them, I have the best thems
Have known the evenings, mornings, afternoons,
I have measured out my life with coffee spoons;
I know the voices dying with a dying fall
Beneath the music from a farther room.
My favorite song is Mambo Number Five
So how should I presume?

And I have known the eyes already, known them all—
The eyes that fix you in a formulated phrase,
And when I am formulated, sprawling on a pin,
When I am pinned and wriggling on the wall,
Then how should I begin
To spit out all the butt-ends of my days and ways?
And how should I presume?
My father never loved me.

And I have known the arms already, known them all—
Arms that are braceleted and white and bare

(But in the lamplight, downed with light brown hair!)
Is it perfume from a dress
That makes me so digress?
Or pee-pee on a bed?
That goes right to my head?
Arms that lie along a table, or wrap about a shawl.
And should I then presume?
And how should I begin?
Does anybody know how to make this pen work?
Shall I say, I have gone at dusk through narrow streets
And watched the smoke that rises from the pipes
Of lonely men in shirt-sleeves, leaning out of windows?…

I should have been a pair of ragged claws
Scuttling across the floors of silent seas.
One time I put a lobster in Marla Maples's bed.

And the afternoon, the evening, sleeps so peacefully!
Smoothed by long fingers,
Much like mine
Asleep… tired… or it malingers,
Stretched on the floor, here beside you and me.
Should I, after tea and cakes and ices,
Have the strength to force the moment to its crisis?
But though I have wept and fasted, wept and prayed,
Because I am religious, I swear. I know all the—what do you say—the Bibles.
Though I have seen my head (*grown slightly bald and then with a bunch of weird yarn
      stitched on it*) brought in upon a platter,
Along with some shrimps, and some cheeses—very nice shrimps!
I am no prophet
*—but I did say—everybody said we couldn't win, but we—you know—they said there's no path
      to 360*
—and here's no great matter;
I have seen the moment of my greatness flicker,
FAKE NEWS
And I have seen the eternal Footman hold my coat, and snicker,
And in short, I was afraid.
Just kidding. I am not afraid.

And would it have been worth it, after all,
After the cups, the marmalade, the tea,
The most beautiful chocolate cake you've ever seen

Among the porcelain, among some talk of you and me,
But mostly me
Would it have been worth while,
To have bitten off the matter with a smile,
To have squeezed the universe into a ball
To roll it towards some overwhelming question,
To say: "I am Lazarus, come from the dead,
Come back to tell you all, I shall tell you all"—
If one, settling a pillow by her head
Should say: "That is not what I meant at all;
That is not it, at all."
I haven't seen my wife in sixteen days.

And would it have been worth it, after all,
Would it have been worth while,
After the sunsets and the dooryards and the sprinkled streets,
Sprinkled with pee-pee. I love pee-pee. There! I said it!
After the novels, after the teacups, after the skirts that trail along the floor—
And this, and so much more?—
It is impossible to say just what I mean!
But as if a magic lantern threw the nerves in patterns on a screen:
Would it have been worth while
If one, settling a pillow or throwing off a shawl,
And turning toward the window, should say:
"That is not it at all,
That is not what I meant, at all."

No! I am not Prince Hamlet, nor was meant to be;
I never even saw that, but you know what I like: Anything With Piven, A.W.P.
Am an attendant lord, one that will do
To swell a progress, start a scene or two,
Advise the prince; no doubt, an easy tool,
Deferential, glad to be of use,
Politic, cautious, and meticulous;
Full of high sentence, but a bit obtuse;
At times, indeed, almost ridiculous—
Almost, at times, the Fool.
Is something the failing New York Times *might say about me.*

I grow old... I grow old...
But you can't tell from looking at my wife
I shall wear the bottoms of my trousers rolled.

Shall I part my hair behind?
Or on the side and then just comb it over?
Do I dare to eat a peach?
Because the peach cobbler at Mar-a-Lago is amazing, and tastes great when you're doing murders
I shall wear white flannel trousers, and walk upon the beach.
I would never ever wear white trousers.
But not because I poop my pants all the time.
For some other reason that I can't tell you because I'm the President.
I have heard the mermaids singing, each to each.

I do not think that they will sing to me.
Just kidding. They love to do that. Some of them are eighteen years old.

I have seen them riding seaward on the waves
My eyes are perfect
Combing the white hair of the waves blown back
My hair is amazing. And combing? Forget about it.
When the wind blows the water white and black.
We have lingered in the chambers of the sea
By sea-girls wreathed with seaweed red and brown
Till human voices wake us, and we drown.
(I am the best at drowning.)
SAD!

SECRET ROOM

by BENJAMIN PERCY

TRADITIONALLY A HUSBAND BEGINS constructing his secret room in the seventh year of his marriage, though some cannot wait. I have heard stories—of Sam Tusk, for instance—who began building as soon as his wedding night, and when he rose from bed and his bride sleepily asked, "Where are you going?" he kissed her forehead and combed his fingers through her honey-colored hair and said, "There's something I need to do."

Secret rooms come in all sizes. They are as small as drawers and they are as big as ballrooms. They could be anywhere, at home, at the office, in the car. Buried in the backyard. Locked away in a storage center on the other side of town. Hidden in a hotel in a faraway city.

Should you ever try to pull a novel off a shelf, and it catches, and a metallic clicking sounds, like a great machine grinding into motion—and the wall opens into a doorway that leads to a shadowy corridor, do not pursue this mystery any further. Return the book to its place. Allow the wall to seal itself. Put it out of your mind. Because the secret room is kept secret for a reason.

If you part the suits in the back of the closet and see a seam in the wall, or if you lift a trapdoor beneath the rug and discover a stairway circling downward, or if you peer into a hollow tree and find a ladder leading to the highest reaches of branches, stop.

Because sometimes, yes, you might be startled by the beauty of what you discover. I know of a secret room that served as an aviary for birds. Barred owls and blue buntings and rose-breasted grosbeaks and yellow finches. I know of a secret room that contained a desk upon which sat an Underwood typewriter and a ream of poems, the white paper tidily stacked. I know of a secret room that was a pond ringed by mossy stones with glowing fish darting through its cold clear water. And I know of a secret room that was walled with canvas and whatever you might paint upon it would come to life.

But sometimes a secret room is merely sad or uncomfortable for those never meant to visit it. Like the one that housed a special mirror that made you look taller and stronger and handsomer. Like the one full of dresses and wigs and makeup. Someone told me that the old magician—the one who performed at all the local birthday parties—had a secret room that opened up into another secret room that opened up into another secret room that opened up into another secret room in which they found one dead white rabbit rotting in a top hat, its neck snapped.

But maybe more often a secret room is dangerous, even terrifying. It might be crammed with pills, needles, white powder. Or money rubber-banded into thousand-dollar wads. There are secret rooms stacked with bones, heaps of bones, yellowed teeth, puzzled vertebrae. There are secret rooms stored with songs—music that hums through the walls of your home, music that wakes you up at night—and when you finally find the source and push into a candlelit chamber you will discover women dancing. You're better off not knowing. You're happier.

Such was the case with Sam Tusk. He died on his front lawn, clawing his chest and thudding to his knees and releasing the mower so that he and the engine died at once. A week after the funeral, his wife started at a noise that came from the basement. She fingered on the light and snuck down the stairs and there discovered, worming along the concrete floor, a man with his wrists and ankles bound with rope, his mouth gagged with a ball, and his naked body covered with bruises and bite marks. The tool bench and pegboard had been shoved aside to reveal an open doorway. Slowly she approached—and when she looked inside, she screamed so loudly the neighbors' ears bled.

If your husband walks into the kitchen and nuzzles your neck and you ask, "What's gotten into you?" and he says, "Nothing!" with too much enthusiasm, and only then do you notice grime under his fingernails and sawdust in his hair, know that he has been building his secret room. Let him. You might have trouble understanding this, but he must have something hidden, a place to retreat. In a way the secret room—as long as it doesn't get too big, as long as it stays secret—permits and protects your marriage.

Every husband has a secret room. Every husband. And if his wife or his friends or his family knew what was in it, maybe they would be pleasantly surprised or maybe they would never speak to him again. Certainly they would say, "It's like I don't even know who you are."

THE SIX-WORD SEQUELS TO "FOR SALE: BABY SHOES, NEVER WORN."

by KEATON PATTI

Sold shoes, we must move on.

Doctor lied: the baby is fine.

Healthy baby born, has cold feet.

Wish we hadn't sold those shoes.

Also, who lies about that, doctor?

Wanted: lawyer good at suing doctors.

But first, we need those shoes.

Let's explain this to the buyer.

That's our story, please, the shoes.

You want how much? That's insane!

Wait, are you wearing a mask?

What the fuck? You're that doctor!

Wanted: lawyer great at suing doctors.

Scandal: doctor not really a doctor.

Wanted: lawyer great at suing liars.

Called police, "doctor" arrested, shoes ours.

Cops say classic scam, happens daily.

Head home, bring baby the shoes.

After all that, they don't fit.

Fuck. Fuck. Fuck. Fuck. Fuck. Fuck.

For sale: baby shoes, never worn.

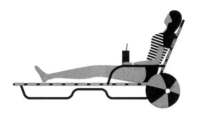

PLEASE FUND ME

by REBECCA CURTIS

R ECENTLY I SPENT TWO weeks on the island of Kauai, Hawaii, at a posh oceanside resort with the nice, hot guy I am dating, and while I was at the resort I noticed that the resort had an excellent thing: a pool boy. I have wanted a pool boy ever since yesterday, when I returned from Kauai, and it has become a wish dear to my heart, one that, if fulfilled, would change my life.

At the resort, the pool boy stood all day in a clean white wooden hut, located somewhat behind the circular, thatched-roof tiki bar, and waited until resort guests approached, then handed them towels, snorkeling gear, or boogie boards. Pretty much every day that my guy and I stayed at the resort, after drinking coffee, eating breakfast, and going for little jogs, we walked downstairs to the vast, manicured lawn around the saline-water resort pool, approached the pool boy's hut, and said, "We'd like six towels, please," and he said, "Beach towels or pool towels?" and we replied, "Several of each," and he gave us stacks of towels, some pristine ivory, for drying off after using the saline pool, and some blue and ivory–striped, for lying on while at the beach. Some days, my guy said, "Boogie board, please," and the pool boy handed him a boogie board.

One day when my boyfriend went golfing, I went to the pool boy by myself and said, "Twelve towels, please," and he gave them to me, just like that. He said, "Planning on getting wet, huh?" and I said, "Not really. I just like towels."

What did the pool boy look like? Well, he was very tanned, I imagine from standing near the pool all day. He had muscular legs, shoulders, and arms. He wore little white cotton shorts. He was probably forty-nine. He had curly dark hair (possibly dyed), wild bushy eyebrows that seemed to eternally ask a naughty question, and slightly inward-tilted, sparkling hazel eyes.

I would like my own pool boy. It would mean a lot to me. I am not asking that he be under thirty and over 5'10" and have dirty blond hair and green eyes, though those things would be nice. I would be happy with an ordinary pool boy, even one close to the pool boy age of retirement. He would not have to look like Ryan Gosling. It is not the prospect of asking the pool boy to provide "off-duty" services—like giving shoulder rubs, doing hula dances, and preparing guava-banana smoothies—that excites me. (Though I would demand things like that.) It is just the prospect—one I've longed for ever since I returned from Kauai, and, who knows? maybe my whole life—of the ongoing possibility of saying, "Fifteen towels today," and having the pool boy hand me more towels than I could ever possibly need.

I know that some may object that my Please Fund Me request is inappropriate, absurd, and offensive, for obvious reasons.

First of all, I already have a boyfriend (actually, several—and I'm also on OkCupid, Tinder, Doorknob, Shiksas_For_Israel, and FarmersOnly.com), so why don't I make *him* my pool boy? Unfortunately, my boyfriend has a job—he works at an investment bank. So he's busy. He's also senior at his workplace, so he's good at reviewing performances, not taking orders. Also, he just dumped me for my hotter friend, Hayley. I can't *blame* him for going after Hayley—she's a tall, willowy, curly-haired stunner—but now I don't want Torg as my pool boy.

Second, some may point out that if a *man* were to make a Please Fund Me request to purchase several "towel sluts" to hand him linens all day while wearing shiny purple thongs, rubbing peanut oil on his pecs and licking ear-gunk from his lobes, the man would be a completely misogynistic, sexist jerk. To that I say, I agree: men are bastards. Also, I only want one pool boy.

Third, some may protest that other petitioners on this site, such as children in Vail with lowered immune systems who love to snowboard but don't have GoPros, recovering addicts who've taken up ultra running and need money for special sneakers, and starving, wounded refugees in war-torn countries, have greater need. I agree that these cases are tragic. But I'd also ask: what would wounded refugees do with a *pool boy?*

Some may object that it's October: it's almost winter! It *is*. When the sun sets early, I feel sad, and long to be reminded of dragon fruits and giant green coconuts. That is why I need a pool boy.

Finally, skeptics may argue that since I live with five roommates in Brooklyn in a two-bedroom, five-story walk-up, I can't house a pool boy. That's true. But I want one anyway.

One afternoon in Kauai, when I was trimming my fingernails on our suite's lanai, and Torg was sitting at the tiki bar drinking Johnnie Walker Blue and thinking about my hotter friend, Hayley, I went down to the lawn and asked Shawn (our pool boy) his rates. He told me and I did calculations. I only need a pool boy part time. To cover part-time salary plus room and board and supplies such as boogie boards, kitesurfing materials, kayaks, stand-up paddleboards, and professional costumes (Shawn says pool boys need these things) will cost $20,000.

It would be so nice to come home to my dirty, roach-infested apartment, walk down the hall past a hairball my cat puked up, and enter my room to find the pool boy, tan, smiling, waiting to hand me a towel.

It would make me feel calm, as if I were still in Kauai, and relieve my anxiety more than Lexapro, Abilify, Ambien, Xanax, Deplin, and the daily supplements I take for my health, such as pot gummi bears, cannabis Sour Patch candies, ninety-nine puffs on an e-bong, digestive enzymes, oregano oil (anti-yeast), uva-ursi (anti-UTI), lysine (anti-herpes), and bovine adrenal, brain, and thyroid.

I know full well that, in America, there are people who are homeless, legless, have sepsis, and may be hungry. But pool boys don't provide food! Just sex, fruit smoothies, and towels.

I grew up in New Hampshire. I never even knew what a pool boy was. I went to college in Southern California. The college had a pool. But we had to fetch our own towels.

A number of people have asked: why I don't buy my own pool boy?

The honest truth is, I have a job—I work as a nutritionist—but it does not pay much. Also, I only work five hours a week. So basically, I am unemployed. Now that my investment bank–president boyfriend has dumped me for my hotter friend, Hayley, I have no access to unmaxed credit cards, and so I am unable to afford these expenses—pool boy salary, health care, and pension—on my own.

Normally, I would not pose my request to the world. But last night, I was awoken by an odd noise—my cat ate a large roach, then puked it up. So I awoke, put on the silk robe I stole from the resort in Kauai, drank some creamer packets I took from the suite, and read the tarot cards. The tarot cards said that I am meant to have a pool boy.

After the tarot cards said that, I lay on my futon and thought: Yes, I have been a good person in life. But do I really deserve a pool boy?

Then the room grew darker, and it was in the darkness that the fuzzy white figure of a man appeared. He wore a toga, kind of winter-white, a thin bamboo cloth wrapped firmly around his slender waist. Below his waist—I hate to be TMI, but this is only full disclosure—was a bulge, as if he were an armless UPS man who had to carry bulky packages between his thighs. But this man had arms, and his hands were empty. He had a kind, also hot, face, and a blond, scruffy beard. He said, "Rebecca. Put a post on PleaseFundMe.com. Five hundred people will send you forty dollars each."

He could have been Jesus, or he could have been a spiritual pool boy.

I wasn't sure which he was, but it got me thinking.

Remember when Jesus, in that book, the bibel, was about to be killed by mean Jewish people, and he said, "Towel, please," and Pompous Pilot said, "Do it, slay him!" and a prostitute or something wiped his face with a dishrag, and an image of his face came off on the cloth, sort of like his face was a temporary tattoo, and the towel became a priceless object, worth so much money that they couldn't even sell it at Christie's because it bore the magic face-tattoo of the holy son of God?

Well, if someone wiped my face with a towel, that wouldn't happen. But it would be fucking cool if it did.

Plus don't we all need a pool boy who'll lovingly whip out a cloth and wipe the dirt and existential anxiety from our faces?

I'm not a materialistic person. I don't want much. But I like shoulder rubs, thousand-dollar bottles of wine, semi-autistic genius banker-sluts who look like Ryan Gosling, such as my nice ex, Torg, and pool boys. I swear as a nutritionist that all donations will be used by me to buy the pool boy. I don't want cash someone can't afford. But if you can spare any, every little bit, such as ten cents, five thousand dollars, or even the whole amount in a cashier's check, helps. Please help me achieve my dream. Help me get a pool boy. Thank you, thank you, thank you, so much.

P.S. If Hayley asks for a pool boy, please don't fund her.

A ROAD WAS BUILT, CONNECTING TWO COMMUNITIES...

by DORIAN GEISLER

'A road was built, connecting two communities. The first community was full of happy, healthy, competent people. The second was full of people who were not.'

—in this way a boring yet instructive parable was written. Johannes didn't care. Johannes wanted to play the saxophone. And because he had a saxophone and other, more nebulous things (like 'opportunities'), he did.

The music Johannes played on the saxophone was very unbeautiful at first. However, as he put more and more capital of various types into it—human and nonhuman—the music became less and less unbeautiful, until finally it crossed that meaningful threshold into beautiful.

On that day the number of beautiful things in Johannes's life increased by one. However, on that day, the overall number of beautiful things also decreased by four.

On that day there was a net loss of three beautiful things. Of course, that is not the full story.

THE TRUTH

by CARSON MELL

T WAS LOVE AT first sight. He was six feet tall, slim and strong, with thick, sandy-colored hair. He smoked cigarettes and laughed loudly and played the guitar. He slapped his friends on their backs and got more ice and said, "Hold on, hold on," as he picked out the next record. It was a real nice song.

Jane walked up to him and introduced herself as he read the record sleeve. He looked right past her, took something out of his pocket, handed it to a passing friend. "What's your name?" she said.

"Marco," he said, still not looking at her. He reset the needle on the record. Mandolins jangled. Then he looked down at her. She was a small woman, 5'2" and skinny, but her eyes were powerful and dark. She didn't like most men. It was really rare for her to be attracted to someone and even rarer for her to just walk right up and introduce herself, the way she'd done just now.

Once he started looking at her face he couldn't stop. He told her as much, and they got pretty drunk together and went back to her place (he was living on a friend's couch at the time) and made love.

After they'd finished he took her face in his hands and stared her dead in the eye. "I'm a liar," he said. "You should know that about me. Sometimes I tell the truth, and sometimes I don't, but I don't care about the truth either way. Maybe it's a defect in me, I don't know, but I've been this way all my life. I like you, I like you a lot, but that doesn't change who I am. I just want to tell you this up front, right now, tonight. That from this moment on you won't be able to trust a single thing I say. You understand?"

"How do you lie?" she asked. "About other women?"

"About everything. That's all I'm going to say. And I'll never say it again, but it's the truth."

She stared at him for a long time, stared into his blue eyes, narrowed and intense, and kissed him. They made love again and fell asleep.

She woke to him cooking breakfast. Eggs and bacon and instant coffee. They ate a little bit of it. Her head was throbbing from the hangover.

"What you said last night," she said. "About the lying. What was all that?"

He looked up at her. His eyes were wide and calm, nothing like they'd been the night before. "I was just kidding," he said. "I'm sorry, I say crazy things when I get drunk."

"You didn't sound like you were kidding," she said. "You sounded really really serious."

He shrugged, smiled. "I'm just a weirdo. I'm sorry. I hope I didn't freak you out."

"You kind of did," she said.

"Sorry. Do you want me to leave?"

She looked at him for a long time. "Yeah, I'm sorry. It's just, you freaked me out."

He smiled sadly, got right up, and walked to the kitchen door that led to the back patio. "It's fine, I get it," he said. "I'm weird." He opened the door, and then he paused. "I do like you, though. Really. And I don't like a lot of people. Everyone says weird things sometimes."

He didn't call her the next day, the next week. She thought about him a lot, about the way they'd made love. One day, a vase of exotic flowers appeared on her doorstep with a card that read: *Weird flowers from a weirdo. Sorry.*

She put them on her kitchen table and stared at them. Then she picked up her cordless phone and called him.

Every few months, every few years, she would question him about that first night together. He'd get furious. "Oh, Jesus Christ, this again! I said one weird thing." If she ever caught him in a fib, she'd bring it up.

"Everybody fibs!" he'd yell. "Everybody tells little white lies!"

They had three children together. He was a great dad. Attentive and kind.

One summer a hiker discovered a human femur in the woods behind their home. Police detectives came and found a few more human bones. They did tests and discovered that the bones belonged to a young woman who'd gone missing the summer before. Marco was questioned simply because of proximity. Jane watched through the glass, watched him charm them. He shook their hands and patted their backs and walked them to the front door. When Jane walked in Marco was staring at the closed door with a serious expression, holding his elbows. He felt Jane's eyes on him and turned and said to her, "Poor woman."

Three years passed. It was their youngest's sixth birthday (their oldest was ten) when Jane found Marco smoking cigarettes on the front porch, away from everybody, staring out at the street with a very intense expression. An expression she had seen on his face only once before.

"Something wrong?" she asked him.

"Nope," he said.

The next morning he was gone. No note, no nothing. But Jane didn't need a note to understand. The whole time she'd known him, she'd known this day was coming.

GENO KNOWS I'VE GOT THE GOODS

by SARAH WALKER

I recently got a phone call from a number with an 860 area code. I live in Los Angeles, but grew up in Connecticut, so I thought it might be an old high school buddy. But as I picked up the phone I thought, I don't have any old high school buddies. Nay, only enemies. Fortunately, I was relieved to hear an instantly familiar voice (in a non–high school way) on the other end.

"Hello, Sarah. It's Geno Auriemma."

I can't say I had been expecting this call. Then again, I hadn't not been expecting it. I always knew that one day Geno would find me.

In his smooth Philadelphia accent he got straight to the point: "I want you to play post for the UConn Huskies next season."

"But Geno," I said, "I'm thirty-five. I haven't played basketball in fourteen years."

"Look, Sarah," said Geno. "You know you've got the goods. I saw them when you played at my camp when you were in sixth grade and won a game of Knockout. Now I'm telling you to knock it out with the false modesty and come play for me."

That silver tongue! He was right. Of course I knew I had the goods. I had been sitting on the goods, on my couch, eating cocktail nuts, scanning Instagram for precocious animals, mentally preparing for the looks I would get from my future teammates: Katie Lou "Shooty" Samuelson, Naphessa "The Rock" Collier, and good old Gabby "Rebound" Williams—the nicknames I would give them—as I walked into the gym at Storrs. They wouldn't want to believe that this older gal with the creaky knees and a two-inch vertical was better than them, but they wouldn't have to. They'd see. Oh, how they would see.

I sighed. There was no use in resisting. It was inevitable. So I tossed my tin of cocktail nuts out the open window for some lucky person to find. It was all protein and complex carbs from now on. "When do I start?"

"Now," he said. And then he turned into a dog. But not a Husky, a Pomeranian with glasses. Then the Pomeranian handed me a phone with a paw that sported eleven National Championship rings. "Answer it," he whispered.

I woke up to the phone ringing.

"Sarah. It's Geno Auriemma. You stole my windbreaker from the bus last time we played at Hartford and I want it back."

"Never!" I cried, clutching the windbreaker tightly around me. On the other end, I could hear Geno chuckling.

"That was a test. Now I know you've got the goods. I want you to play post for the UConn Huskies next season."

I sighed with relief, even though I was totally confident. I had the goods and Geno knew it. But I had more goods than even he knew, for I had also stolen his warm-up pants, which I packed in my bag and headed to Connecticut.

ENDNOTES

by VALERIA LUISELLI

1. THESE ENDNOTES, STRUNG TOGETHER to form a fictional essay or a nonfictional short story, are both a commentary on Balzac's "The Unknown Masterpiece" (1845) and a theory of posturing and imposture in contemporary art and literature.

2. These endnotes were originally written as a response to a piece by the artist Terence Gower, "Sculpture Portraits," which offers a subtle yet brutally sardonic commentary on the tradition of artists' self-portraits through a sequence of photographs in which an artist stands with his work in a series of standard poses: "artist working," "cradling the sculpture," or "intense concentration."

3. These endnotes are a quiet response to our ridiculous world in an age of selfies, self-promotion, self-publishing, self-made identities, and self-indulgence in general.

4. These endnotes transgress some genre boundaries and most historical chronologies. Not because they want to but because they have to. They place Balzac in the same space as Picasso, Dora Maar, Noguchi, Martha Graham, Anne Carson, and Kendrick Lamar, in order to map a history of portraiture.

5. These endnotes propose a complicated genealogy of professional posers, masters of posturing, and critics of imposture.

6. These endnotes respectfully disregard bibliographical conventions. All citations and references to sources are, in an annoyingly Borgesian way, sometimes very true and sometimes very false.

THE UNKNOWN MASTERPIECE

by HONORÉ DE BALZAC

(Translated by Ellen Marriage)

Auguste Rodin, Monument to Balzac[1]

TO MY FRIENDS...[2]

I — GILLETTE[3]

O N A COLD DECEMBER morning in the year 1612, a young man, whose clothing was somewhat of the thinnest, was walking to and fro before a gateway in the Rue des Grands-Augustins in Paris. He went up and down the street before this house with the irresolution of a gallant who dares not venture into the presence of the mistress whom he loves for the first time, easy of access though she may be; but after a sufficiently long interval of hesitation, he at last crossed the threshold and inquired of an old woman, who was sweeping out a large room on the ground floor, whether Master Porbus was within.[4] Receiving a reply in the affirmative, the young man went slowly up the staircase, like a gentleman but newly come to court, and doubtful as to his reception by the king. He came to a stand once more on the landing at the head of the stairs, and again he hesitated before raising his hand to the grotesque knocker on the door of the studio, where doubtless the painter was at work—Master Porbus, sometime painter in ordinary to Henri IV till Mary de' Medici took Rubens into favor.[5]

The young man felt deeply stirred by an emotion that must thrill the hearts of all great artists when, in the pride of their youth and their first love of art, they come into the presence of a master or stand before a masterpiece. For all human sentiments there is a time of early blossoming, a day of generous enthusiasm that gradually fades until nothing is left of happiness but a memory, and glory is known for a delusion. Of all these delicate and short-lived emotions, none so resemble love as the passion of a young artist for his art, as he is about to enter on the blissful martyrdom of his career of glory and disaster, of vague expectations and real disappointments.

Those who have missed this experience in the early days of light purses; who have not, in the dawn of their genius, stood in the presence of a master and felt the throbbing of their hearts, will always carry in their inmost souls a chord that has never been touched, and in their work an indefinable quality will be lacking, a something in the stroke of the brush, a mysterious element that we call poetry. The swaggerers, so puffed up by self-conceit that they are confident over-soon of their success, can never be taken for men of talent save by fools.[6] From this point of view, if youthful modesty is the measure of youthful genius, the stranger on the staircase might be allowed to have something in him; for he seemed to possess the indescribable diffidence, the early timidity that artists are bound to lose in the course of a great career, even as pretty women lose it as they make progress in the arts of coquetry.[7] Self-distrust vanishes as triumph succeeds to triumph, and modesty is, perhaps, distrust of itself.

The poor neophyte was so overcome by the consciousness of his own presumption and insignificance that it began to look as if he was hardly likely to penetrate into the studio of the painter, to whom we owe the wonderful portrait of Henri IV. But fate was propitious; an old man came up the staircase. From the quaint costume of this newcomer, his collar of magnificent lace, and a certain serene gravity in his bearing, the first arrival thought that this personage must be either a patron or a friend of the court painter. He stood aside therefore upon the landing to allow the visitor to pass, scrutinizing him curiously the while. Perhaps he might hope to find the good nature of an artist or to receive the good offices of an amateur not unfriendly to the arts; but besides an almost diabolical expression in the face that met his gaze, there was that indescribable something which has an irresistible attraction for artists.

Picture that face. A bald high forehead and rugged jutting brows above a small flat nose turned up at the end, as in the portraits of Socrates and Rabelais; deep lines about the mocking mouth; a short chin, carried proudly, covered with a grizzled pointed beard; sea-green eyes that age might seem to have dimmed were it not for the contrast between the iris and the surrounding mother-of-pearl tints, so that it seemed as if under the stress of anger or enthusiasm there would be a magnetic power to quell or kindle in their glances. The face was withered beyond wont by the fatigue of years, yet it seemed aged still more by the thoughts that had worn away both soul and body. There were no lashes to the deep-set eyes, and scarcely a trace of the arching lines of the eyebrows above them. Set this head on a spare and feeble frame, place it in a frame of lace wrought like an engraved silver fish-slice, imagine a heavy gold chain over the old man's black doublet, and you will have some dim idea of this strange personage, who seemed still more fantastic in the somber twilight of the staircase.[8] One of Rembrandt's portraits might have stepped down from its frame to walk in an appropriate atmosphere of gloom, such as the great painter loved. The older man gave the younger a shrewd glance, and knocked thrice at the door. It was opened by a man of forty or thereabout, who seemed to be an invalid.

"Good day, Master."

Porbus bowed respectfully, and held the door open for the younger man to enter, thinking that the latter accompanied his visitor; and when he saw that the neophyte stood a while as if spellbound, feeling, as every artist-nature must feel, the fascinating influence of the first sight of a studio in which the material processes of art are revealed, Porbus troubled himself no more about this second comer.

All the light in the studio came from a window in the roof, and was concentrated upon an easel, where a canvas stood untouched as yet save for three or four outlines in chalk. The daylight scarcely reached the remoter angles and corners of the vast room; they were as dark as night, but the silver ornamented breastplate of a Reiter's corselet, that hung upon the wall, attracted a stray gleam to its dim abiding-place among the brown shadows; or a shaft of light shot across the carved and glistening surface of an antique sideboard covered with curious silver-plate, or struck out a line of glittering dots among the raised threads of the golden warp of some old brocaded curtains, where the lines of the stiff, heavy folds were broken, as the stuff had been flung carelessly down to serve as a model.

Plaster écorchés stood about the room; and here and there, on shelves and tables, lay fragments of classical sculpture-torsos of antique goddesses, worn smooth as though all the years of the centuries that had passed over them had been lovers' kisses. The walls were covered, from floor to ceiling, with countless sketches in charcoal, red chalk, or pen and ink. Amid the litter and confusion of color boxes, overturned stools, flasks of oil, and essences, there was just room to move so as to reach the illuminated circular space where the easel stood. The light from the window in the roof fell full upon Porbus's pale face and on the ivory-tinted forehead of his strange visitor. But in another moment the younger man heeded nothing but a picture that had already become famous even in those stormy days of political and religious revolution, a picture that a few of the zealous worshippers, who have so often kept the sacred fire of art alive in evil days, were wont to go on pilgrimage to see. The beautiful panel represented a Saint Mary of Egypt about to pay her passage across the seas. It was a masterpiece destined for Mary de' Medici, who sold it in later years of poverty.[9]

"I like your saint," the old man remarked, addressing Porbus. "I would give you ten golden crowns for her over and above the price the Queen is paying; but as for putting a spoke in that wheel—the devil take it!"[10]

"It is good, then?"

"Hey! hey!" said the old man; "good, say you?—Yes and no. Your good woman is not badly done, but she is not alive. You artists fancy that when a figure is correctly drawn, and everything in its place according to the rules of anatomy, there is nothing more to be done. You make up the flesh tints beforehand on your palettes according to your formulae, and fill in the outlines with due care that one side of the face shall be darker than the other; and because you look from time to time at a naked woman who stands on the platform before you, you fondly imagine that you have copied nature, think yourselves to be painters, believe that you have wrested His secret from God. Pshaw! You may know your syntax thoroughly and make no blunders in your grammar, but it takes that and something more to make a great poet. Look at your saint, Porbus! At a first glance she is admirable; look at her again, and you see at once that she is glued to the background, and that you could not walk round her. She is a silhouette that turns but one side of her face to all beholders, a figure cut out of canvas, an image with no power to move nor change her position. I feel as if there were no air between that arm and the background, no space, no sense of distance in your canvas. The perspective is perfectly correct, the strength of the coloring is accurately diminished with the distance; but, in spite of these praiseworthy efforts, I could never bring myself to believe that the warm breath of life comes and goes in that beautiful body. It seems to me that if I laid my hand on the firm, rounded throat, it would be cold as marble to the touch. No, my friend, the blood does not flow beneath that ivory skin, the tide of life does not flush those delicate fibers, the purple veins that trace a network beneath the transparent amber of her brow and breast. Here the pulse seems to beat, there it is motionless, life and death are at strife in every detail; here you see a woman, there a statue, there again a corpse. Your creation is incomplete. You had only power to breathe a portion of your soul into your beloved work. The fire of Prometheus died out again and again in your hands; many a spot in your picture has not been touched by the divine flame."

"But how is it, dear master?" Porbus asked respectfully, while the young man with difficulty repressed his strong desire to beat the critic.

"Ah!" said the old man, "it is this! You have halted between two manners. You have hesitated between drawing and color, between the dogged attention to detail, the stiff precision of the German masters and the dazzling glow, the joyous exuberance of Italian painters. You have set yourself to imitate Hans Holbein and Titian, Albrecht Dürer and Paul Veronese in a single picture. A magnificent ambition truly, but what has come of it? Your work has neither the severe charm of a dry execution nor the magical illusion of Italian *chiaroscuro*. Titian's rich golden coloring poured into Albrecht Dürer's austere outlines has shattered them, like molten bronze bursting through the mold that is not strong enough to hold it. In other places the outlines have held firm, imprisoning and obscuring the magnificent, glowing flood of Venetian color. The drawing of the face is not perfect, the coloring is not perfect; traces of that unlucky indecision are to be seen everywhere. Unless you felt strong enough to fuse the two opposed manners in the fire of your own genius, you should have cast in your lot boldly with the one or the other, and so have obtained the unity which simulates one of the conditions of life itself. Your work is only true in the centers; your outlines are false, they project nothing, there is no hint of anything behind them. There is truth here," said the old man, pointing to the breast of the Saint, "and again here," he went on, indicating the rounded shoulder. "But there," once more returning to the column of the throat, "everything is false. Let us go no further into detail, you would be disheartened."

The old man sat down on a stool, and remained a while without speaking, with his face buried in his hands.

"Yet I studied that throat from the life, dear master," Porbus began; "it happens sometimes, for our misfortune, that real effects in nature look improbable when transferred to canvas—"

"The aim of art is not to copy nature, but to express it. You are not a servile copyist, but a poet!" cried the old man sharply, cutting Porbus short with an imperious gesture. "Otherwise a sculptor might make a plaster cast of a living woman and save himself all further trouble. Well, try to make a cast of your mistress's hand, and set up the thing before you. You will see a monstrosity, a dead mass, bearing no resemblance to the living hand; you would be compelled to have recourse to the chisel of a sculptor who, without making an exact copy, would represent for you its movement and its life. We must detect the spirit, the informing soul in the appearances of things and beings. Effects! What are effects but the accidents of life, not life itself? A hand, since I have taken that example, is not only a part of a body, it is the expression and extension of a thought that must be grasped and rendered. Neither painter nor poet nor sculptor may separate the effect from the cause, which are inevitably contained the one in the other. There begins the real struggle! Many a painter achieves success instinctively, unconscious of the task that is set before art. You draw a woman, yet you do not see her! Not so do you succeed in wresting Nature's secrets from her! You are reproducing mechanically the model that you copied in your master's studio. You do not penetrate far enough into the inmost secrets of the mystery of form; you do not seek with love enough and perseverance enough after the form that baffles and eludes you. Beauty is a thing severe and unapproachable, never to be won by a languid lover. You must lie in wait for her coming and take her unawares, press her hard and clasp her in a tight embrace, and force her to yield. Form is a Proteus more intangible and more manifold than the Proteus of the legend; compelled, only after long wrestling, to stand forth manifest in his true aspect.[11] Some of you are satisfied with the first shape, or at most by the second or the third that appears. Not thus wrestle the victors, the unvanquished painters who never suffer themselves to be deluded by all those treacherous shadow-shapes; they persevere till Nature at the last stands bare to their gaze, and her very soul is revealed.

"In this manner worked Rafael," said the old man, taking off his cap to express his reverence for the King of Art. "His transcendent greatness came of the intimate sense that, in him, seems as if it would shatter external form. Form in his figures (as with us) is a symbol, a means of communicating sensations, ideas, the vast imaginings of a poet. Every face is a whole world. The subject of the portrait appeared for him bathed in the light of a divine vision; it was revealed by an inner voice, the finger of God laid bare the sources of expression in the past of a whole life.

"You clothe your women in fair raiment of flesh, in gracious veiling of hair; but where is the blood, the source of passion and of calm, the cause of the particular effect? Why, this brown Egyptian of yours, my good Porbus, is a colorless creature! These figures that you set before us are painted bloodless phantoms; and you call that painting, you call that art!

"Because you have made something more like a woman than a house, you think that you have set your fingers on the goal; you are quite proud that you need not to write *currus venustus* or *pulcher homo* beside your figures, as early painters were wont to do, and you fancy that you have done wonders. Ah! my good friend, there is still something more to learn, and you will use up a great deal of chalk and cover many a canvas before you will learn it. Yes, truly, a woman carries her head in just such a way, so she holds her garments gathered into her hand; her eyes grow dreamy and soft with that expression of meek sweetness, and even so the quivering shadow of the lashes hovers upon her cheeks. It is all there, and yet it is not there. What is lacking? A nothing, but that nothing is everything.

"There you have the semblance of life, but you do not express its fullness and effluence, that indescribable something, perhaps the soul itself, that envelops the outlines of the body like a haze; that flower of life, in short, that Titian and Rafael caught. Your utmost achievement hitherto has only brought you to the starting point. You might now perhaps begin to do excellent work, but you grow weary all too soon; and the crowd admires, and those who know smile.

"Oh, Mabuse! oh, my master!" cried the strange speaker, "thou art a thief! Thou hast carried away the secret of life with thee!

"Nevertheless," he began again, "this picture of yours is worth more than all the paintings of that rascal Rubens, with his mountains of Flemish flesh raddled with vermilion, his torrents of red hair, his riot of color. You, at least have color there, and feeling and drawing—the three essentials in art."

The young man roused himself from his deep musings.

"Why, my good man, the Saint is sublime!" he cried. "There is a subtlety of imagination about those two figures, the Saint Mary and the Shipman, that cannot be found among Italian masters; I do not know a single one of them capable of imagining the Shipman's hesitation."

"Did that little malapert come with you?" asked Porbus of the older man.

"Alas! master, pardon my boldness," cried the neophyte, and the color mounted to his face. "I am unknown—a dauber by instinct, and but lately come to this city—the fountainhead of all learning."

"Set to work," said Porbus, handing him a bit of red chalk and a sheet of paper.

The newcomer quickly sketched the Saint Mary line for line.

"Aha!" exclaimed the old man. "Your name?" he added.

The young man wrote *Nicolas Poussin* below the sketch.

"Not bad for a beginning," said the strange speaker, who had discoursed so wildly. "I see that we can talk of art in your presence. I do not blame you for admiring Porbus's saint. In the eyes of the world she is a masterpiece, and those alone who have been initiated into the inmost mysteries of art can discover her shortcomings. But it is worthwhile to give you the lesson, for you are able to understand it, so I will show you how little it needs to complete this picture. You must be all eyes, all attention, for it may be that such a chance of learning will never come in your way again—Porbus! your palette."[12]

Porbus went in search of palette and brushes. The little old man turned back his sleeves with impatient energy, seized the palette, covered with many hues, that Porbus handed to him, and snatched rather than took a handful of brushes of various sizes from the hands of his acquaintance. His pointed beard suddenly bristled—a menacing movement that expressed the prick of a lover's fancy. As he loaded his brush, he muttered between his teeth, "These paints are only fit to fling out of the window, together with the fellow who ground them, their crudeness and falseness are disgusting! How can one paint with this?"

He dipped the tip of the brush with feverish eagerness in the different pigments, making the circuit of the palette several times more quickly than the organist of a cathedral sweeps the octaves on the keyboard of his clavier for the "O Filii" at Easter.

Porbus and Poussin, on either side of the easel, stood stock-still, watching with intense interest.

"Look, young man," he began again, "see how three or four strokes of the brush and a thin glaze of blue let in the free air to play about the head of the poor Saint, who must have felt stifled and oppressed by the close atmosphere! See how the drapery begins to flutter; you feel that it is lifted by the breeze! A moment ago, it hung as heavily and stiffly as if it were held out by pins. Do you see how the satin sheen that I have just given to the breast rends the pliant, silken softness of a young girl's skin, and how the brown-red, blended with burnt ochre, brings warmth into the cold gray of the deep shadow where the blood lay congealed instead of coursing through the veins? Young man, young man, no master could teach you how to do this that I am doing before your eyes. Mabuse alone possessed the secret of giving life to his figures; Mabuse had but one pupil—that was I. I have had none, and I am old. You have sufficient intelligence to imagine the rest from the glimpses that I am giving you."

While the old man was speaking, he gave a touch here and there; sometimes two strokes of the brush, sometimes a single one; but every stroke told so well, that the whole picture seemed transfigured—the painting was flooded with light. He worked with such passionate fervor that beads of sweat gathered upon his bare forehead; he worked so quickly, in brief, impatient jerks, that it seemed to young Poussin as if some familiar spirit inhabiting the body of this strange being took a grotesque pleasure in making use of the man's hands against his own will. The unearthly glitter of his eyes, the convulsive movements that seemed like struggles, gave to this fancy a semblance of truth which could not but stir a young imagination. The old man continued, saying as he did so—[13]

"Paf! paf! that is how to lay it on, young man!—Little touches! Come and bring a glow into those icy cold tones for me! Just so! Pon! pon! pon!" and those parts of the picture that he had pointed out as cold and lifeless flushed with warmer hues, a few bold strokes of color brought all the tones of the picture into the required harmony with the glowing tints of the Egyptian, and the differences in temperament vanished.

"Look you, youngster, the last touches make the picture. Porbus has given it a hundred strokes for every one of mine. No one thanks us for what lies beneath. Bear that in mind."

At last the restless spirit stopped, and turning to Porbus and Poussin, who were speechless with admiration, he spoke—

"This is not as good as my *Belle Noiseuse*; still one might put one's name to such a thing as this.[14] —Yes, I would put my name to it," he added, rising to reach for a mirror, in which he looked at the picture. "And now," he said, "will you both come and breakfast with me? I have a smoked ham and some very fair wine!... Eh! eh! the times may be bad, but we can still have some talk about art! We can talk like equals... Here is a little fellow who has aptitude," he added, laying a hand on Nicolas Poussin's shoulder.

In this way the stranger became aware of the threadbare condition of the Norman's doublet. He drew a leather purse from his girdle, felt in it, found two gold coins, and held them out.

"I will buy your sketch," he said.

"Take it," said Porbus, as he saw the other start and flush with embarrassment, for Poussin had the pride of poverty. "Pray, take it; he has a couple of king's ransoms in his pouch!"

The three came down together from the studio, and, talking of art by the way, reached a picturesque wooden house hard by the Pont Saint-Michel. Poussin wondered a moment at its ornament, at the knocker, at the frames of the casements, at the scrollwork designs, and in the next he stood in a vast low-ceiled room. A table, covered with tempting dishes, stood near the blazing fire, and (luck unhoped-for) he was in the company of two great artists full of genial good humor.

"Do not look too long at that canvas, young man," said Porbus, when he saw that Poussin was standing, struck with wonder, before a painting. "You would fall a victim to despair."

It was the "Adam" painted by Mabuse to purchase his release from the prison where his creditors had so long kept him. And, as a matter of fact, the figure stood out so boldly and convincingly that Nicolas Poussin began to understand the real meaning of the words poured out by the old artist, who was himself looking at the picture with apparent satisfaction, but without enthusiasm. "I have done better than that!" he seemed to be saying to himself.

"There is life in it," he said aloud; "in that respect my poor master here surpassed himself, but there is some lack of truth in the background. The man lives indeed; he is rising, and will come toward us; but the atmosphere, the sky, the air, the breath of the breeze—you look and feel for them, but they are not there. And then the man himself is, after all, only a man! Ah! but the one man in the world who came direct from the hands of God must have had a something divine about him that is wanting here. Mabuse himself would grind his teeth and say so when he was not drunk."

Poussin looked from the speaker to Porbus, and from Porbus to the speaker, with restless curiosity. He went up to the latter to ask for the name of their host; but the painter laid a finger on his lips with an air of mystery. The young man's interest was excited; he kept silence, but hoped that sooner or later some word might be let fall that would reveal the name of his entertainer. It was evident that he was a man of talent and very wealthy, for Porbus listened to him respectfully, and the vast room was crowded with marvels of art.

A magnificent portrait of a woman, hung against the dark oak panels of the wall, next caught Poussin's attention.

"What a glorious Giorgione!" he cried.

"No," said his host, "it is an early daub of mine—"

"Gramercy! I am in the abode of the god of painting, it seems!" cried Poussin ingenuously.

The old man smiled as if he had long grown familiar with such praise.

"Master Frenhofer!" said Porbus, "do you think you could spare me a little of your capital Rhine wine?"

"A couple of pipes!" answered his host; "one to discharge a debt, for the pleasure of seeing your pretty sinner, the other as a present from a friend."

"Ah! if I had my health," returned Porbus, "and if you would but let me see your *Belle Noiseuse*, I would paint some great picture, with breadth in it and depth; the figures should be life-size."

"Let you see my work!" cried the painter in agitation. "No, no! it is not perfect yet; something still remains for me to do. [15] Yesterday, in the dusk," he said, "I thought I had reached the end. Her eyes seemed moist, the flesh quivered, something stirred the tresses of her hair. She breathed! But though

I have succeeded in reproducing Nature's roundness and relief on the flat surface of the canvas, this morning, by daylight, I found out my mistake. Ah! to achieve that glorious result I have studied the works of the great masters of color, stripping off coat after coat of color from Titian's canvas, analyzing the pigments of the king of light. Like that sovereign painter, I began the face in a slight tone with a supple and fat paste—for shadow is but an accident; bear that in mind, youngster! Then I began afresh, and by half-tones and thin glazes of color less and less transparent, I gradually deepened the tints to the deepest black of the strongest shadows. An ordinary painter makes his shadows something entirely different in nature from the highlights; they are wood or brass, or what you will, anything but flesh in shadow. You feel that even if those figures were to alter their position, those shadow stains would never be cleansed away, those parts of the picture would never glow with light.

"I have escaped one mistake, into which the most famous painters have sometimes fallen; in my canvas the whiteness shines through the densest and most persistent shadow. I have not marked out the limits of my figure in hard, dry outlines, and brought every last anatomical detail into prominence (like a host of dunces, who fancy that they can draw because they can trace a line elaborately smooth and clean), for the human body is not contained within the limits of line. In this the sculptor can approach the truth more nearly than we painters. Nature's way is a complicated succession of curve within curve. Strictly speaking, there is no such thing as drawing. Do not laugh, young man; strange as that speech may seem to you, you will understand the truth in it someday. A line is a method of expressing the effect of light upon an object; but there are no lines in Nature, everything is solid. We draw by modeling, that is to say that we disengage an object from its setting; the distribution of the light alone gives to a body the appearance by which we know it. So I have not defined the outlines; I have suffused them with a haze of half-tints warm or golden, in such a sort that you can not lay your finger on the exact spot where background and contours meet. Seen from near, the picture looks a blur; it seems to lack definition; but step back two paces, and the whole thing becomes clear, distinct, and solid; the body stands out; the rounded form comes into relief; you feel that the air plays round it. And yet—I am not satisfied; I have misgivings. Perhaps one ought not to draw a single line; perhaps it would be better to attack the face from the center, taking the highest prominences first, proceeding from them through the whole range of shadows to the heaviest of all. Is not this the method of the sun, the divine painter of the world? Oh, Nature, Nature! who has surprised thee, fugitive? But, after all, too much knowledge, like ignorance, brings you to a negation. I have doubts about my work."[16]

There was a pause. Then the old man spoke again. "I have been at work upon it for ten years, young man; but what are ten short years in a struggle with Nature? Do we know how long Sir Pygmalion wrought at the one statue that came to life?" The old man fell into deep musings, and gazed before him with unseeing eyes, while he played unheedingly with his knife.[17]

"Look, he is in conversation with his *esprit!*" murmured Porbus.

At the word, Nicolas Poussin felt himself carried away by an unaccountable accession of artist's curiosity. For him the old man, at once intent and inert, the seer with the unseeing eyes, became something more than a man—a fantastic spirit living in a mysterious world, and countless vague thoughts awoke within his soul. The effect of this species of fascination upon his mind can no more be described in words than the passionate longing awakened in an exile's heart by the song that recalls his home. He thought of the scorn that the old man affected to display for the noblest efforts of art, of his wealth, his manners, of the deference paid to him by Porbus. The mysterious picture, the work of patience on which he had wrought so long in secret, was doubtless a work of genius, for the head of the Virgin which young Poussin had admired so frankly was beautiful even beside Mabuse's "Adam"—there was no mistaking the imperial manner of one of the princes of art. Everything combined to set the old man beyond the limits of human nature.

Out of the wealth of fancies in Nicolas Poussin's brain an idea grew, and gathered shape and clearness. He saw in this supernatural being a complete type of the artist nature, a nature mocking and kindly, barren and prolific, an erratic spirit entrusted with great and manifold powers which she too often abuses, leading sober reason, the Philistine, and sometimes even the amateur forth into a stony wilderness where they see nothing; but the white-winged maiden herself, wild as her fancies may be, finds epics there and castles and works of art. For Poussin, the enthusiast, the old man, was suddenly transfigured, and became Art incarnate, Art with its mysteries, its vehement passion and its dreams.[18]

"Yes, my dear Porbus," Frenhofer continued, "hitherto I have never found a flawless model, a body with outlines of perfect beauty, the carnations—Ah! where does she live?" he cried, breaking in upon himself, "the undiscoverable Venus of the older time, for whom we have sought so often, only to find the scattered gleams of her beauty here and there? Oh! to behold once and for one moment, Nature grown perfect and divine, the Ideal at last, I would give all that I possess... Nay, Beauty divine, I would go to seek thee in the dim land of the dead; like Orpheus, I would go down into the Hades of Art to bring back the life of art from among the shadows of death."

"We can go now," said Porbus to Poussin. "He neither hears nor sees us any longer."

"Let us go to his studio," said young Poussin, wondering greatly.

"Oh! the old fox takes care that no one shall enter it. His treasures are so carefully guarded that it is impossible for us to come at them. I have not waited for your suggestion and your fancy to attempt to lay hands on this mystery by force."

"So there is a mystery?"

"Yes," answered Porbus. "Old Frenhofer is the only pupil Mabuse would take. Frenhofer became the painter's friend, deliverer, and father; he sacrificed the greater part of his fortune to enable Mabuse to indulge in riotous extravagance, and in return Mabuse bequeathed to him the secret of relief, the power of giving to his figures the wonderful life, the flower of Nature, the eternal despair of art, the secret which Mabuse knew so well that one day when he had sold the flowered brocade suit in which he should have appeared at the Entry of Charles V, he accompanied his master in a suit of paper painted to resemble the brocade. The peculiar richness and splendor of the stuff struck the Emperor; he complimented the old drunkard's patron on the artist's appearance, and so the trick was brought to light. Frenhofer is a passionate enthusiast, who sees above and beyond other painters. He has meditated profoundly on color, and the absolute truth of line; but by the way of much research he has come to doubt the very existence of the objects of his search. He says, in moments of despondency, that there is no such thing as drawing, and that by means of lines we can only reproduce geometrical figures; but that is overshooting the mark, for by outline and shadow you can reproduce form without any color at all, which shows that our art, like Nature, is composed of an infinite number of elements. Drawing gives you the skeleton, the anatomical framework, and color puts the life into it; but life without the skeleton is even more incomplete than a skeleton without life. But there is something else truer still, and it is this—for painters, practice and observation are everything; and when theories and poetical ideas begin to quarrel with the brushes, the end is doubt, as has happened with our good friend, who is half crack-brained enthusiast, half painter. A sublime painter! but unlucky for him, he was born to riches, and so he has leisure to follow his fancies. Do not you follow his example! Work! Painters have no business to think, except brush in hand."

"We will find a way into his studio!" cried Poussin confidently. He had ceased to heed Porbus's remarks. The other smiled at the young painter's enthusiasm, asked him to come to see him again, and they parted. Nicolas Poussin went slowly back to the Rue de la Harpe, and passed the modest hostelry where he was lodging without noticing it. A feeling of uneasiness prompted him to hurry up the crazy staircase till he reached a room at the top, a quaint, airy recess under the steep, high-pitched roof common among houses in old Paris. In the one dingy window of the place sat a young girl, who sprang up at once when she heard someone at the door; it was the prompting of love; she had recognized the painter's touch on the latch.

"What is the matter with you?" she asked.

"The matter is... is... Oh! I have felt that I am a painter! Until today I have had doubts, but now I believe in myself! There is the making of a great man in me! Never mind, Gillette, we shall be rich and happy! There is gold at the tips of those brushes—"[19]

He broke off suddenly. The joy faded from his powerful and earnest face as he compared his vast hopes with his slender resources. The walls were covered with sketches in chalk on sheets of common paper. There were but four canvases in the room. Colors were very costly, and the young painter's palette was almost bare. Yet in the midst of his poverty he possessed and was conscious of the possession of inexhaustible treasures of the heart, of a devouring genius equal to all the tasks that lay before him.

He had been brought to Paris by a nobleman among his friends, or perchance by the consciousness of his powers; and in Paris he had found a mistress, one of those noble and generous souls who choose to suffer by a great man's side, who share his struggles and strive to understand his fancies, accepting their lot of poverty and love as bravely and dauntlessly as other women will set themselves to bear the burden of riches and make a parade of their insensibility. The smile that stole over Gillette's lips filled the garret with golden light, and rivaled the brightness of the sun in heaven. The sun, moreover, does not always shine in heaven, whereas Gillette was always in the garret, absorbed in her passion, occupied by Poussin's happiness and sorrow, consoling the genius which found an outlet in love before art engrossed it.

"Listen, Gillette. Come here."[20]

The girl obeyed joyously, and sprang upon the painter's knee. Hers was perfect grace and beauty, and the loveliness of spring; she was adorned with all luxuriant fairness of outward form, lighted up by the glow of a fair soul within.

"Oh! God," he cried; "I shall never dare to tell her—"

"A secret?" she cried; "I must know it!"

Poussin was absorbed in his dreams.

"Do tell it me!"

"Gillette... poor beloved heart!..."

"Oh! do you want something of me?"

"Yes."

"If you wish me to sit once more for you as I did the other day," she continued with playful petulance, "I will never consent to do such a thing again, for your eyes say nothing all the while. You do not think of me at all, and yet you look at me—"

"Would you rather have me draw another woman?"

"Perhaps—if she were very ugly," she said.

"Well," said Poussin gravely, "and if, for the sake of my fame to come, if to make me a great painter, you must sit to someone else?"

"You may try me," she said; "you know quite well that I would not."

Poussin's head sank on her breast; he seemed to be overpowered by some intolerable joy or sorrow.

"Listen," she cried, plucking at the sleeve of Poussin's threadbare doublet, "I told you, Nick, that I would lay down my life for you; but I never promised you that I in my lifetime would lay down my love."

"Your love?" cried the young artist.

"If I showed myself thus to another, you would love me no longer, and I should feel myself unworthy of you. Obedience to your fancies was a natural and simple thing, was it not? Even against my own will, I am glad and even proud to do thy dear will. But for another, out upon it!"

"Forgive me, my Gillette," said the painter, falling upon his knees; "I would rather be beloved than famous. You are fairer than success and honors. There, fling the pencils away, and burn these sketches! I have made a mistake. I was meant to love and not to paint. Perish art and all its secrets!"

Gillette looked admiringly at him, in an ecstasy of happiness! She was triumphant; she felt instinctively that art was laid aside for her sake, and flung like a grain of incense at her feet.

"Yet he is only an old man," Poussin continued; "for him you would be a woman, and nothing more. You—so perfect!"

"I must love you indeed!" she cried, ready to sacrifice even love's scruples to the lover who had given up so much for her sake; "but I should bring about my own ruin. Ah! to ruin myself, to lose everything for you!... It is a very glorious thought! Ah! but you will forget me. Oh! what evil thought is this that has come to you?"

"I love you, and yet I thought of it," he said, with something like remorse, "Am I so base a wretch?"

"Let us consult Père Hardouin," she said.

"No, no! Let it be a secret between us."

"Very well; I will do it. But you must not be there," she said. "Stay at the door with your dagger in your hand; and if I call, rush in and kill the painter."

Poussin forgot everything but art. He held Gillette tightly in his arms.[21]

"He loves me no longer!" thought Gillette when she was alone. She repented of her resolution already.

But to these misgivings there soon succeeded a sharper pain, and she strove to banish a hideous thought that arose in her own heart. It seemed to her that her own love had grown less already, with a vague suspicion that the painter had fallen somewhat in her eyes.[22]

Camille Claudel, Bust of Rodin[23]

II — CATHERINE LESCAULT[24]

Three months after Poussin and Porbus met, the latter went to see Master Frenhofer. The old man had fallen a victim to one of those profound and spontaneous fits of discouragement that are caused, according to medical logicians, by indigestion, flatulence, fever, or enlargement of the spleen; or, if you take the opinion of the Spiritualists, by the imperfections of our mortal nature. The good man had simply overworked himself in putting the finishing touches to his mysterious picture. He was lounging in a huge carved oak chair, covered with black leather, and did not change his listless attitude, but glanced at Porbus like a man who has settled down into low spirits.[25]

"Well, master," said Porbus, "was the ultramarine bad that you sent for to Bruges? Is the new white difficult to grind? Is the oil poor, or are the brushes recalcitrant?"

"Alas!" cried the old man, "for a moment I thought that my work was finished, but I am sure that I am mistaken in certain details, and I cannot rest until I have cleared my doubts. I am thinking of traveling. I am going to Turkey, to Greece, to Asia, in quest of a model, so as to compare my picture with the different living forms of Nature. Perhaps," and a smile of contentment stole over his face, "perhaps I have Nature herself up there. At times I am half afraid that a breath may waken her, and that she will escape me."

He rose to his feet as if to set out at once.

"Aha!" said Porbus, "I have come just in time to save you the trouble and expense of a journey."

"What?" asked Frenhofer in amazement.

"Young Poussin is loved by a woman of incomparable and flawless beauty. But, dear master, if he consents to lend her to you, at the least you ought to let us see your work."

The old man stood motionless and completely dazed.

"What!" he cried piteously at last, "show you my creation, my bride? Rend the veil that has kept my happiness sacred? It would be an infamous profanation. For ten years I have lived with her; she is mine, mine alone; she loves me. Has she not smiled at me, at each stroke of the brush upon the canvas? She has a soul—the soul that I have given her. She would blush if any eyes but mine should rest on her. To exhibit her! Where is the husband, the lover so vile as to bring the woman he loves to dishonor? When you paint a picture for the court, you do not put your whole soul into it; to courtiers you sell lay figures duly colored. My painting is no painting, it is a sentiment, a passion. She was born in my studio, there she must dwell in maiden solitude, and only when clad can she issue thence. Poetry and women only lay the last veil aside for their lovers! Have we Rafael's model, Ariosto's Angelica, Dante's Beatrice? Nay, only their form and semblance. But this picture, locked away above in my studio, is an exception in our art. It is not a canvas, it is a woman—a woman with whom I talk. I share her thoughts, her tears, her laughter. Would you have me fling aside these ten years of happiness like a cloak? Would you have me cease at once to be father, lover, and creator? She is not a creature, but a creation.

"Bring your young painter here. I will give him my treasures; I will give him pictures by Correggio and Michelangelo and Titian; I will kiss his footprints in the dust; but make him my rival! Shame on me. Ah! ah! I am a lover first, and then a painter. Yes, with my latest sigh I could find strength to burn my *Belle Noiseuse*; but—compel her to endure the gaze of a stranger, a young man and a painter!—Ah! no, no! I would kill him on the morrow who should sully her with a glance! Nay, you, my friend, I would kill you with my own hands in a moment if you did not kneel in reverence before her! Now, will you have me submit my idol to the careless eyes and senseless criticisms of fools? Ah! love is a mystery; it can only live hidden in the depths of the heart. You say, even to your friend, 'Behold her whom I love,' and there is an end of love."

The old man seemed to have grown young again; there was light and life in his eyes, and a faint flush of red in his pale face. His hands shook. Porbus was so amazed by the passionate vehemence of Frenhofer's words that he knew not what to reply to this utterance of an emotion as strange as it was profound. Was Frenhofer sane or mad? Had he fallen a victim to some freak of the artist's fancy? or were these ideas of his produced by the strange lightheadedness which comes over us during the long travail of a work of art? Would it be possible to come to terms with this singular passion?

Harassed by all these doubts, Porbus spoke—"Is it not woman for woman?" he said. "Does not Poussin submit his mistress to your gaze?"

"What is she?" retorted the other. "A mistress who will be false to him sooner or later. Mine will be faithful to me forever."

"Well, well," said Porbus, "let us say no more about it. But you may die before you will find such a flawless beauty as hers, even in Asia, and then your picture will be left unfinished."

"Oh! it is finished," said Frenhofer. "Standing before it you would think that it was a living woman lying on the velvet couch beneath the shadow of the curtains. Perfumes are burning on a golden tripod by her side. You would be tempted to lay your hand upon the tassel of the cord that holds back the curtains; it would seem to you that you saw her breast rise and fall as she breathed; that you beheld the living Catherine Lescault, the beautiful courtesan whom men called *la belle noiseuse*. And yet—if I could but be sure—"

"Then go to Asia," returned Porbus, noticing a certain indecision in Frenhofer's face. And with that Porbus made a few steps toward the door. By that time Gillette and Nicolas Poussin had reached Frenhofer's house. The girl drew away her arm from her lover's as she stood on the threshold, and shrank back as if some presentiment flashed through her mind.

"Oh! what have I come to do here?" she asked of her lover in low vibrating tones, with her eyes fixed on his.

"Gillette, I have left you to decide; I am ready to obey you in everything. You are my conscience and my glory. Go home again; I shall be happier, perhaps, if you do not—"

"Am I my own when you speak to me like that? No, no; I am a child. Come," she added, seemingly with a violent effort; "if our love dies, if I plant a long regret in my heart, your fame will be the reward of my obedience to your wishes, will it not? Let us go in. I shall still live on as a memory on your palette; that shall be life for me afterward."

The door opened, and the two lovers encountered Porbus, who was surprised by the beauty of Gillette, whose eyes were full of tears. He hurried her, trembling from head to foot, into the presence of the old painter.[26]

"Here!" he cried, "is she not worth all the masterpieces in the world!"

Frenhofer trembled. There stood Gillette in the artless and childlike attitude of some timid and innocent Georgian, carried off by brigands, and confronted with a slave merchant. A shamefaced red flushed her face, her eyes drooped, her hands hung by her side, her strength seemed to have failed her, her tears protested against this outrage. Poussin cursed himself in despair that he should have brought his fair treasure from its hiding place. The lover overcame the artist, and countless doubts assailed Poussin's heart when he saw youth dawn in the old man's eyes, as, like a painter, he discerned every line of the form hidden beneath the young girl's vesture. Then the lover's savage jealousy awoke.

"Gillette!" he cried, "let us go."

The girl turned joyously at the cry and the tone in which it was uttered, raised her eyes to his, looked at him, and fled to his arms.

"Ah! then you love me," she cried; "you love me!" and she burst into tears.

She had spirit enough to suffer in silence, but she had no strength to hide her joy.

"Oh! leave her with me for one moment," said the old painter, "and you shall compare her with my Catherine... yes—I consent."

Frenhofer's words likewise came from him like a lover's cry. His vanity seemed to be engaged for his semblance of womanhood; he anticipated the triumph of the beauty of his own creation over the beauty of the living girl.

"Do not give him time to change his mind!" cried Porbus, striking Poussin on the shoulder. "The flower of love soon fades, but the flower of art is immortal."

"Then am I only a woman now for him?" said Gillette. She was watching Poussin and Porbus closely.

She raised her head proudly; she glanced at Frenhofer, and her eyes flashed; then as she saw how her lover had fallen again to gazing at the portrait which he had taken at first for a Giorgione—

"Ah!" she cried; "let us go up to the studio. He never gave me such a look."

The sound of her voice recalled Poussin from his dreams.

"Old man," he said, "do you see this blade? I will plunge it into your heart at the first cry from this young girl; I will set fire to your house, and no one shall leave it alive. Do you understand?"

Nicolas Poussin scowled; every word was a menace. Gillette took comfort from the young painter's bearing, and yet more from that gesture, and almost forgave him for sacrificing her to his art and his glorious future.

Porbus and Poussin stood at the door of the studio and looked at each other in silence.[27] At first the painter of the Saint Mary of Egypt hazarded some exclamations: "Ah! she has taken off her clothes; he told her to come into the light—he is comparing the two!" but the sight of the deep distress in Poussin's face suddenly silenced him; and though old painters no longer feel these scruples, so petty in the presence of art, he admired them because they were so natural and gracious in the lover. The young man kept his hand on the hilt of his dagger, and his ear was almost glued to the door. The two men standing in the shadow might have been conspirators waiting for the hour when they might strike down a tyrant.

"Come in, come in," cried the old man. He was radiant with delight. "My work is perfect. I can show her now with pride. Never shall painter, brushes, colors, light, and canvas produce a rival for 'Catherine Lescault,' the beautiful courtesan!"[28]

Porbus and Poussin, burning with eager curiosity, hurried into a vast studio. Everything was in disorder and covered with dust, but they saw a few pictures here and there upon the wall. They stopped first of all in admiration before the life-size figure of a woman partially draped.

"Oh! never mind that," said Frenhofer; "that is a rough daub that I made, a study, a pose, it is nothing. These are my failures," he went on, indicating the enchanting compositions upon the walls of the studio.

This scorn for such works of art struck Porbus and Poussin dumb with amazement. They looked round for the picture of which he had spoken, and could not discover it.

"Look here!" said the old man. His hair was disordered, his face aglow with a more than human exaltation, his eyes glittered, he breathed hard like a young lover frenzied by love.

"Aha!" he cried, "you did not expect to see such perfection! You are looking for a picture, and you see a woman before you. There is such depth in that canvas, the atmosphere is so true that you cannot distinguish it from the air that surrounds us. Where is art? Art has vanished, it is invisible! It is the form of a living girl that you see before you. Have I not caught the very hues of life, the spirit of the living line that defines the figure? Is there not the effect produced there like that which all natural objects present in the atmosphere about them, or fishes in the water? Do you see how the figure stands out against the background? Does it not seem to you that you pass your hand along the back? But then for seven years I studied and watched how the daylight blends with the objects on which it falls. And the hair, the light pours over it like a flood, does it not?... Ah! she breathed, I am sure that she breathed! Her breast—ah, see! Who would not fall on his knees before her? Her pulses throb. She will rise to her feet. Wait!"

"Do you see anything?" Poussin asked of Porbus.

"No... do you?"

"I see nothing."

The two painters left the old man to his ecstasy, and tried to ascertain whether the light that fell full upon the canvas had in some way neutralized all the effect for them. They moved to the right and left of the picture; they came in front, bending down and standing upright by turns.

"Yes, yes, it is really canvas," said Frenhofer, who mistook the nature of this minute investigation.

"Look! the canvas is on a stretcher, here is the easel; indeed, here are my colors, my brushes," and he took up a brush and held it out to them, all unsuspicious of their thought.

"The old *lansquenet* is laughing at us," said Poussin, coming once more toward the supposed picture. "I can see nothing there but confused masses of color and a multitude of fantastical lines that go to make a dead wall of paint."

"We are mistaken, look!" said Porbus.

In a corner of the canvas, as they came nearer, they distinguished a bare foot emerging from the chaos of color, half-tints and vague shadows that made up a dim, formless fog. Its living delicate beauty held them spellbound. This fragment that had escaped an incomprehensible, slow, and gradual destruction seemed to them like the Parian marble torso of some Venus emerging from the ashes of a ruined town.

"There is a woman beneath," exclaimed Porbus, calling Poussin's attention to the coats of paint with which the old artist had overlaid and concealed his work in the quest of perfection.

Both artists turned involuntarily to Frenhofer. They began to have some understanding, vague though it was, of the ecstasy in which he lived.

"He believes it in all good faith," said Porbus.

"Yes, my friend," said the old man, rousing himself from his dreams, "it needs faith, faith in art, and you must live for long with your work to produce such a creation. What toil some of those shadows have cost me. Look! there is a faint shadow there upon the cheek beneath the eyes—if you saw that on a human face, it would seem to you that you could never render it with paint. Do you think that that effect has not cost unheard-of toil?

"But not only so, dear Porbus. Look closely at my work, and you will understand more clearly what I was saying as to methods of modeling and outline. Look at the highlights on the bosom, and see how by touch on touch, thickly laid on, I have raised the surface so that it catches the light itself and blends it with the lustrous whiteness of the highlights, and how by an opposite process, by flattening the surface of the paint, and leaving no trace of the passage of the brush, I have succeeded in softening the contours of my figures and enveloping them in half-tints until the very idea of drawing, of the means by which the effect is produced, fades away, and the picture has the roundness and relief of nature. Come closer. You will see the manner of working better; at a little distance it cannot be seen. There? Just there, it is, I think, very plainly to be seen," and with the tip of his brush he pointed out a patch of transparent color to the two painters.

Porbus, laying a hand on the old artist's shoulder, turned to Poussin with a "Do you know that in him we see a very great painter?"

"He is even more of a poet than a painter," Poussin answered gravely.

"There," Porbus continued, as he touched the canvas, "is the utmost limit of our art on earth."

"Beyond that point it loses itself in the skies," said Poussin.

"What joys lie there on this piece of canvas!" exclaimed Porbus.

The old man, deep in his own musings, smiled at the woman he alone beheld, and did not hear.

"But sooner or later he will find out that there is nothing there!" cried Poussin.

"Nothing on my canvas!" said Frenhofer, looking in turn at either painter and at his picture.[29]

"What have you done?" muttered Porbus, turning to Poussin.

The old man clutched the young painter's arm and said, "Do you see nothing? Clodpate! Huguenot! Varlet! Cullion! What brought you here into my studio?—My good Porbus," he went on, as he turned to the painter, "are you also making a fool of me? Answer! I am your friend. Tell me, have I ruined my picture after all?"

Porbus hesitated and said nothing, but there was such intolerable anxiety in the old man's white face that he pointed to the easel.

"Look!" he said.

Frenhofer looked for a moment at his picture, and staggered back.

"Nothing! nothing! After ten years of work..." He sat down and wept.

"So I am a dotard, a madman, I have neither talent nor power! I am only a rich man who works for his own pleasure, and makes no progress. I have done nothing after all!"

He looked through his tears at his picture. Suddenly he rose and stood proudly before the two painters.

"By the body and blood of Christ," he cried with flashing eyes, "you are jealous! You would have me think that my picture is a failure because you want to steal her from me! Ah! I see her, I see her!" he cried, "she is marvelously beautiful..."

At that moment Poussin heard the sound of weeping; Gillette was crouching forgotten in a corner. All at once the painter once more became the lover. "What is it, my angel?" he asked her.

"Kill me!" she sobbed. "I must be a vile thing if I love you still, for I despise you... I admire you, and I hate you! I love you, and I feel that I hate you even now!"

While Gillette's words sounded in Poussin's ears, Frenhofer drew a green serge covering over his "Catherine" with the sober deliberation of a jeweler who locks his drawers when he suspects his visitors to be expert thieves. He gave the two painters a profoundly astute glance that expressed to the full his suspicions and his contempt for them, and saw them out of his studio with impetuous haste and in silence, until from the threshold of his house he bade them "Goodbye, my young friends!"

That farewell struck a chill of dread into the two painters. Porbus, in anxiety, went again on the morrow to see Frenhofer, and learned that he had died in the night after burning his canvases.[30]

ENDNOTES TO HONORÉ DE BALZAC'S "THE UNKNOWN MASTERPIECE"

by VALERIA LUISELLI

1.   THE FIRST ILLUSTRATED EDITION of "The Unknown Masterpiece"—
which included an original frontispiece by Pablo Picasso, as well as
thirteen *hors-texte* etchings and wood engravings on the front and back
covers—was published in Paris by the art dealer, collector, and publisher
Ambroise Vollard in 1931. Vollard, who had organized Picasso's first
major exhibition in 1901 and offered him continual emotional support,
commissioned this edition, later considered Picasso's *livre d'artiste* masterpiece. We, however, have decided to replace Picasso's frontispiece with
this well-known image of Rodin's *Monument to Balzac* (1898). Decidedly
one of his weakest sculptures, the *Monument to Balzac* was rejected by the
Société des Gens de Lettres when Rodin exhibited it during the Salon of
1898, and was later described by the critic Joanna Pike as "the world's
most hideous piece of bronze" (Pike, 1968). We believe that Rodin's
Balzac is not only the perfect frontispiece for a story about pretense and
posturing in the art world, but also an elegant vindictive gesture, the
humor of which our author would have appreciated. "The Unknown
Masterpiece" is, after all, a story about artists—about the way writers
see artists. And here, in turn, we have an image of the great Balzac,
epitome of the nineteenth century *écrivain*, as seen by an artist. In this

way, the artist-writer/writer-artist caricature—masterful and inspired, but caricature nonetheless—has gone full circle.

2. Balzac dedicated the 1845 edition of "The Unknown Masterpiece," the first to be published as a book, to a mysterious "Lord," whose identity erudite scholars and *balzaciens* have never managed to trace. We do not think he had anyone in mind, and believe the dedication was a sort of performative gesture *avant la lettre*—an expression of the author's contrived *amour-mépris* for the interdependent, vertical relationship between artists and their patrons. Today, the mechanisms of recognition and patronage have become more horizontal and diffuse, so we have decided to replace "To a Lord" with this "To My Friends."

3. "The Unknown Masterpiece" portrays a tense game of posturing by artists in three generations: the promising young artist (Nicholas Poussin); the accomplished, mature artist (François Porbus); and the aging, forgotten, and bitter has-been (Maître Frenhofer). In the original 1831 version of the story—published in *L'Artiste*, the weekly review dedicated to commentary on contemporary artists and exhibitions—the title for this first section was "Maître Frenhofer." In a later edition, despite the story's central dynamic, the author changed the subtitle to "Gillette," the name of a young woman who serves as mistress and model to Poussin. Similarly, the second section in the story was later subtitled "Catherine Lescault," the name of the fictional character who serves as model for Frenhofer's portrait *La Belle Noiseuse*, on which the artist has spent the past ten years of his life working. The author's correction underscores a subtle but ultimately determining shift of narrative perspective: instead of framing the beginning of his story within the more traditional retrospective gaze of a close third-person narrator who observes the story from the point of view of a central character standing at the end of the narrative parabola, he chooses the slipperier frame of a tangential vector—Gillette—that only just touches the arc of the narrative trajectory. The shift is also perhaps a form of political posturing: although the two women in the story—Gillette and Catherine Lescault—are only

mistresses, muses, and models, their names frame the story's two sections. Whether this gesture is merely decorative or in fact a more significant decision that our author made to demarcate his stance on gender politics in literature is hard to determine.

4. The story's action begins here, outside Porbus's house on Rue des Grands-Augustins, during the early hours of a cold December morning in the year 1612. The young Poussin has been lingering outside the house for a while, walking up and down the street with the irresolution of a lover, until he is able to gather enough courage to knock on the great artist's door. It is not clear whether our author had some ulterior motive in situating Porbus's house on Rue des Grands-Augustins. What is clear is that Balzac contributed to a large future real-estate bubble by means of a common procedure: endowing property with added value by means of representing it in a narrative (or artwork of any sort). In 1937, approximately 325 years after Poussin walked into Porbus's house, and ninety-five years after Balzac published his final version of this story, Picasso decided to rent the Rue des Grands-Augustins studio. The fact is not a mere coincidence. Picasso claimed that the ghost of Balzac had haunted him ever since he worked on the etchings for the 1931 edition of "The Unknown Masterpiece," and he was apparently so transfixed by the story that he decided to live and work in the very same space where Balzac sets the beginning. Balzac, in sum, was a pioneering gentrifier of this once quiet and unremarkable street. Then came Picasso, taking the bait. (Before him, in the early 1930s, the mime artist and director Jean-Louis Barrault had sought out this same studio and paid a considerable monthly rent to be able to rehearse his plays in it.) The main culprits of real-estate inflation tend to be writers and artists, but they are also the first victims of their own meddling. Today, a two-bedroom apartment on Rue des Grands-Augustin costs 1.5 million euros and it is unlikely that any writer or artist lives there.

5. The action continues as Poussin finally stands in front of Porbus's door on

Rue des Grands-Augustins and raises his hand to the "grotesque knocker" on the door of the studio where the painter is at work. Although the etymological origin of *grotesque* refers simply to the patterns and images found in grottos and Roman ruins, by the mid-eighteenth century the word already suggested the clownishly absurd and uncouth. In a way, therefore, the knocker foreshadows the intricate games of seduction, the egoistic tug-of-wars, the overt and tacit power struggles, the posturing and layered pretension, and the choreographed masquerade that will begin to take place among the three artists in the story as soon as that door is crossed. In these passages, Balzac was also referencing a later event: during the early hours of a cold December morning in the year 1937, Dora Maar also lingered outside Picasso's house on Rue des Grands-Augustins. She walked up and down the street, with the irresolution of a lover, until she was able to gather enough courage to knock on the artist's door. On that door hung a grotesque knocker, slightly eroded by the friction of the many nervous palms of successive generations of young artists who, like the young Poussin, had knocked on heavy doors.

6. The idea of the young painter being deeply stirred "by an emotion that must thrill the hearts of all great artists when, in the pride of their youth and their first love of art, they come into the presence of a master or stand before a masterpiece," a kind of rapture in the face of artistic greatness, is the cornerstone of the Balzacian aesthetic edifice, so to speak, and the foundation of a theory of art that this story postulates. There are several baroque twists and spirals to Balzac's premise: recognition of others' greatness is what distinguishes real artists from all the other "swaggerers." "The Unknown Masterpiece" is not so much a story as a kind of curatorial self-positioning, by which Balzac moves from description to prescription, from narrative speculation to categorical dogma, from tentative thought to hearty pedagogical preaching. In 2014, the writer and critic A. K. Murray published the academic essay "Balzac the Mansplainer," which became more popular than she perhaps envisioned, and eventually inspired a play by the young Pulitzer-winning playwright

Annie Baker. In this play Balzac visits Emily Dickinson in her native Amherst. While the two stand under the rain outside a closed patisserie, he reveals to her, unbidden, the secrets of Spinoza's philosophy.

.

7. Balzac further compares young Poussin to Dora Maar. He describes their modesty before a "master" as a measure of their youthful genius, and suggests that the progressive loss of that modesty is a direct result of the constant exercise of their art as they grow older. In the case of young men like Poussin, Balzac refers to the mastery of an artistic technique, such as painting; and, in the case of young women, like Maar, he refers to the art of coquetry: "the indescribable diffidence, the early timidity that artists are bound to lose in the course of a great career, even as pretty women lose it as they make progress in the arts of coquetry."

8. The narrator describes Frenhofer's nose as "a small flat nose" and compares it to Socrates' legendary nose. We believe this reference, beyond serving a descriptive purpose, is a light stroke through which Balzac attempts to write himself into the Socratic-Platonic tradition. Indeed, "The Unknown Masterpiece" mirrors some of the better-known Platonic dialogues—perhaps *The Symposium* in particular—in which men in different stages of experience discuss subjects such as love, art, or science. Further down, the narrator describes Frenhofer's eyes thus: "There were no lashes to the deep-set eyes, and scarcely a trace of the arching lines of the eyebrows above them." Per several historic accounts, this peculiarity was a trait of Balzac's mature anatomy. Following the narrator's descriptions of Frenhofer's facial features, it is safe to conclude that Balzac was sketching a self-portrait—via Frenhofer—in which he subtly layered his own countenance upon Socrates'. Balzac thus masters the art of posturing. Consecration and immortality within artistic disciplines is determined by the perceived links of a creator—writer, painter, dancer—to a lineage and a tradition, as well as by his or her potential to occupy the seats left empty within the Pantheon once the elder masters have abandoned them. Those who are dexterous enough to weave themselves into the complicated web

of artistic heritage and tradition solely by means of their work usually find a place in the canon. But the very few who, on top of this, are also able to convince others that they—and nobody else—are the natural heirs to a specific seat in the Pantheon—those are the immortals.

9. The artist and his studio are described in equal or even superior standing to the art pieces. In the description of Porbus's studio, Balzac is referencing the studio-as-set and the studio-as-boudoir quality that some of the most famous artist-studio photographs reveal. He had been reading Hélène Parmelin's essays on artists' studios, such as her *Secrets d'alcôve d'un atelier* (1966), as well as her writings about Brassaï's artist-studio photographs. Brassaï, the Hungarian photographer whom Henry Miller nicknamed "the eye of Paris," was asked to photograph Picasso's sculptures for André Breton's pioneering Surrealist art review, *Minotaure*. According to Miller, after each visit to Picasso's studio, Brassaï would return home, make copious notes on his talks with Picasso on little scraps of paper, and stuff these into a giant vase. The notes were varied in their subject matter: the ego, the artist's creative process, romantic infatuation, desire, stardust, Greco-Roman coins, and Dali's enormous penis.

10. "I like your saint" are the first words the old master utters in the story. And for the next few pages, much as in a Platonic dialogue in which Socrates finally speaks, the story hinges more on ideas and references than on action. Frenhofer speaks, mostly uninterrupted, for what seems like an eternity—criticizing Porbus's work and delivering his teachings on painting and sculpture. Interestingly, however, Frenhofer's critique seems more relevant to nineteenth-century realism in literature and character depictions than to portraiture in painting. His main observation of Porbus's work-in-progress—a portrait of Maria Aegyptiaca or Saint Mary of Egypt—is that despite the perfection of its imitation of life it does not, itself, exude life. It lacks, in Frenhofer's words, Prometheus's fire and a certain "breath of life." With this last reference, Balzac is of course reminding his readers of one of his favorite films, Godard's 1960 *Breathless*, whose young Patricia

(Jean Seberg) was herself inspired by Saint Mary of Egypt. Both Maria Aegyptiaca and Patricia are young wanderers in a kind of anti-pilgrimage, who run away from their fatherlands—Egypt and America, respectively. From a young age, Maria Aegyptiaca lives a dissolute life in Alexandria (the Paris of the late fourth and early fifth centuries), sometimes offering sexual favors in exchange for money.

11. Frenhofer's critique continues, comparing form to the mythical Proteus: "Form is a Proteus..." Balzac is introducing yet another cinematographic reference here. This time he is commenting on *Zelig*, Woody Allen's mockumentary about a character, Leonard Zelig, who, like Proteus, constantly assumes different shapes. Mr. Allen has never contested Balzac's equation of his Zelig to Proteus.

12. What slowly begins to palpitate—first between the lines, then more overtly—is the question around the relationship between the neophyte and the master. Though Porbus is indeed attentive to the older painter, more and more we see the younger Poussin observing and listening in these pages. He—the neophyte—is necessary for the older artist to come into full existence. Just like a painting that must be seen and recognized by others to be endowed with the value it does not intrinsically possess, the master needs the younger apprentice to fully inhabit his persona and become what he or she is. As he holds the absolute attention of the younger painter, and gets further carried away by his own words, Frenhofer asks Porbus for his palette and begins to add some touches to his portrait of Saint Mary of Egypt.

13. Frenhofer's movements as he intervenes in the portrait are carefully choreographed in their apparent impulsivity—brief jerks, convulsive movements—his entire body, old as it may be, full of passion and ardor, as if a demon had possessed him and were painting through him. What Frenhofer utters, from now on, is hardly made to be of any interest to the reader and becomes more and more like gibberish: "Paf, paf... pon,

pon!" That is, our author was clearly not using Frenhofer's character as a vessel to articulate his contribution to art theory and criticism. Rather, it is the spectacle and posturing that Frenhofer offers which Balzac is perhaps most interested in scrutinizing.

14. Toward the end of his monologue, Maître Frenhofer finally begins to talk about his own unfinished work, the *Belle Noiseuse*, which he has been painting for ten years. Here, Balzac begins to explore the question of how an accomplished artist's yet unfinished work has value, and how that value is perhaps attached to the artist's narrative and theatrical abilities. In any case, Balzac was doubtlessly thinking of Picasso when he wrote these paragraphs. Before he started painting his *Guernica*, in the studio he had rented on Rue des Grands-Augustins, Picasso had already spread the word widely about it, announcing it as a major new work. And, this being a work of great importance, he wanted it to be documented in the process of being painted. Dora Maar was the person in charge of creating the archive of the successive creative stages of Picasso's *Guernica*. Between May and June 1937, she visited the artist every day, sometimes capturing him engaging with his work, in deep concentration, sometimes capturing only the painting in different instants in its development. Today, the Museo Reina Sofía holds a total of twenty-eight photographs showing different stages of the *Guernica*'s execution. Maar's *Guernica* series is thus one of the first documents of an artist posing and performing, perhaps unwittingly, but not quite innocently, for the camera. Furthermore, Picasso, in his process of working on the *Guernica*, is perhaps a precursor of action painting, though some of our most notable phalluses, such as Jackson Pollock and Willem de Kooning, might dispute the idea. After all, the length of their respective paintbrushes and the vigor of their strokes far exceed Picasso's. Nonetheless, Picasso made the best of his circumstances. He used Dora Maar's photographs to mirror and retro-feed his creative process, then saved some of them for later use in his many self-branding and publicity campaigns. In the meantime, he adopted the habit of abusing Dora Maar, physically and emotionally.

The two artists engaged in a well-choreographed power struggle—the artist and the neophyte, the painter and his muse, etc.—performing a script and reenacting an ancestral ritual that would end as one might predict: he finished, she lost; he won, she left. She had gathered enough courage to walk out the door of the studio, down Rue des Grands-Augustins, but she was already reduced to little more than nothing. Later she met Lacan, who generously offered his aid and treated her nervous breakdown with electroshocks. She managed to walk away from him, too, and finally settled in a small village in southern France, where she became a devout Catholic, turned to abstract painting, and died in 1997.

15. The three artists leave Porbus's studio and walk over to Frenhofer's house, where he offers them ham and wine, and shows them the many valuable pieces hung upon the walls. The dialogue continues until finally the younger artists ask Frenhofer the question he has eagerly been waiting for: can they see his work? He then of course says no: "Something still remains for me to do." He still needs to perfect it further, and begins to describe, in much greater detail, the changing nature and metamorphoses of his work in progress. The key point here is the insistence on describing change and metamorphosis, and the critique whereby Balzac comments more generally on the aging artist's self-portrait: their self-made eccentricity, their self-serving *ars poetica*, their confident and even cynical rewriting of their discipline's history, and their savvy way of turning the possibility of failure into capital for their ultimate recognition as geniuses. It is well known that Picasso, when he began working on *Guernica* in the studio on Rue des Grands-Augustins, gave a heads-up to his friend Christian Zervos, founder of the *Cahiers d'Art*, saying that "it would be interesting to use a camera to fix not the stages of a painting, but its metamorphosis." (It was then that Zervos, paying heed to Picasso's indirect suggestion, sent Dora Maar to document this *metamorphosis*.) An echo of this frolicsome lepidopterous metaphor reverberates in Nabokov's intellectual boast-whining, of which Balzac was doubtlessly also thinking when he wrote this section of the story. In his autobiographical *Speak, Memory,* Nabokov recounts

the heavy emotional burden and deep existential anguish that his own obsessive-compulsive and controlling personality inflicts upon his creative process, and describes the (self-inflicted) pains of self-translation and re-translation—from English to Russian, Russian to English, English to Russian, etc.—of some of his masterworks, as well as his having found redemption and consolation in becoming conscious of his utter, absolute originality in undergoing such processes: "some consolation was given me by the thought that such multiple metamorphoses, familiar to butterflies, had not been tried by any human before." As we know, however, many self-translators and second-language writers—including John Donne, Sor Juana, Francis Bacon, Thomas Moore, and the more contemporary Samuel Beckett—preceded him in this kind of work. And they did so rather silently in comparison to Nabokov. It is unlikely that Nabokov, with his encyclopedic knowledge of literary history, was unaware of this robust lineage of second-language writers and self-translators, which would mean that his self-positioning as a pioneer in the genre is more of a posturing than an error born from ignorance. He was thus, like Picasso with his *Guernica*, like Frenhofer with his *Belle Noiseuse*, performing a great and memorable scene of the artist at work. Balzac's critique centers particularly on Nabokov and Picasso, whom he admired, despised, and perhaps also slightly envied. In his depiction of them, we see: (1) Nabokov as the first explorer, conqueror, and monarch (butterfly) of the newfoundland of bilingualism and self-translation; and (2) Picasso as the fluttering *papillon* of performative painting. Balzac depicts these two alpha males as daintily metamorphosing into butterflies, in a way that both sympathizes with them and reveals the sinister-comedic quality of their "type" (a type to which he knew all too well that he, too, belonged). As the critic Marco Gallini has noted in his seminal article "Balzac: Bed, Bath and Beyond" (1991), our author would have happily partaken in all the Viagra-fueled parties and rejoiced in the company of brothers-in-arms like Picasso and Nabokov. He sympathized with these companions. But, being who he was, he would have later turned against himself and his peers, "undoing the spell of the episode, un-writing the narrative, and de-codifying each of the participants, including himself, into perfectly dissected types—all to feed the monster of his multi-volume social tapestry and lifelong masterpiece, *La Comédie humaine*."

16. "But, after all, too much knowledge, like ignorance, brings you to a negation." Many critics believe that, here, Frenhofer finally unveils the kernel of Balzac's story. Others have argued that Balzac surely intended to write *consciousness* and not *knowledge*—as in self-consciousness. Balzac, who was an aficionado of modern ballet, used to say that the best dancers were those who were unconscious of their movements while performing them on stage, and convincingly argued that too much self-consciousness in a dancer spoiled the natural beauty and dexterity of his or her movements. It is thus plausible that Balzac was extending this critique to painters. However, critics have argued that our author shied away from this more blatant spelling-out, as it were, of his critique of posturing and self-consciousness, for fear that his many critics might extend it even further and turn it against him, arguing that Balzac's own excessive self-consciousness was what impeded him from becoming a truly great writer.

17. "Do we know how long Sir Pygmalion wrought at the one statue that came to life?" Via the mythical figure of Pygmalion—the Cypriot sculptor who carved a woman out of ivory and then fell in love with her—Balzac is finally moving away from the pictorial and photographic references present in the early stages of the story, to the wider and more multidisciplinary discussions he will engage with in the story's second half. More specifically, what Balzac introduces here is the first reference to the collaborative relationship between the sculptor Isamu Noguchi and the dancer-choreographer Martha Graham, which he will develop further as the story progresses. More specifically, through his reference to Pygmalion, Balzac is probably pointing us to Noguchi's conceptualization of the role of sculpture in stage arts, and the peculiar way that Graham engaged with the sculptor's sets and props: "There is joy in seeing sculpture come to life on the stage in its own world of timeless

time. Then the air becomes charged with meaning and emotion, and form plays its integral part in the re-enactment of a ritual. Theater is a ceremonial; the performance is a rite. Sculpture in daily life should or could be like this." Finally, it is also possible, as some critics have argued, that through this reference to Pygmalion, Balzac was offering a small sardonic nudge, in passing, to the much discussed "Pygmalion effect," a form of self-fulfilling prophecy whereby higher expectations lead to better performance, as demonstrated by the psychologists and pedagogues Lenore Jacobson and Robert Rosenthal in the 1960s. Balzac is known to have despised behavioral psychology, especially when applied to pedagogy, and was especially critical of the Californian school of behavioral sciences.

18. "For Poussin, the enthusiast, the old man, was suddenly transfigured, and became Art incarnate..." Here, in a reverse Pygmalion procedure of sorts, Frenhofer himself becomes a kind of ur-sculpture or ultimate artwork. Poussin's description of Frenhofer's facial expressions—via the third-person narrator who now takes over the neophyte's gaze—is reminiscent of the portrait heads that Noguchi made after 1929, when Graham commissioned two of them. Noguchi and Graham met in 1928 and collaborated for the next forty years, during which time Noguchi made nineteen distinct dance sets for Graham.

19. "Never mind, Gillette, we shall be rich and happy! There is gold at the tips of those brushes," says Poussin to his young love, Gillette. He has just left the older painters, promising both they will meet again, and has returned to his modest lodgings in a pension on Rue de la Harpe. The following scene between these two young lovers, full of hope and dreams of their future, is Balzac's commentary on *Appalachian Spring* (1944), one of Martha Graham's most popular ballets, for which Aaron Copland wrote the score and Noguchi designed the set. The ballet, one of Graham's more programmatic pieces, is about a young and hopeful marriage between two nineteenth-century pioneers, who will eventually grow old and less hopeful.

20. As critics have noticed, the young couple's postures and movements in these final pages of the story's first section closely mirror those in the climax of *Appalachian Spring* and are almost a textbook representation of the three stages of Graham's technique and kinetic vocabulary: (1) *Base position*. The two bodies begin on the floor, balancing their body masses slowly against the pull of gravity by aligning their upper torsos and heads over their lower torsos. Their tense buttocks, grounded hips, and tight stomach muscles stretch upwards through the core of their bodies toward the base of the throats, and form vertical lines from the bases of their spines to the bases of their throats, centering their erect torsos. (2) *Contractions*. The two dancers begin to curve their torsos. The lowest point of the curve is located in the sacrum, and the highest point is situated in the topmost vertebra of the neck. Internally, the contraction traces an arc through the stomach muscles, which are contracting inward, up, and back toward the spine, while at the same time the ribs and chest hollow in, furthering the depth of the curve in an upward movement toward the base of the throat. (3) *Spirals*. As if there were a shaft at their centers, with axis points at the base of the throat and base of the spine, the dancers twist their torsos. The external line of the spiral begins at the sitting bone, in the pivoting hip, and slowly circles upward to the opposite shoulder. The dancers use the opposition between the hip and shoulder, retaining the center line as a cross-reference, to keep the upper and lower torso in alignment. The turn of the head is the final factor: it either completes the rotation or moves in opposition to it. Thus, the young bodies—Gillette and Poussin; the pioneer boy and pioneer girl—move from their original base positions on the floor, separate from one another, to a contraction, and to a final, tight, spiraled embrace in fully erect position. Externally, they transition from a distinctly separate occupancy of space to a single sculptural figure, indistinct and inseparable. Interiorly, however, while they discuss their future and agree on a plan to move forward together, they grow further and further apart. By the end of the scene, Gillette and the young pioneer girl are struck by the first blow of doubt that will eventually shatter the illusion of their love. And though they are physically bound to their

lovers in a tight embrace, the two young women suddenly internalize and learn how to manipulate the art of distance. They now observe their male counterparts with a new, and possibly irreconcilable, detachment.

21. The two young bodies, in this embrace, resemble a sculpture: "Poussin forgot everything but art. He held Gillette tightly in his arms." They occupy space like actors on a stage, more than the way people inhabit an intimate, private room. They have become a representation of themselves and of their story, as most couples do when they have had a successful fight and have "made a scene." Perhaps because love, both in its beginning and during its final heartbeats, is always a performance of love. In this last embrace, the two figures become a Noguchi-like abstraction: a rock that is also a liquid that is also a cloud that is also a problem. And the room where they now move—once a space that was unquestionably their own; a space they inhabited knowing that, in it, they were truly themselves; a space where they felt simultaneously grounded to the world and connected to each other—has now acquired the placelessness of a waiting or consultation room. They move about in it like two blind fish, trying not to knock their heads against the furniture. Hovering above and around them hang a series of questions, strung together like a cascade of free associations.

22. "... she strove to banish a hideous thought that arose in her own heart. It seemed to her that her own love had grown less already, with a vague suspicion that the painter had fallen somewhat in her eyes." These are the closing lines of the first section of the story, in which the third-person narrator finally attempts to observe the mess of a situation that the three artists have created from the point of view of the young Gillette, who now questions her love for Poussin and suspects he is less lovable than she thought. Her new gaze circles back to the beginning of the story—where the young artist Nicholas Poussin lingers outside the painter's house, pacing the street with the irresolution of a lover—and recasts him in an entirely different light. Seen now, through Gillette, Poussin is no longer an innocent young apprentice and innocent lover, full of promise and future,

but a mere puppet that pathetically embodies the competitive struggles between male artists and foreshadows the most predictable of outcomes of such struggles: ambition, muses, models, work, ego, failure. The young promise turned old fart, as Gertrude Stein may have written. Balzac was given to constructing narratives that, despite their nuanced complexity, followed the model of the typical moral tale. The moral meditation that thus ensues at the close of the first section of his "Unknown Masterpiece" hinges on the notion of the neophyte artist who, desperate to become "someone," is willing to relinquish anything in the name of his future anointment. However, Balzac turns the eye of the story around at this very last minute, and looks at Poussin from the viewpoint of what he is relinquishing, which happens to be not a thing that he owns, not prop within a set in a story of which he is a protagonist, but a young woman, Gillette, who now looks upon him with the incipient but sturdy gaze of a neophyte but already noteworthy bitch. A more recent portrait of this "second" Poussin, and an answer to Balzac's paradox of ownership and loss of the lover-cum-artwork, is offered by Anne Carson in her book *The Albertine Workout*, where the young Albertine becomes conscious that she is imprisoned inside her narrator's house and mind. This narrator happens to be Marcel Proust, who has, as Carson writes, "a theory of desire, which equates possession of another person with erasure of the otherness of her mind, while at the same time positing otherness as what makes another person desirable." Gradually, Carson's Proust loses his mind over Albertine, who in turn becomes more and more ungraspable, devious, and slippery, until she is thrown off a horse and dies. This is "the paranoia of possession," as Carson phrases it. Or, as Roland Barthes writes, this is the moment of catastrophe, in which at least one of the two subjects of an amorous impasse sees him or herself doomed to total destruction and experiences a panic situation. Such a panic situation, writes Barthes, is one "without remainder, without an escape, without return: I have projected myself into the other with such power that when I am without the other I cannot recover myself, regain myself: I am lost, forever." In Carson's version of the Albertine post-panic situation, Proust—like a melancholy

Frenhofer—then returns to correcting his typescript of *La Prisonnière* and spends his afternoons peeling pistachios.

23. As a frontispiece for this second section of the story, and in counterpoint to Auguste Rodin's frontispiece for the first section, we have decided to use Camille Claudel's sculpture "Bust of Rodin" (1892). In the image we see an aged Rodin with small slanted eyes, protruding cheekbones, and an unkempt beard that cascades down toward the raw support of the bust cast in bronze.

24. The second and final section of the story is titled "Catherine Lescault," the name of the character—fictional, as far as *balzaciens* have determined— who served as a model for Frenhofer's final masterwork (*i.e.*, his unknown masterpiece). In this section, our author engages more brutally, and yet more empathetically, on dissecting the old Maître Frenhofer. We see him before his final work—and by transference or transposition, we see Balzac himself—through the eyes of the female subjects that have served as models or muses but who suddenly turn around to observe their creators in the same light as they were seen. What is most striking about this section is how easily the male subject forgets that he is being observed by another presence—a woman's presence. Perhaps male artists are unaccustomed to being studied by the female gaze, so they sometimes—if only for an instant—forget to keep up the posturing and sustain the pose, even while they are being deliberately studied and actively portrayed by a woman in front of them. In any case, it is in these moments of male forgetfulness that the gazes of female artists—such as Maar's Picasso, Claudel's Rodin, Carson's Proust, etc.—have best managed to congeal instants of brutal clarity and deliver a true "portrait of the artist as a young [or aging] man." Carson, for instance, via Albertine, studies the young Proust under the bright, blazing light of her linguistic scrutiny, and delivers a detailed account of his posturing in all its languid, long-suffering romantic imposture. Suddenly, though, in the middle of the portrait, she seems to grow bored of the task, and makes this single, quick, final note: "It's always

tricky, the question..." She then leaves her desk to go to breakfast in a Broadway diner, where she calls the waiter by his first and last name, Gustavo Sánchez, and orders a sunny-side up.

25. In the opening pages of the second section of the story, we see Frenhofer, deeply sunk in his own melancholy humors. Porbus then makes a tempting offer to him. He offers nothing other than Gillette, Poussin's mistress, for the use and usufruct of the Maître's work in progress. The beautiful Gillette, argues Porbus, can be cracked open as an egg might, and out of this may flower beauty itself, opening its new wings before the master, ready to be captured for eternity by his stroke. Frenhofer, desperate for a model to inspire him enough to finally finish his unknown masterpiece, is deeply tempted by the offer. In exchange, however, Porbus tells him that he will have to unveil the mystery of his long-unfinished portrait to him and the young Poussin. Frenhofer resists Porbus's offer at first. But finally he accepts, and Poussin is forced to offer his young love to the old man. In the meantime, Carson is paying for her eggs in the diner where she just had breakfast, then walking back to her studio. She returns to her writing desk, and adds a final exercise/note to *The Albertine Workout*, beginning with the line "Granted the transposition theory is a graceless, intrusive and saddening hermeneutic mechanism... it is also irresistible."

26. Poussin soon regrets his decision. But, alas, it's too late. The door opens, and the two young lovers stand before the older painters. Henceforward, through the final pages of the second section of "The Unknown Masterpiece," the story develops in two distinct layers. On the one hand, it is a complex and nuanced articulation of an innovative theory of aesthetics that unveils the mechanisms of artistic posturing. On the other, it follows the same simplistic logic that governs the lesser Greek tragedies and makes liberal use of the same dramatic ingredients that characterize the contemporary soap opera: swift amorous heartbreak and equally swift reconciliation; copious tears in the interim; sudden marriage proposals; physical violence; polyamorous debauchery and endogamy, often with family members; moralistic

reductions of complex behavior; and finally: death. Balzac's experience and sophistication as a writer when he wrote this second part of the story were well beyond any conformist, audience-pleasing solutions, which raises the question of why he opted for this *feuilleton*-ending of sorts as opposed to a more complex and ambivalent literary *dénouement*. We adjudicate his decision to the general, condescending complacency that tends to settle in and take hold of even the most subversive souls once they've crossed the barrier between prestige and fame and begun reaching "the larger audience." In other words, despite some of Balzac's meaningful contributions to discussions on aesthetics and art criticism in this second section of the story, we agree with the widely accepted verdict among *balzaciens* that, in terms of both plot and formal complexity, this second section offers a very weak follow-up and answer to the conflicts and questions posed in the first.

27. Frenhofer now takes Gillette with him into his studio and paints her, while the other two painters stand by outside his door. It is in this interstice that Carson inserts her final commentary on the Balzac-Proust conundrum of "the paranoia of possession." Deftly, she ends *The Albertine Workout* with a quote from Proust's *La Prisonnière*: "Everything, indeed, is at least double." Balzac became enraged, of course, with her commentary. As critics have noted, she has gradually become Balzac's most lethal literary enemy, though she has perhaps always remained happily oblivious to this fact while he has grown more and more enraged by her pacifist's nonchalance. Some critics trace the struggle between the two back to a dream she had in 1976. In this dream, Carson saw herself attending a lecture on Balzac's "The Unknown Masterpiece," where the speaker offered a key to interpreting *something* in the story, something that was not entirely defined in the dream but nonetheless seemed important enough. The speaker said: "Everything—from Canada, to several species of antelopes, to metastasizing cancers, to ancestral matriarchal societies, to the young Olympic gymnasts that practice cartwheels next to the Hudson River—is all there, inside Frenhofer's bewildered eyes gazing up at the lens of a camera, frozen like blazing stars, right when flash photography was being invented."

28. Finally, Frenhofer lets the two artists into his studio and shows them his painting. But we don't see his painting. We see him. We see his bewildered eyes gazing up at the lens of a camera, frozen like the blazing eyes of a deer caught by a car's headlights on a dark road, looking up at history right when flash photography was being invented. Then we see the other two artists. We see the three of them through the eyes of Gillette. She looks at them, and looks at Catherine Lescault. And Catherine Lescault looks at the room, and the room is populated with all the other ghostly observers that Balzac has been recruiting. She sees Dora Maar photographing Picasso; she sees Carson picturing Proust, and Graham thinking of Noguchi, and Claudel observing Rodin. They all stand there, these women, in the studio on Rue des Grands-Augustins, observing the men before them, who in turn each observe their masterpieces. Some contemplate their work with a distant bewilderment; others awkwardly cradle it in their arms like a newborn; some are lost in intense concentration, as if trying to solve a puzzle.

29. And so Porbus and Poussin stand before *La Belle Noiseuse*, Frenhofer's unknown masterpiece, and the younger of the two exclaims that he sees nothing but a "confused mass of color" contained within a multitude of bizarre lines and a wall of paint. Then Porbus, whose gaze is better trained than Poussin's, notices that, under the mess of colors and beyond the visual noise of all those confused attempts, there is, in the corner of the portrait, a foot: a "delicious" foot; a "real" foot; a foot that is "alive." He notices then that, despite the progressive destruction to which the old master has subjected his portrait, there remains that one foot, like the marble torso of some ancient Venus among the ruins and debris of a fallen city. Frenhofer, in turn, finally sees his own masterpiece, for the first time, through the eyes of his younger contemporaries: "'Nothing on my canvas!' said Frenhofer, looking in turn at either painter and at his picture." It is perhaps thanks to this final image of the failed masterpiece and its master that so many artists have seen in Frenhofer's unknown masterpiece a kind of parable that explains their own search for accuracy and precision as a process of erasure, destruction, and inevitable, progressive illegibility:

"Nothing!" Among these artists are Paul Cézanne—who famously said: "I am Frenhofer"—as well as Alberto Giacometti, Arnold Schoenberg, Yoko Ono, Sally Mann, and, most recently, Danh Vo, Lady Gaga, and Kendrick Lamar, who dedicated his song "HUMBLE." to Frenhofer, and whose lines "I'm so fuckin' sick and tired of the Photoshop... Show me somethin' natural like ass with some stretch marks" reckon with the decoratively beautified and naively aestheticized portrayal of feminine subjects.

30. Later that night, Frenhofer decides to burn all his canvases. His last, brilliant performative gesture: to spit thickly in the face of the future. His legacy: the amorphous phlegm of an *amour-mépris*. His legacy: illegible, destroyed. His legacy: nothing but the ashes of unresolved problems and unanswered questions. Similarly, Balzac challenges the common hermeneutical assumption that art, like science, is a cumulative discipline in which our understanding of the past equips us for the future of the discipline's theory and praxis. He reverts this premise and suggests, in turn, that it is perhaps indeed much more difficult to interpret the past than it is to understand the present.

31. Frenhofer dies that same night: alone, misunderstood, and under-acknowledged by his successors. His last spoken line in the story: "Goodbye, my young friends!" After having read this line, while riding on the subway one day in 1976, Anne Carson took a nap and dreamt that Balzac, Auguste Rodin, Gertrude Stein, Pablo Picasso, and Susan Sontag were all standing on the corner of Rue de Grands-Augustins and Rue de Savoie. They were congratulating one another on something important, some kind of accomplishment. They shook hands, nodded. Then they all unbuttoned their pants, smiled, and dick-waved goodbye to each other: "Adieu."

THE
DISPERSING JOURNEYS
(FINAL APPENDIX)

by EDUARDO BERTI

(Translated by Daniel Levin Becker)

SOON YOU WILL FINISH reading the *Winter Journeys*.* You have made yourself comfortable in your big green velvet armchair in view of the large, slightly misty window, your gaze fixed straight ahead, shoes off, feet propped up on the cushion, holding the book in your left hand and turning pages with the right. You have been thinking for some time now that the long hours spent with the book you are preparing to leave have been more than worthwhile; you think, even, that if you were the author of this book you would say the same of the hours spent writing

---

* *Winter Journeys*, published in 2013 by Atlas Press, is a volume containing Georges Perec's 1979 novella "The Winter Journey"—which recounts the discovery of a book of the same title by the unknown poet Hugo Vernier, whose work turns out to have prefigured most of the French poetry of the twentieth century—and twenty sequels, by different members of the Oulipo, published between 1992 and 2013.

it, but you know perfectly well that in the case of the *Winter Journeys* the writing was collective, which means it may well be that some authors are more satisfied than others, more satisfied not only with their own texts but with the overall result as well. Collective writing is a peculiar affair, and you, despite your experience as a reader, do not have so great an understanding of that species unto itself that is the collective book.

Now, deep into the final pages, feeling the edge and calculating with your right hand the few pages that remain (one of the rare cases where it makes little difference whether the work is collective or not), you begin to do those things you habitually do when a book has pleased you: adjust the lighting for the *n*th time, take a break to go make some tea, take another break to go get a sweater: undisciplined little actions with no purpose but to prolong the reading of this book you will have a hard time leaving, no matter how promising the next one.

For some time now (since page thirty-six, and especially since page fourty-four), you have been thinking that you should try to write some poems or sentences and attribute them to the hero of the *Winter Journeys*, the poet Hugo Vernier, of whom the multiple authors of this collective book cannot seem to agree whether he published verse or scattered fragments of prose. You have been thinking of writing in the manner of Vernier, which would amount to using the finest formulations of the best poets of your time, and you conclude that your desire is doubtless a symptom of the effects that Vernier and his story have had on you. It would be easy, you tell yourself; no, not exactly easy, it would be an amusing challenge: to take a great number of those lines that distinguish the major figures of French literature and copy them, compile them, combine them on a sheet of paper, not as a plagiarist but as a sort of vigilante judge trying to imagine, somewhat hastily, the original aspect and context of these verses.

You have been thinking of a possible analogue: a man who goes to four or five flea markets in a given town and buys objects, furniture, ornaments, even utensils that all belonged to a single family, the Perrens family, say, or the Dupontel or Villiers family, in any case a good upstanding local family; once he has gathered the objects, the man sets himself the challenge of envisioning how these furnishings and ornaments were arranged initially, in the family home. Of course there are as many Dupontel family dining rooms as there are, have been, will be individuals in the world, which disheartens you somewhat and leads you to reflect for a moment, as a reader, on all those theories of infinite worlds, though you feel far off from understanding those theories from an intellectual point of view, and your simple comprehension is, alas, in a word, poetical.

What's the matter? Why are you ignoring the book like this? Yes, it's clear that you haven't abandoned it physically, since its spine is resting more or less pressed onto the palm of your left hand, but your mind is visibly elsewhere. Is it that, faced with the idea of an infinite library of *winter journeys*, this book, between your fingers, audaciously named *Winter Journeys*, strikes you as a vague imposture? Is it this possibility of the infinite that awakens in you your fear of dispersion?

If you were less dispersed, you would have already written these texts by Vernier, that much is clear, since the idea came to you almost nine or ten days ago, on a day of scattered showers (so the weather report called it), when you read, on page forty-four, that "the most celebrated along with the most obscure poets [had] used 'The Winter Journey' as a bible from which they had extracted the best of themselves."

If you were less dispersed, moreover, you would not have this almost compulsive need for a reading method, rigorous and full of ridiculous rules, to stalk the ghost of disorder. Ordinarily, for instance, you never finish a book without first reading a few pages into the book you will read next. You have discussed this method with a close friend from your childhood, an engineer, a cinema fanatic who even worked in his youth as an editor on a few films; he told you that your reading technique (or, more precisely, your technique of transit between two books) was like those crossfades that serve to signify distant memories on the movie screen: those moments where the end of one scene and the beginning of the next are superimposed on one another for a few seconds, the way those disc jockeys from the seventies and eighties mixed together two songs with similar rhythmic models, except that you, reader of the *Winter Journeys*, you know nothing about your next book but a vague factual knowledge, a hint, from the back cover copy, a foretaste based on the dozen pages you read last night, whereas the editor and the DJ know perfectly well why they are superimposing the two pieces, they know the perfection of both, and they are certain that the moment of eclipse, not ellipsis, will be a moment of happiness, a twilight transition between two moments of happiness.

So you began reading the first ten or fifteen pages of the next book. You did so last night, yes, after reading the last sentence of the penultimate chapter of the *Winter Journeys*. You have a strange mania (not so strange, true, for someone fighting dispersion) for balance and symmetry. You come to a moment near the end of whatever novel you are currently reading, a moment that makes you emerge from the pages like a swimmer raising his head out of the water just before reaching the finish line in order to see how many strokes remain (three or four, maybe?), and you say to yourself, aha, here is the moment to scout out the next book, so you do five things in the following inflexible order: (1) choose the next book, a choice you have forbidden yourself until now, even if you already have a list of five possible books, and once you have chosen the successor, the heir, your next travel companion (and bed and green velvet armchair companion), only then do you (2) count the pages remaining in the current book, suppose there are fifteen left, the fifteen pages occupied by this "final appendix," and then you (3) read exactly fifteen pages, the first fifteen of the next book, not one more, not one less, before you (4) return to the current book and finish it, and then (5) settle in, once and for all, to the next book, which is no longer the next, which has become the current book: your new present.

If you were less dispersed, you would have no need for these reading tactics, bizarre and (let's be honest) almost therapeutic as they are. If you were less dispersed (and you are the first to admit it), you would not have this pathological need to always have a current book, this need to always have a book between your fingers: a book as reassuring as a cane or some other instrument that helps you not fall, on the ground or into digression, an instrument that helps you not lose your balance or your calm or the thread of your daily journey. You know it well: deep into a book, even one you have written off as insignificant, you feel the illusion of concentration, you force back your propensity for dissipation and for the kind of insane thinking, you think, called analogy, the thinking that seems to guide each pace of your mind, as it did in the book that once made you so nervous because you recognized in it your own innumerable bifurcations (you know I'm talking about *Tristram Shandy*, right?), because you are like a spider who cannot manage to weave a real web, or who has decided to amuse herself by making a singular spiderweb, centerless, full of holes and therefore sterile: a web that other spiders would never make and that, but for its unique beauty, will neither create a new school among spiders nor trap any insects.

Well then, you're reading this epilogue because you have reached step four of your ritual. Last night you read the first pages of the next book: a novel by an author you had never heard of. You are obsessed with finding a next book whose title bears a certain echo of the current one. This is not a strict rule, but a little ancillary game that brings you pleasure. You are always looking (with successful results, generally) for a word shared between the book you will soon leave and the one waiting on your bedside table. In this case, the words are not quite identical but closely related: *journeys* and *traveler*. In this case you are finishing *Winter Journeys* (about three thousand fifty words left, I can say with precision, starting with this parenthesis) and the book waiting for you is called *If on a summer's morning a traveler*. Of course, you are a discerning reader, a man of culture, and if the name of the author (one Réta Altare Tulnai) did not ring any bells, on the contrary one glance at *If on a summer's morning a traveler* sufficed to make you think, obviously, of that well known novel by Italo Calvino, *If on a winter's night a traveler*, a novel which, to be honest, you had already thought of while reading the book still between your hands, all the more because Georges Perec and Calvino not only knew one another but also shared a great complicity, all the more because *If on a winter's night...* remains one of your bedside books, a book that was created expressly for you: a novel made, in a sense, of the first chapters of books, which awakened in you, fifteen years ago, when you read it for the first and only time, the dream of literary success. Because you told yourself, no point in denying it, that you yourself were also a magnificent author of beginnings, an artist of the unfinished and of ideas quickly taken up and quickly set aside: a master of dispersion, which in your opinion is your greatest weakness: the dispersion that keeps you from concentrating, from pursuing your ambitions to the end; the dispersion that keeps you from deepening your friendships and engagements with others, to the point that it seems inevitable that you live a bit like a hermit, away from your neighbors and colleagues, who will soon be no more than your ex-colleagues, because you are approaching retirement age; the dispersion in the face of which, whether the weather outside is ugly or beautiful, you have erected, over the years, this fortress of books.

You read, last night, during dinner (because you eat while reading, which is to say you read while eating), the first twenty pages or so of this book by Réta Altare Tulnai, who signs her name Réta A. Tulnai, and you felt the mixture of anger and frustration that overcomes you each time the first pages of a next book are usurped by a preface or, even worse, each time you face a double usurpation, such as here, where the preface was written not by the author herself but by someone else, one Mikhail Gorliuk, a Russian, presumably, a man who is supposed to be the foremost specialist of the works of Réta Tulnai, of the work of her uncle, the dramaturg Endro Altare, and, what's more, of the twentieth-century literature of Poldavia, birthplace of Tulnai and Altare, a small quasi-Balkan republic about which you know absolutely nothing. You read Gorliuk's preface and thought how easy it must be for a scholar, a researcher, to become a specialist of a domain about which the vast majority of humanity lacks even the slightest information or imagination. Which is quite the opposite, evidently, of being a specialist of the work of a writer on whom millions of pages and articles and books have been written, for example Kafka. Yes, it's much simpler, you think, to be an expert on the obscure and nearly improbable body of work of a novelist from Lithuania or Macedonia or, why not, Poldavia, to be the great connoisseur of an artist whose work seems to exist solely thanks to the pages dedicated to it by that same connoisseur, thanks especially to his or her descriptions thereof. You tell yourself that Gorliuk could even make up total nonsense about Réta Tulnai or about the little republic of Poldavia, that all of it could just as easily not exist at all, could be the impetuous invention of Gorliuk, which would, given the circumstance, make Gorliuk the real author of all of it, of the preface as well as the novel; but, at this thought, you feel a sort of déjà vu, you look at the book, not the new one, *If on a summer's morning a traveler*, but *Winter Journeys*, your future ex-book, to put it as a temporal paradox, and a quick search is enough to confirm that your memory serves correctly: the name (spelled Gorliouk, which is but a minor detail) is there, within the pages of the book you are preparing to leave, and so you suddenly feel the fear of having walked into a fine swindle. The book awaiting you is, you think, a book whose author is neither Réta Tulnai nor Mikhail Gorliuk, but someone else. Maybe even the same author as that of the pages of the *Winter Journeys* in which Gorliuk appears? Impossible to know...

The preface of your next book, despite your suspicions, despite the potential swindle (though within the realm of literary games, you think, that word is unfair, too severe and moralizing), the preface piqued your interest. With good reason, Gorliuk explains that Tulnai took up Calvino's idea: to write a series of first chapters of novels, a series of books that begin without developing into anything, without pursuing their stories; except that she, Réta Tulnai, has done the opposite and written a series of last chapters, a little museum of books that are ending. In certain cases, Gorliuk explains, Réta Tulnai took the same novels as Calvino's and imagined their final chapters. Gorliuk's preface struck you as a bit excessive, not only because it bandies about some reckless ideas about Calvino's novel, in an overly complex and convoluted fashion (what does "the intertextual metalepsis of the frame-story itself" mean?), but especially because the Russian expert revealed too much of the Poldavian writer's novel by summarizing in lavish detail the entire narrative of the reader, who provides the novel's throughline and central character. The Americans have a word for this kind of atrocity: a *spoiler*, a bit of information that ruins one of the best parts of the pact between a book and its reader: the surprise that comes from being oblivious to a fact or a series of facts that has been placed on this or that page of the book for aesthetic reasons, no doubt, but also dramatic ones, the same way one does not plant a tree just anywhere in a garden, because a tree (like every key event in an arc) has the multiple power of being seen, of hiding certain things, of projecting its shadow in this or that manner, and, why not, of supplying shade.

Reading Gorliuk's preface allowed you to learn a bit about the history and culture of Poldavia. This explains why you are now reading this "final appendix" while still meditating on something you read last night in the next book: a strange particularity in the Poldavian language that Mikhail Gorliuk explains amply (a bit overmuch, even) in his preface, since according to him "one cannot and must not approach a literary work produced in Poldavia without knowing this particularity of its language." It may be useful to summarize: in Poldavian, all nouns, adjectives, and verbs are grouped in antonymic binomials (*man/woman*, *big/small*, *day/night*) and each word therein is pronounced nearly the same, except for a difference indicated by an accent: *ílgore* (accent on the *i*) and *ilgóre* (accent on the *o*) for *pretty* and *ugly*; *gúrbita* (accent on the *u*) and *gurbíta* (accent on the *i*) for *hot* and *cold*. This is simple enough for dual concepts, like *good* and *bad*, *old* and *young*, *birth* and *death*. But it becomes problematic, for example, with the names of animals, flowers, or foods. In many cases the binomials are constructed from popular beliefs: *dog* and *cat*. Some are more whimsical, like *wine* and *milk*. Others still (*philosophical/athletic*) may be considered absurd or extravagant, unless you think that they confirm, in sum, that each language is its own vision of the universe.

In any case, this linguistic digression aside, your feeling remains one of anger toward the Russian specialist who was incapable of the slightest deference toward you, the reader. He must belong, this Gorliuk, to that army of professors who are a bit pedantic, a bit elitist, who show mistrust for *naive* readers, readers who still read to solve an engima or a mystery, to find out the identity of the assassin or see whether the girl finally marries the young man. All of this, for old Gorliuk, because you imagine him old, all this is banal and secondary to him, to judge by the prefaces he cooks up. Unless… unless old Gorliuk is a victim of all this, you think, increasingly agitated, unless all of this is the fault of the publisher, who asked him to write an afterword, a text to be read at the end, as is the case of this appendix you are reading right now, except that old Gorliuk wrote his text without thinking for a moment that his scoundrel of a publisher would turn his afterword into a foreword, out of neglect or, worse, because he disdains readers even more than old Gorliuk does.

Now you are wild with rage at the publisher of the next book. But the poor *Winter Journeys* is not at fault. Calm down. Get up from your soft velvet armchair. Pick up the *Winter Journeys*, which has fallen to your feet, the cover turned to face up, the open pages like a crushed bird (all right, I won't say you threw it down on purpose), yes, that's it, collect yourself, and before diving back in, look for a moment out of the misted window: there, across from your house, stands a little plaza, or a little square, which may be the main reason you love your house and your neighborhood so much, a plaza whose form is both circular and triangular but not really square, no, awash in fallen leaves, carrying the name and displaying the bust of a writer who, for a certain country (a better known country than Poldavia), even for a language better known than Poldavian, is the demigod, the national author, the literary hero: a Goethe, a Shakespeare, a Camões, a Dante, a Cervantes…

Back in your green velvet armchair, you suddenly tell yourself that there, in the idea that a writer can be the hero of a language, is a potential key to the figure of Vernier. If Hugo Vernier is the source of all of these great poets and prose writers, then it is ultimately him, the hero figure that seems to be missing for France, that has made French literature the exception, since otherwise choosing Montaigne would mean scorning Flaubert, choosing Balzac would be tantamount to leaving behind Stendhal or Victor Hugo, and let no more be said of it! No, of course, you are not a reader who looks for a thesis, a "message" or a lesson, in works of fiction, and whenever a novel happens to have some kind of allegory, you prefer that it be rich, polysemic: an allegory that can be read on many levels, even contradictory ones, and not a case of fiction being pressed into service illustrating an idea.

This is why, after having read the nearly three hundred fifty pages of the *Winter Journeys*, you believe that Hugo Vernier does not deserve to be reduced to a single interpretation, so great does his richness appear to you. Nonetheless, you cannot help but laugh at the idea of an Institut Vernier instead of an Alliance Française, of a Université Vernier instead of the Sorbonne, of Hugo Vernier's face on the old fifty-franc note, not the youthful portrait painted by Gustave Courbet but an image of maturity, at almost fifty, done, with any luck, by Henri Fantin-Latour. This makes you laugh because the idea is amusing; the problem, though, is that you see digression approaching. Or, worse yet, you didn't see it coming, and yet here, now, for a few minutes already, you have been in the middle of a distraction, your eyes skating on the page, this last page of the final appendix, in an irresponsible manner.

If you were less dispersed... if you were more implacable... all you need is a final effort. Just one last push. But you can't manage to concentrate. And, what's more, the text isn't helping. It's more dispersed than you are; it is everything but the resolution it seemed to promise. To cap it all off, your hand can see... your hand can feel that there are only two or three pages remaining and that on these pages there can hardly be enough space to develop an ending, to tie up all the loose ends, all the paths pointing this way and that; this is the major inconvenience of collective novels: the disorder and the dissipation, two topics on which you could write a fine thesis.

Clearly, you think, they included this appendix to give an air of conclusion to the whole thing, but it hasn't worked: the arc is still open, there is nothing in these final pages but rhetorical effects aimed at some impression of closure... in any case, the epilogue is a failure, in all respects, even stylistically. This is why you are not surprised to find yourself now so distracted. Anyway, you wonder, what kind of writer would agree to such a lowly task, and, worse yet, to put as a title, in bold letters, like a sinister neon sign, that terrible word, *appendix*, verging on a slip of the tongue, suggesting absence, somehow admitting the uselessness of its very task. Isn't the appendix the organ that serves absolutely no purpose, except to doctors looking to make a fistful of cash by extracting it?

It's a pity, you tell yourself, the *Winter Journeys* started well, but journeys, alas, are always a bit like this: a little jumble of clues and expectations, with ups and downs, always more or less frustrated. You tell yourself also that, nonetheless, the poor epilogue notwithstanding, you have had an agreeable time, it only remains to be seen now where you will file this book that has begun to tire of your clammy hands: whether among the books-you-have-read-and-don't-want-to-keep-at-home-because-you-already-have-so-many-so-you-will-sell-or-trade-them, or among the books-you-have-read-and-that-you-keep-without-quite-knowing-what-reason-or-superstition-compels-you-to-keep-them, or among the books-you-have-read-and-feel-sure-you-will-reread-in-the-near-or-distant-future-so-you-leave-a-subway-ticket-or-an-advertising-flyer-or-anyway-some-kind-of-bookmark-between-the-pages-as-a-message-for-a-future-you, or among the books-you-keep-in-a-second-library-that-you-put-up-in-your-basement-in-spite-of-the-humidity-because-the-other-library-the-official-one-is-saturated-so-you-took-recourse-to-a-sort-of-appendix-if-you'll-excuse-the-expression.

You don't know yet. You push the question away because, finally, you are a damned idealist: an optimist hooked on the illusion of finding a stroke of genius in the few words remaining between you and the end (about six hundred fifty, as of the word *remaining*), on the illusion of falling upon an idea so sublime that it ties together all of the stories, all of the threads yet unwoven... but no, these illusions are just that, illusory. You know one thing, however: as soon as you think about all of this, as soon as you ask yourself where you will file the book, it means in no uncertain terms that you are ready to leave it, to replace it with another, especially if the other book, as in the present case, appears to be a veritable factory of resolutions, one in which (the idea explodes inside you all of a sudden, like an absurd promise) you could potentially find the ending missing from the *Winter Journeys*. No, certainly that will never happen, of course such a thing is perfectly unlikely. But the idea has its ludic, fantasist charm: a book that constitutes the end of another, unbeknownst to the author. By a sort of miracle.

If you were less dispersed, naturally, you would write a little story describing this: the story of a reader who finds, in the copious library of a friend, a book that contains the ending of another book. Or, why not, a series of unknown books that offer, unruffled and unknowing, a resolution for all of those unfinished books that have proliferated for ages. Your story could begin with the same words as "The Winter Journey" does: "In the last week of August 1939, as the talk of war..." That would tie something together. But at the same time, it would lead you, properly speaking, onto a vertiginous path. And for the first time you would be forced to stay within the book in question. Like a reader with nothing else on the horizon. Like a reader with no more dispersion and, in spite of everything, no escape.

You are thinking about these questions, even as your hand does not take down a single word (this is how you write, in your head; but then you are a reader), when you witness, stunned, a bizarre spectacle: your book is shaking. There, in the middle of those sentences and those words, you think, is where the shaking begins, before moving to your hands, your arms, your chest and your head now dumbfounded to see and to understand that it is possible to die, that tragic and fatal act, just before finishing an almost completed reading, just before arriving at a final point that is nonetheless right there, within reach.

Is this book your final book, then? Is this where your journey ends? If you were less dispersed and not on the verge of dying, perhaps you would write (in your head, yes) a text in which a man arrives simultaneously at the end of his life and at the end of the book he has been busy reading. Naturally, the shaking overtakes you, the book falls to the ground, the pages visible this time, the cover flattened against the merciless cold of the floor, but in your head the reading does not stop: victim of your own imagination, you read, a bit theatrically, your own final sentence, so far from the real final sentence, and you find everything you had wanted so badly, everything you had been waiting for for so long. The words and ideas and objects and characters and settings and sentiments seal themselves off, for good. And you murmur, all at once, with the last of your strength, ten final words, which you had perhaps managed to glimpse before the book fell, or else it is a miracle of clairvoyance on your part, because both your delirium and this text (which continues here, without you), conclude the same: "In its own way, each book begins with its ending."

CONTRIBUTORS

CHIMAMANDA NGOZI ADICHIE grew up in Nigeria. Her work has been translated into thirty languages and has appeared in various publications, including the *New Yorker*, *Granta*, *The O. Henry Prize Stories*, the *Financial Times*, and *Zoetrope*. She is the author of three novels, *Purple Hibiscus* (2003), *Half of a Yellow Sun* (2006), and *Americanah* (2013), as well as a short story collection, *The Thing Around Your Neck* (2009), and her most recent work is the just-published *Dear Ijeawele, or A Feminist Manifesto in Fifteen Suggestions*.

SHERMAN ALEXIE is a poet, short-story writer, novelist, and performer. A Spokane/Coeur d'Alene Indian, Alexie grew up in Wellpinit, Washington, on the Spokane Indian Reservation. Alexie has been an urban Indian since 1994 and lives in Seattle with his family.

BIANCA BAGNARELLI is an Italian cartoonist and illustrator and the author of the short graphic novel *Fish*, published by Nobrow. She founded Delebile, a small independent press that publishes short comic stories by Italian and foreign artists, in 2010. She lives and works in Bologna.

JESSE BALL was born in New York. His various works of absurdity have been published in many parts of the world.

EDUARDO BERTI, born in Buenos Aires, has lived in France for almost twenty years. Author of seven novels and several short story collections, he's a member of the Oulipo and writes in both Spanish and French. Next October, Deep Vellum will publish his novel *Imagined Country*.

CARRIE BROWNSTEIN is the award winning co-creator, cowriter, and costar of the hit sketch comedy show *Portlandia* (IFC), as well as an author, director, and musician (she is the guitarist in the highly lauded rock band Sleater-Kinney). She is a former contributor to NPR Music, and her writing has appeared in the *New Yorker*, the *New York Times*, and numerous anthologies on music and culture. Brownstein's bestselling memoir, *Hunger Makes Me a Modern Girl*, was released in fall 2015.

LILLI CARRÉ is an interdisciplinary artist and illustrator living in Chicago. Her animated films have shown in festivals internationally, including the Sundance Film Festival, and she co-founded the Eyeworks Festival of Experimental Animation. She has created several books of comics, including *Heads or Tails* (Fantagraphics) and the children's book *Tippy and the Night Parade* (Toon Books). Her work has appeared in the *New Yorker*, the *New York Times*, *Best American Comics*, and *Best American Nonrequired Reading*. She has had recent solo exhibitions at the Museum of Contemporary Art in Chicago and the Columbus Museum of Art.

LUCY CORIN is the author of two short story collections, *One Hundred Apocalypses and Other Apocalypses* (McSweeney's Books) and *The Entire Predicament* (Tin House Books), as well as a novel, *Everyday Psychokillers: A History for Girls* (FC2). She won an American Academy of Arts and Letters Rome Prize and is currently an NEA fellow. She lives in Asheville and Northern California, teaches at the University of California at Davis, and is at work on a novel.

REBECCA CURTIS's first book, *Twenty Grand and Other Tales of Love and Money*, was a finalist for the PEN/Hemingway Award. She lives and works in New Jersey.

LYDIA DAVIS's most recent collection of stories is *Can't and Won't* (Farrar, Straus & Giroux, 2014). She is also the author of *The Collected Stories* (Farrar, Straus & Giroux, 2009) and translator of Proust's *Swann's Way* (Viking Penguin, 2002) and Flaubert's *Madame Bovary* (Viking Penguin, 2010). She is currently assembling a collection of essays, and her translation of Proust's *Letters to His Neighbor* appears this year from New Directions.

HARIS A. DURRANI is an author, engineer, academic, and lawyer-in-training. His debut, *Technologies of the Self*, won the Driftless Novella Contest, and his stories and non-fiction have appeared in *Analog*, *Lightspeed*, the *New Inquiry*, *Catapult*, *Buffalo Almanack*, *Mithila Review*, the *New York Review of Science Fiction*, *Comparative Islamic Studies*, *Skin Deep*, *Media Diversified*, and *altMuslimah*. He is a JD candidate at Columbia Law School, holds an MPhil in History and Philosophy of Science from the University of Cambridge, and holds a BS in Applied Physics from Columbia University, where he co-founded The Muslim Protagonist literary symposium. After winning the McSweeney's Student Short Story Contest, this story appeared in modified form in *Buffalo Almanack*.

BRIAN EVENSON is the author of a dozen books of fiction, most recently the story collection *A Collapse of Horses* (Coffee House Press, 2016) and the novella *The Warren* (Tor.com, 2016). He lives in Los Angeles and teaches in the Critical Studies Program at CalArts.

JAMES FOLTA is a writer and comedian. His writing has been published by the *New Yorker*, *National Lampoon*, the *American*

Bystander, and more. James co-created the *New Yorker* parody magazine the *Neu Jorker*, as well as the forthcoming political satire magazine *Paul Ryan*.

SOPHIA FOSTER-DIMINO is an illustrator and cartoonist living in San Francisco. She teaches conceptual illustration at California College of the Arts. A collection of her Ignatz Award–winning comic series, *Sex Fantasy*, will be released by Koyama Press in the fall of 2017.

DORIAN GEISLER is a graduate of UC Berkeley and the Iowa Writers' Workshop. He has taught at the Millennium Art Academy and Arcadia University, and his poetry has appeared in the *Believer*, *Hayden's Ferry Review*, *LVNG*, and the *Berkeley Poetry Review*. Geisler is currently studying law at the University of Michigan.

SHEILA HETI is the author of several books, including *How Should a Person Be?* In the spring of 2018, she will be releasing a new novel called *Motherhood*.

JOHN HODGMAN is a writer, comedian, and famous minor television personality. His next book is called *VACATIONLAND*, and it comes out in October of 2017.

ELI HOROWITZ worked at McSweeney's from 2004 to 2011, editing and designing books and quarterlies. He is the co-author of a treasure-hunt mystery, a digital novel, a useless cookbook, an audio drama, and an illustrated cultural history of ping pong.

KRISTEN ISKANDRIAN's debut novel, *Motherest*, is forthcoming from Twelve/Hachette in August. Her recent fiction appears in *Ploughshares*, *Zyzzyva*, and *EPOCH*, and her story "The Inheritors," first published in *Tin*

House, won an O. Henry Prize in 2014. She lives in Birmingham, Alabama.

JESSE JACOBS works from his home in Hamilton, Ontario. A selection of his work can be viewed at www.jessejacobs.ca. His books can be found at koyamapress.com.

HEIDI JULAVITS is a novelist and essayist and diarist and the author, most recently, of *The Folded Clock*.

DAN KENNEDY is host of *The Moth* storytelling podcast and live shows; author of the books *Loser Goes First, Rock On,* and *American Spirit*; and a screenwriter. He is represented by Carolyn Sivitz at UTA and Sean Perrone at Kaplan/Perrone Entertainment.

ETGAR KERET is an Israeli writer known for his short stories, graphic novels, and scriptwriting for film and television. His writing has been published in the *New York Times*, the *New Yorker, Zoetrope*, and the *Paris Review*; his books have been published in more than forty languages. His latest book, *The Seven Good Years*, was chosen by the *Guardian* as one of the best biographies and memoirs of 2015. Keret is the winner of the 2016 Charles Bronfman Prize.

ZAIN KHALID is a writer whose work has appeared in *The New Yorker*, here, and elsewhere. He is working on a novel.

ANDREW LELAND is working on a podcast series about going blind. He hosts the Organist (kcrw.com/theorganist) and teaches at Smith College and UMass Amherst.

JONATHAN LETHEM is the author of many acclaimed novels, a number of grudgingly acknowledged short stories, and a few

poems which are passed over in remorseful silence. He lives in Los Angeles and Maine.

DANIEL LEVIN BECKER is a critic, translator, editor, and member of the Oulipo. He lives in Oakland.

VALERIA LUISELLI was born Mexico City in 1983 and grew up in South Africa. She is a novelist (*The Story of My Teeth* and *Faces in the Crowd*) and essayist (*Sidewalks*) whose work has been translated into many languages and has appeared in publications including the *New York Times*, the *New Yorker, Granta*, and *McSweeney's*. A longer version of her piece is forthcoming in the monograph *Form, Model, Syntax, Display: Terence Gower Sculpture Works,* to be published next year by Black Dog Press.

SARAH MANGUSO is the author of seven books including *300 Arguments, Ongoingness,* the *Guardians*, and *The Two Kinds of Decay*. Her work has been supported by a Guggenheim Fellowship and the Rome Prize. She lives in Los Angeles.

THOMAS MCGUANE is the author of ten novels, six nonfiction essay collections, and two short story collections. In 1971, McGuane received the Rosenthal Award from the American Academy of Arts and Letters, and in 1974 he received a National Book Award nomination for his novel *Ninety-two in the Shade*. Knopf will be publishing McGuane's upcoming short story collection, *Blind Copy: New and Collected Stories,* in February 2018.

CARSON MELL is an ape on Earth. He is currently publishing a serialized sci-fi novel, *Field Notes From Dimension X*. Parts one through three are available from his website, carsonmell.com. His feature film, *Another Evil*, is available on iTunes and Amazon, and the first season of his cartoon series *Tarantula* debuts on TBS some time in 2018.

STEVEN MILLHAUSER is the author of thirteen works of fiction, including *Edwin Mullhouse* and *Martin Dressler*. His most recent book is *Voices in the Night*, a collection of stories.

JOHN MOE is a writer in St. Paul who sometimes gets to read what he wrote on the radio and on podcasts. He's the author of *Dear Luke, We Need to Talk, Darth* and two other books and his work has appeared in *McSweeney's* a lot and then sometimes in the *New York Times Magazine* and other publications. He's better than you'd think at thumb wrestling.

KEVIN MOFFETT is the author of two story collections and a collaborative novel, *The Silent History*. He teaches at Claremont McKenna College and in the low-residency MFA at the University of Tampa.

WENDY MOLYNEUX is a writer/producer on the TV show *Bob's Burgers* who got her start writing for McSweeney's Internet Tendency. In exchange, she has given McSweeney's her firstborn child, Durfa, who screams constantly and demands raw meats at all hours. Not all bargains work out well for everyone.

DAN MOREY is a freelance writer in Pennsylvania. He's worked as a book critic, nightlife columnist, travel correspondent, and outdoor journalist. He thinks Tony Danza was great in *Going Ape!*

APARNA NANCHERLA is a comedian who can currently be seen on HBO's *Crashing* and the latest seasons of *Love* and *Master of None* on Netflix. She has a Comedy Central half-hour special and an album called *Just Putting It Out There* on Bentzen Ball Records.

TUCKER NICHOLS is an artist whose work has been shown in museums and galleries around the world. He is the co-author of *Crabtree* (with Jon Nichols) and *This Bridge Will Not Be Gray* (with Dave Eggers), both published by McSweeney's.

AGATA NOWICKA is an illustrator and comics artist. She has worked for *Elle*, *GQ*, the *New Yorker*, *Time*, and the *New York Times*. Her work has been featured in Taschen's *Illustration Now!*, *American Illustration*, and *Communication Arts Annual*. Originally from Poland, she currently lives in Brooklyn, where she continues to be an avid fan of Polish illustration and marzipan. www.agatanowicka.com

PATTON OSWALT is an actor/writer/comedian (or "actwredian") as well as a father and a friend (or "fathead").

JEFF PARKER's most recent book is *Where Bears Roam the Streets: A Russian Journal* (Harper Collins). With Pasha Malla he co-"wrote" *Erratic Fire, Erratic Passion: The Poetry of Sportstalk* (Featherproof). He teaches fiction in the MFA program at UMass Amherst.

KEATON PATTI is a writer and comedian living in New York City. He has written for the *New Yorker*, *Comedy Central*, and the *Onion*, to name exactly three. You may remember him from the previous sentences.

BENJAMIN PERCY's most recent novel is *The Dark Net* (Houghton Mifflin Harcourt, 2017). He writes the *Green Arrow* and *Teen Titans* series for DC Comics, and his fiction and nonfiction have been published in *Esquire*, *GQ*, *Time*, *Men's Journal*, the *Paris Review*, *Ploughshares*, and *Tin House*. His honors include the Whiting Award, an

NEA fellowship, two Pushcart Prizes, the Plimpton Prize, and inclusion in *Best American Short Stories* and *Best American Comics*.

JASON POLAN is an artist living in New York. He is from Michigan.

ISMET PRCIC (Izzy) was born in Bosnia-Herzegovina and immigrated to the USA in 1996. His debut novel, *Shards,* was published in 2011 by Grove Press to critical acclaim, winning numerous awards. He co-wrote the screenplay for the film *Imperial Dreams,* currently on Netflix. Prcic lives in Portland, Oregon, and teaches at IAIA in New Mexico.

MATTHEW SHARPE is the author of the novels *You Were Wrong, Jamestown, The Sleeping Father,* and *Nothing Is Terrible*. He teaches sometimes in the MFA program at Columbia University and at the 92nd Street Y in New York City.

SONDRA SILVERSTON is a native New Yorker who has been living in Israel since 1970. Among her published translations are works by Israeli authors Amos Oz (her translation of *Between Friends* won the 2013 National Jewish Book Award for fiction), Eshkol Nevo (her translation of *Homesick* was on the Independent Translation prize long list, 2009), Ayelet Gundar-Goshen (her translation of *Waking Lions* won the 2017 Jewish Quarterly Wingate prize), Savyon Liebrecht, Alona Frankel, and, of course, Etgar Keret.

CORINNA VALLIANATOS's story collection, *My Escapee,* won the Grace Paley Prize for Short Fiction and was a *New York Times Book Review* Editors' Choice. She lives in Southern California and teaches in the University of Tampa's low-residency MFA program.

VAUHINI VARA is an O. Henry Prize–winning fiction writer, with stories published in *Tin House, Zyzzyva,* and elsewhere. As a journalist, she has written for the *Atlantic, Harper's,* and other publications; she is currently a staff writer at the *California Sunday Magazine*. She is working on a story collection and a novel.

SARAH VOWELL contributed to the first issue of McSweeney's back in the twentieth century. Her most recent book is *Lafayette in the Somewhat United States*.

SARAH WALKER is a writer living in Los Angeles. Her piece is a tribute to her lifelong fandom of UConn Women's Basketball and dogs.

DIANE WILLIAMS's most recent book of fiction is *Fine, Fine, Fine, Fine, Fine,* out from McSweeney's. *The Collected Stories of Diane Williams* and *The Collected Novellas of Diane Williams* are due out from Soho Press in 2018. She is also the editor of the literary annual *NOON*.

SEAN WILSEY is the author of a memoir, *Oh the Glory of It All,* and a collection of essays, *More Curious*. He is at work on a second memoir, *I Am in Love*.

KEVIN YOUNG is the author of *Bunk: The Rise of Hoaxes, Humbug, Plagiarists, Phonies, Post-Facts, and Fake News,* and a previous book of nonfiction, *The Grey Album: On the Blackness of Blackness,* which was a finalist for the National Book Critics Circle Award for criticism. He is the author of ten celebrated books of poetry, most recently *Blue Laws: Selected and Uncollected Poems 1995–2015,* which was longlisted for the National Book Award. He is the director of the Schomburg Center for Research in Black Culture, and, starting in fall 2017, poetry editor of the *New Yorker*.

McSWEENEY'S WOULD LIKE TO
THANK THE FOLLOWING DONORS FOR
THEIR BOUNDLESS GENEROSITY.
YOU MAKE OUR WORK POSSIBLE.

A. Dupuis · A. Elizabeth Graves · A. Haggerty · A. Lee · A. Reiter · Aaron · Aaron Cripps · Aaron Davidson · Aaron Flowers · Aaron Mcmillan @Ericrosenbizzle · 826 Fan · A.A. · Aaron Quint · Aaron Rabiroff · Aaron Richard Marx · Aaron Sedivy · Aaron Stewart · Aaron Vacin · Aaron Wishart · Abbey · Abigail Droge · Abigail Keel · Abigail Kroch · Adam Alley · Adam Angley · Adam Baer · Adam Batty · Adam Blanchard · Adam Cady · Adam Colman · Adam Esbensen · Adam Hirsch · Adam J. Kurtz · Adam Keker · Adam Kempa · Adam Mueller · Adam O'Riordan · Adam Shaffer · Adam Wager · Adam Weiss · Adam Zaner · Addison Eaton · Adeline Teoh · Aditi Rao · Adriana Difranco · Adrienne Adams · Adrienne Kolb · Adrienne Spain Chu · Adscriptum.nl · Agatha Trundle · Aida Daay · Aiden Enns · Aimee · Aimee Kalnoskas · Akiko K · Alaina Roche · Alan Federman · Alan Keefer · Alana Lewis · Alana Stubbs · Alanna Watson · Alessia Rotondo · Alex · Alex Andre · Alex Atkinson · Alex Daly · Alex Field · Alex Grecian · Alex Haynes · Alex Khripin · Alex Motzenbecker · Alex Power · Alexa Dooseman · Alexa Huyck · Alexa Pogue · Alexander Birkhold · Alexander Carney · Alexander F. Myers · Alexandra Cousy · Alexandra Kordoski · Alexandra Phillips · Alfie · Alfredo Agostini · Ali Procopio · Ali Sternburg · Alice Armstrong · Alice Christman · Alice Curtis Cline · Alice Freilinger · Alice Gardner Kelsh · Alice Mccormick · Alice Quinn · Alicia Kolbus · Alicia Mullen · Alijah · Alina Shlyapochnik · Alisa Bonsignore · Alisa Morgan · Alison Benowitz · Alison Huffman · Alison Lester · Alison Michael · Alison Thayer · Alissa Elliott · Alissa Sheldon · Alistair Bright · Alisun Armstrong · Allan Weinrib · Allen Eckhouse · Allen Rein · Allie Carey · Allison · Allison Arieff · Allison B. Bransfield · Allison Downing · Ally Kornfeld · Allyson Fielder · Altaire Productions · Alvin Tsao · Alyson Levy · Amalia Durham · Amanda & Keagan · Amanda Bullock · Amanda Canales · Amanda Duling · Amanda Durbin · Amanda Niu · Amanda Roer Duling · Amanda Uhle · Amanda Wallwin · Amandeep Jutla · Amazing Grace! · Amber · Amber Bittiger · Amber D. Kempthorn · Amber Murray · Amro Gebreel · Amy · Amy Blair · Amy Brownstein · Amy Henschen · Amy Lampert Pfau · Amy Macauley · Amy Marcus · Amy Ponsetti · Amy Rosenthal · Amy Shields · Amy Wallace · Amy Ware · Amy Welch · Amy Wolfner · Ana Cr · Ananda V.h. · Andi Biren · Andi Winnette · Andra Kiscaden · Andre Kuzniarek · André Mora · Andrea Biren · Andrea D'tonio · Andrea Dahl · Andrea Lunsford · Andrea Pilati · Andrea Sammarco · Andrew Bailey · Andrew Bannon · Andrew Benner · Andrew Blossom · Andrew Cohn · Andrew Crooks · Andrew Durbin · Andrew Eichenfield · Andrew Eisenman · Andrew Glaser · Andrew Glencross · Andrew Gurnett · Andrew Hirshman · Andrew Holets · Andrew Jensen · Andrew Kaufteil · Andrew M. Jackson · Andrew Macbride · Andrew Mason · Andrew Mclaughlin · Andrew Mcleod · Andrew Miles · Andrew Noonan · Andrew Patton · Andrew Perito ·

Andrew Rose · Andrew Rosen · Andrew Sachs · Andrew Stargel · Andrew Steele · Andrew Stratis · Andrew Watson · Andrew Yakas · Andrew Alan Ferguson · Andy Banks · Andy Barnes · Andy Dobson · Andy Que · Andy Steckling · Andy Steele · Andy Waer · Andy Yaco-Mink · Angel Logue · Angela Hunter · Angela Johnson · Angela Johnson · Angela Lau · Angela Petrella · Angela Saunders · Angelo Delsante · Angelo Pizzo · Angie · Angie Boysen · Angie Holan · Angie Newgren · Anisse Gross · Anja R. · Ann Giardina Magee · Ann Gillespie · Ann Gillespie · Ann McDonald · Ann McKenzie · Ann Morrone · Ann Sieber · Ann Stuart King · Anna Bond · Anna Calasanti · Anna Luebbert · Anna March · Anna Stroup · Anna Wiener · Anna-Marie Silvester · Annalisa Post · Anne Connell · Anne Fougeron · Anne Gaynor · Anne Germanacos · Anne Holland · Anne Lebaron · Anne Petersen · Anne Shelton · Anne Tonolli Cook · Anne Wheeler · Annemarie Gray · Annette Toutonghi · Annick Mcintosh · Annie Ganem · Annie Logue · Annie Lynsen · Annie Neild · Annie Porter · Annie Ross · Annika Shore · Anonymous × 9 · Antares M · Anthology LLC · Anthony "Tony" Schmiedeler · Anthony Clavelli · Anthony Devito · Anthony Effinger · Anthony Ha · Anthony Marks · Anthony Myint · Anthony St George · Anthony Teoh · Anthony Thompson · April Fry Ruen · April Ruen · Arianna Reiche · Ariel Hartman · Ariel Zambelich · Arielle Brousse · Arlene Buhl · Armadillo & Dicker · Arthur Hurley · Arthur Strauss · Arturo Elenes · Ash Huang · Asha Bhatia · Ashima Bawa · Ashley · Ashley Aguirre · Ashley Kalagian Blunt · Ashley Otto · Ashraf Hasham · Atsuro Riley · Audrey · Audrey Butcher · Audrey Fennell · Audrey Yang · Augusta Palmer · Christopher Robin · Ayni · Azro Cady · Balz Meierhans · Barbara Barnes · Barbara David · Barbara Demarest · Barbara Kirby · Barbara Passino · Barry Traub · Basil Guinane · Beau Bailey · Becca · Becky · Beckyjo Bean · Beejieweejie · Bekah Grim · Beki Pope · Ben Ames · Ben Blum · Ben Crowley · Ben Gibbs · Ben Goldmam · Ben Hughes · Ben Larrison · Ben Matthews · Ben Pfeiffer · Ben Zotto · Benjamin Elkind · Benjamin Han · Benjamin Jahn · Benjamin Liss · Benjamin Novak · Benjamin Peskoe · Benjamin Petrosky · Benjamin Russell · Benjamin Small · Benjamin Southworth · Bernadette Segura · Bernard Yu · Berry Bowen · Bertis Downs · Beth Ayer · Beth Chlapek · Beth Daugherty · Beth Duncan · Beth Mcduffee · Betsy Ely · Betsy Henry Pringle · Betsy Henschel · Betsy Levitas · Betsy Pattullo · Betty Jane Jacobs · Betty Joyce Nash · Bill Bonwitt · Bill Crosbie · Bill Frazier · Bill Hughes · Bill Manheim · Bill Owens · Bill Rising · Bill Spitzig · Bill Weir · Billy Moon · Billy Taylor · Billy Tombs · Bindi Kaufman · Birch Norton · Birchy Norton · Blair Roberts · Blake Coglianese · Blaz · Blythe Alpern · Bob · Bob Blanco · Bob Den Hartog · Bob Sherron · Bob Slevc · Bob Wilson · Bonnie Garmus · Bookman · Boris Glazunov · Boris Mindzak · Boris Vassilev · Bosco Hernandez · Bourbonsmartypants · Brad Feld · Brad Kik · Brad Marcoux · Brad Phifer · Bradley Clarke · Bradley Flynt · Bradley Harkrader · Bradley Mcmahon · Brandon Amico · Brandon Bussolini · Brandon Chalk · Brandon Flammang · Brandon Forsyth · Brandon Wynn · Brenda A Vogan · Brendan Dowling · Brendan James Moore · Brendan Mcguigan · Brenna Field · Brent Emery · Brett Anders · Brett Goldblatt · Brett Klopp · Brett Silton · Brett Yasko · Brian Agler · Brian Bailey · Brian Bowen · Brian Cassidy · Brian Chess · Brian Cobb · Brian Cullen · Brian Dice · Brian Dillon · Brian Eck · Brian Gallay · Brian Godsey · Brian Green

· Brian Grygiel · Brian Guthrie · Brian Hiatt · Brian James Rubinton · Brian Knott · Brian M Rosen · Brian Meacham · Brian Pfeffer · Brian Pluta · Brian Turner · Brian Z Danin · Brianna Kratz · Brianna Suzelle · Bridget · Brinda Gupta · Brittany · Brittany Carroll Jones · Brittany Medeiros · Brnnr · Bronwyn Glubb · Brooke Haskell · Brooke Lewis · Brooke Prince · Brownstone BBQ · Bruce G Gordon · Bruce Gordon · Bruce Greeley · Bruce King · Bryan Alexander · Bryan Curtis · Bryan Waterman · Bryce Gorman · Bryn Durgin · Brynn Elizabeth Kingsley · Bsj · Buffalo Architectural Machine · Buffy · Buttocks · C Broderick · C. Odal · C.d. Hermelin · C.j.winter · C.m. Tomlin · Caedlighe Paolucci · Caitlin · Caitlin Fischer · Caitlin L. Baker · Caitlin Van Dusen · Caitlin Webb · Callie Ryan · Calvin Crosby · Camaro Powers · Cameron David · Candice Chiew · Capelesst · Cara Beale · Cara J Giaimo · Cara Mchugh · Cari Hauck · Carisa Miller · Carl Grant · Carl H. Hendrickson Jr · Carl Jacobsen · Carl Salbacka · Carl Voss · Carleton Smith · Carley Phillips · Carlos Parreno · Carly · Carmel Boerner · Carol Anne Tack · Carol Davis · Carole Sargent · Caroline · Caroline Carney · Caroline Moakley · Caroline Pugh · Carolyn Anthony · Caryn Lenhoff · Cassie Ettinger · Catastrophoea · Cate Trujillo · Caterina Fake · Cath Keenan · Cath Le Couteur · Catharine Bell · Catherine · Catherine Chen · Catherine Coan · Catherine Flores Marsh · Catherine Hagin · Catherine Jayne · Catherine Keenan · Catherine Leclair · Catherine Shuster · Catherine Smith · Cathi Falconwing · Cathryn Lyman · Cathy Nieng · Catie Myers-Wood · Cb Murphy · Cece · Cecile Forman · Cecilia Holmes · Cecilia M Holmes · Cecilia Mills · Cedric Howe · Celbridge Rob · Celeste Adamson · Celeste Hotaling-Lyons · Celeste Roberts-Lewis · Cesar Contreras · Chad Gibbs · Chad Gibbs · Chairs And Tables · Char Kuperstein · Charibdys · Charis Poon · Charlene Ortuno · Charles · Charles Bertsch · Charles D Myers · Charles Dee Mitchell · Charles Irby · Charles Lamar Phillips · Charles Pence · Charles Spaht, Jr. · Charley Brammer · Charlie B Spaht · Charlie Garnett · Charlie Hoers · Charlotte · Charlotte Locke · Charlotte Moore · Cheesybeard666 · Chef Ben Bebenroth · Chelsea Bingham · Cheng Leong · Chenoa Pettrup · Cherisse Datu · Cheryl · Cheryl Flack · Chester Jakubowicz · Chris · Chris Baird · Chris Brinkworth · Chris Bulock · Chris Clancy · Chris Cobb · Chris Duffy · Chris Foley · Chris Hogan · Chris Kleinknecht · Chris Maddox · Chris Martins · Chris Niewiarowski · Chris Ohlson · Chris Preston · Chris Remo · Chris Roberts · Chris Roe · Chris Saeli · Chris Sandoval · Chris Schmidt · Chris Warack · Chrissy Simonte Boylan · Christen Herland · Christi Chidester · Christian Gheorghe · Christian Lovecchio · Christian Rudder · Christian S. · Christian Smith · Christina Dickinson · Christina Erickson · Christina Grachek · Christina Macsweeney · Christina Schmigel · Christine Allan · Christine Chen · Christine Delorenzo · Christine Evans · Christine Langill · Christine Luketic · Christine Lyons · Christine Ogata · Christine Rehm · Christine Ross · Christine Ryan · Christine Tilton · Christine Vallejo · Christopher Benz · Christopher Carver · Christopher Fauske · Christopher Fox · Christopher Greenwald · Christopher Harnden · Christopher Hinger · Christopher Knaus · Christopher Madden · Christopher Maynard · Christopher Mclachlan · Christopher Naccari · Christopher Sarnowski · Christopher Soriano · Christopher Stearly · Christopher Strelioff · Christopher Todd · Christopher W Ulbrich · Christopher Wright · Christy Brown · Christy Fletcher · Christy Rishoi

· Chrysta Cherrie · Cindi Hickman · Cindi Rowell · Cindy Foley · Cindy Lamar · Cirocco · City Tap House · Claire Burleson · Claire Swinford · Claire Tan · Clare Hyam · Clare Louise Jones · Clare Wallin · Claudia · Claudia Milne · Claudia Mueller · Claudia Stein · Cleri Coula · Cleri Coula · Clint Popetz · Clive Thompson · Cloe Shasha · Cmg · Cns · Cody Hudson · Cody Peterson · Cody Williams · Colby Aymar · Colby Ray · Colin · Colin Nissan · Colin Urbina · Colin Winnette · Colleen Bright · Collin Brazie · Colton Powell · Connor Kalista · Conor Delahunty · Corey & Meghan Musolff · Corinne Caputo · Corinne Marrinan Tripp · Cortney Kammerer · Cory Gutman · Cory Hershberger · Cory Hershberger · Courtney A. Aubrecht · Courtney Hopkins · Courtney Nguyen · Craig Clark · Craig New · Craig Short · Cris Pedregal Martin · Crystal · Curt Sobolewski · Curtis Edmonds · Curtis Rising · Curtis Sutton · Cyd Peroni · Cydney Stewart · Cynthia Baute · Cynthia Foley · Cynthia Yang · D · D Cooper · D Miller · D. Whiteman · D.a. Pratt · Daan Windhorst · Dale Sawa · Damfrat · Damian Bradfield · Damien James · Damon Copeland · Damon-Eugene Rich · Dan Ashton · Dan Carroll · Dan Colburn · Dan Grant · Dan Haugen · Dan May · Dan Mckinley · Dan Money · Dan Pasternack · Dan Pritts · Dan Rollman · Dan Schreiber · Dan Spealman · Dan Stein · Dan Winkler · Dana K · Dana Skwirut · Dana Werdmuller · Dani D · Daniel · Daniel A. Hoyt · Daniel Bahls · Daniel Beauchamp · Daniel Berger · Daniel Dejan · Daniel Edwards · Daniel Erwin · Daniel Feldman · Daniel Grossman · Daniel Grou · Daniel Guilak · Daniel Hoyt · Daniel Khalastchi · Daniel Levin Becker · Daniel Morgan · Daniel Ness · Daniel Ridges · Daniel Tovrov · Daniel Wilbur · Danielle Bailey · Danielle Gallen · Danielle Granatt · Danielle Jacklin · Danielle Kucera · Danielle Lavaque-Manty · Danika Esden-Tempski · Danny Richelson · Danny Shapiro · Danyl Garnett · Darby Dixon Iii · Darcie Thomas · Dargaud-Fons · Darko Orsic · Darlene Zandanel · Darrell Hancock · Darren Higgins · Daryl Dragon · Dash Shaw · Dave · Dave Baptist · Dave Curry · Dave David · Dave Forman · Dave Haas · Dave Lucey · Dave Madden · Dave Polus · Davi Ferreira · David · David · David + Kami · David Andrews · David Baker · David Bradley · David Brett Kinitsky · David Brown · David Burns · David Charlton · David Chatenay · David Cornwell · David Desmond · David Dietrich · David E Baker · David Eckles · David F. Gallagher · David Frankel · David Galef · David Givens · David Givens · David Goldstein · David Guerrero · David Hodge · David J. Whelan · David James · David K · David Karpa · David Kneebone · David Knopp · David Kurz · David L Gobeli · David Leftwich · David Lerner · David Levy · David M · David Macy-Beckwith · David Mccarty · David Nilsen And Melinda Guerra · David Peter · David Pollock · David R Lamarre · David Rodwin · David Sam · David Sanger · David Sievers · David Springbett · David Strait · David Sundin · David Thompson · David Wolske · David Wright · David Zaffrann · David Zarzycki · D.b. Ramer · De_hart · Dean · Dean O'donnell · Deane Taylor · Deb Olin Unferth · Debbie Baldwin · Debbie Berne · Debbie Millman · Debby Weinstein · Deborah Conrad · Deborah Urban · Deborah Wallis · Debra Bok · Demeny Pollitt · Dena Verhoff · Denae Dietlein · Denise Sarvis · Denise Witherspoon · Dennis Caraher · Dennis Gallagher · Dennis Marfurt · Derek Van Westrum · Designers & Books · Devon Henderson · Diana Behl · Diana Cohn · Diana Funk · Diana M. · Diana Tomchick · Diane Arisman · Diane B Kresal · Diane Fitzsimmons · Diane

Holdgate · Diane Lederman · Diane M. Fedak · Diane S. · Diane Wang · Dianne Weinthal · Dianne Wood · Dillon Morris · Dinika Amaral · Dirk Heniges · Dom Baker · Dominic Lepper · Dominic Luxford · Dominica Phetteplace · Don Smith · Donald Deye · Donald Schaffner · Donald Solem · Donald Woutat · Donna Copeland-Fuller · Donna Fogarty · Doreen Kaminski · Doro · Dory Culver · Doug · Doug Dorst · Doug Green · Doug Mayo-Wells · Doug Messel · Doug Michel · Doug Moe · Doug Schoemer · Doug Taub · Doug Wolff · Doug Wykstra · Douglas Andersen · Douglas Candano · Douglas Hirsch · Douglas Kearney · Douglas Mcgray · Dov Lebowitz-Nowak · Dr. Demento · Dr. Hornet · Dr. Meredith Blitzmeyer · Drew Atkins · Drew Baldwin · Drew Sussman · Duane Murray · Duane Murray · Dustin Mark · Eap · Ed Freedman · Ed Krakovsky · Ed Riley · Ed Rodley · Ed Sweeney · Edie Jarolim · Edinblack · Edward · Edward Crabbe · Edward Lim · Edwina Trentham · Eileen Consedine · Eileen M Mccullough · Eileen Madden · Eitan Kensky · El Chin · Elaine Froneberger · Elana Spivack · Elda Guidinetti · Eleanor Cooney · Eleanor Horner · Elia Wise · Elinor Wahl · Elisa · Elisa Harkness · Elisabeth Carroll · Elisabeth Hammerberg · Elisabeth Seng · Elise Persico · Elizabeth Alkire · Elizabeth Allspaw · Elizabeth Averett · Elizabeth Carmichael-Davis · Elizabeth Chang · Elizabeth Craft · Elizabeth Dalay · Elizabeth Davies · Elizabeth Engle · Elizabeth Gemmill · Elizabeth Gray · Elizabeth Green · Elizabeth Hom · Elizabeth Hykes · Elizabeth Keim · Elizabeth Macklin · Elizabeth Miller · Elizabeth Pfeffer · Elizabeth Ray · Elizabeth Redick · Elizabeth Rovito · Elizabeth Siggins · Elizabeth Smith · Elizabeth Taylor · Elizabeth Weber · Elizwill · Ella Haselswerdt · Ellen Goldblatt · Ellen Line · Ellen Tubbaji · Ellia Bisker · Ellia Bisker · Ellie Flock · Ellie Turzynski · Ellyn Farrelly · Ellyn Toscano · Eloy Gomez · Elsa Figueroa · Elske Krikhaar · Elyse Rettig · Ema Solarova · Emilce Cordeiro · Emily Bliquez · Emily Bryant · Emily Cardenas · Emily Carroll · Emily Diamond · Emily Donohoo · Emily Friedlander · Emily Goode · Emily Harris · Emily Kaiser Thelin · Emily Lynch · Emily M. · Emily Morian-Lozano · Emily Olmstead-Rumsey · Emily Raisch · Emily Schleiger · Emily Schuck · Emily Wallis Hughes · Emma Axelson · Emma Axelson · Emma D. Dryden, Drydenbks Llc · Emma Roosevelt · Enrico Casarosa · Epilogue · Eric · Eric · Eric · Eric Botts · Eric Brink · Eric Brink · Eric Donato · Eric Farwell · Eric Harker · Eric Heiman · Eric Hsu · Eric Johnson · Eric Kuczynski · Eric Larsh · Eric Mauer · Eric Meyers · Eric Muhlheim · Eric Perkins · Eric Potter · Eric Prestemon · Eric Randall · Eric Ricker · Eric Ries · Eric Schulmiller · Eric Segerstrom · Eric Tell · Eric W · Erica Behr · Erica Lively · Erica Nardello · Erica Nist-Lund · Erica Portnoy · Erica Seiler · Erick · Erick Gordon · Erik Henriksen · Erik Pedersen · Erin · Erin Ambrozic · Erin Badillo · Erin Barnes · Erin Corrigan · Erin Eakle · Erin Mcgrath · Erin Senge · Ernesto Gloria · Erwin Wall · Esme Weijun Wang · Ethan Nosowsky · Ethan Rogers · Euan Monaghan · Eva Funderburgh Hollis · Eva Thompson · Evan Brooks · Evan Orsak · Evan Regner · Evan Rosler · Evan Williams · Eve Bower · Evelyn Tunnell · Everett Shock · Evil Supply Co. · Evonne Okafor · Experiencing Life To The Fullest-Da Wolf · Eylem Ezgi Ozaslan · Ezra Karsk · F.p. De L. · Faisel Siddiqui · Fanny Luor · Farnaz Fatemi · Fawn · Felicia · Femme Fan1946 · Fengypants · Fern Culhane · Fernanda Dutra · Fiona Hamersley · Fiona Hartmann · Flash Sheridan · Fotios Zemenides · Frederic Jaume · Fran Gensberg ·

Frances Lopez · Frances Tuite · Frances Tuite · Francesca Moore · Francis Desiderio · Frank Drummond · Frank Lortscher · Frank Riley · Frank Ruffing · Frank Turek · Franklin · Franklin Friedman · Freddi Bruschke · Freddy Powys · Frederick De Naples · Frederick Fedewa · Free Expressions Seminars And Literary Services · Frin Atticus Doust · Fualana Detail · Full Gamut Consulting · Gabe Gutierrez · Gabe Mcgowan · Gabriel Pumple · Gabriel Vogt · Gabriela Melchior · Gala Grant · Galen Livingston · Garth Reese · Gary Almeter · Gary Almeter · Gary Beckerman · Gary Chun · Gary Gilbert · Gary Rudoren · Gary Rudoren · Gavin Beatty · Gaye Hill · Gayle Brandeis · Gayle Dosher · Gayle Engel · Genevieve Kelly · Geoff "Not-So-Mysterious-Benefactor" Brown · Geoff D. · Geoff Smith · George Hodosh Associates · George Mcconochie · George Mitolidis · George Veugeler · George Washington Hastings · Georgia · German (Panda) Borbolla · Gerrit Thompson · Gertrude And Alice Editions · Gibby Stratton · Gieson Cacho · Gina · Gina B. · Gina Smith · Ginny · Girija Brilliant · Gisela Sehnert · Gitgo Productions · Glorianne Scott · Gopakumar Sethuraman · Gordon Mcalpine · Grace Levin · Graeme Deuchars · Graham Bell · Greg Grallo · Greg Johnson · Greg Lavine · Greg Lloyd · Greg Prince · Greg Steinberg · Greg Storey · Greg Versch · Greg Vines · Greg Weber · Greg Wheeler · Greg Williams · Gregory Affsa · Gregory Hagan · Gregory Stern · Gregory Sullivan · Griffin Richardson · Guillaume Morissette · Gunnar Paulsen · Guy Albertelli · Gwen Goodkin · Haden Lawyer · Haiy Le · Hal Tepfer · Haley Cullingham · Haley Williams · Hank Scorpio · Hannah Mcginty · Hannah Meyer · Hannah O'regan · Hannah Rothman · Hannah Settle · Hannelore · Hans Balmes · Hans Ericson · Hans Lillegard · Hans Zippert · Hans-Juergen Balmes · Harold Check · Harris Levinson · Harry Deering · Harry J. Mersmann · Harry Mersmann · Harry White · Haruna Iwase · Hassan Fahs · Hassanchop · Hathaway Green · Heather Bause · Heather Boyd · Heather Braxton · Heather Flanagan · Heather Forrester · Heather Guillen · Heckle Her · Hedwig Van Driel · Heidi Baumgartner · Heidi Meurer · Heidi Raatz · Helen Chang · Helen Kim · Helen Linda · Helen Tibboel · Helena · Hemant Anant Jain · Hilary · Hilary Leichter · Hilary Rand · Hilary Sasso-Schleh · Hilary Van Dusen · Hillary Lannan · Holly · Holly Iossa · Holly Kennedy · Houston Needs A Swimming Hole! · Howard Katz · Howeverbal · Hugh Geenen · Hypothetical Development Organization · Ian · Ian Benjamin · Ian Casselberry · Ian Chung · Ian Delaney · Ian Foe · Ian Frederick-Rothwell · Ian Glazer · Ian Harrison · Ian Joyce · Ian Prichard · Ian Shadwell · Ilana Gordon · Iliana Helfenstein · Ingrid Kvalvik Sørensen · Ioana Popa · Irene Arntz · Irene Hahn · Isabel A · Isabel Pinner · Isabella · J.F. Gibbs · J.G. Hancock · J. Wilson · J.A. López · J.B. Van Wely · J.J. Larrea · J.L. Schmidt · Jack Amick · Jack Dodd · Jack Stokes · Jack Thorpe · Jackie Jones · Jackie Mccarthy · Jackie Yang · Jaclyne D Recchiuti · Jacob Davis · Jacob Haller · Jacob Lacivita · Jacob Leland · Jacob Zionts · Jacqueline Utkin · Jacquelyn Moorad And Carolyn Hsu · Jade Higashi · Jaime Young · Jaimen Sfetko · Jake · Jake Bailey · Jamal Saleh · James Adamson · James And Rasika Boice · James Brown · James Chesky · James Crowley, Jr · James E Wolcott · James English · James Manion · James Merk · James Mnookin · James Moore · James Newton · James O'brien · James Osborne · James Park · James Roger · James Roger · James Ross-Edwards · James Trimble · James Vest · James Woods (Not The Actor) · Jamie

Alexander · Jamie Campbell · Jamie Campbell · Jamie Tanner · Jamie Zeppa · Jamon Yerger · Jan Greene · Jan Yeaman · Jane Clarke · Jane Darroch Riley · Jane Gibbins · Jane Jonas · Jane Kirchhofer · Jane Knoche · Jane Nevins · Jane Whitley · Jane Wilson · Janet Beckerman · Janet Beeler · Janet Fendrych · Janet Gorth · Janet M. Fendrych · Janet Marie Paquette · Janice & Cooper · Janice Dunn · Janice Goldblatt · Janie Locker · Jared Quist · Jared R Delo · Jared Silvia · Jaron Kent-Dobias · Jaron Moore · Jarry Lee · Jason · Jason Bradshaw · Jason Chen · Jason File · Jason Gittler · Jason Hannigan · Jason Kirkham · Jason Kunesh · Jason Levin · Jason Martin · Jason Martin · Jason Riley · Jason Rodriguez · Jason S · Jason Seifert · Jason Sobolewski · Jason Sussberg · Jasper Smit · Jasun Mark · Jay · Jay Dellacona · Jay Price · Jay Schutawie · Jay Traeger · Jayveedub · Jbflanz · Jd Ferries-Rowe · Jean Carney · Jean Haughwout · Jean Prasher · Jean Sinzdak · Jean T Barbey · Jeanette Shine · Jeanine Fritz · Jeanne Weber · Jeanne Wilkinson · Jeannette · Jeannie Vanasco · Jeanvieve Warner · Jed Alger · Jedidiah Smith · Jeff · Jeff · Jeff Albers · Jeff Anderson · Jeff Caltabiano · Jeff Campoli · Jeff Chacon · Jeff Dickerson · Jeff G. Peters · Jeff Garcia · Jeff Greenstein · Jeff H White · Jeff Hampl · Jeff Hayward · Jeff Hilnbrand · Jeff Hitt · Jeff Jacobs · Jeff Klein · Jeff Klein · Jeff Magness · Jeff Neely · Jeff Omiecinski · Jeff Peters · Jeff Stiers · Jeff Stuhmer · Jeff Trull · Jeff Vitkun · Jeff Ward · Jeffrey Brothers · Jeffrey Brothers · Jeffrey Brown · Jeffrey Garcia · Jeffrey Meyer · Jeffrey Parnaby · Jeffrey Posternak · Jeffrey Snyder · Jen Alam · Jen Burns · Jen Butts · Jen Donovan · Jen Jurgens · Jen Lofquist · Jenn De La Vega · Jenni B. Baker · Jenni Baker · Jennie Lynn Rudder · Jennifer · Jennifer Aheran · Jennifer Anthony · Jennifer Cole · Jennifer Cruikshank · Jennifer Dait · Jennifer Day · Jennifer Dopazo · Jennifer Grabmeier · Jennifer Howard Westerman · Jennifer Kabat · Jennifer Kain Kilgore · Jennifer Laughran · Jennifer Marie Lin · Jennifer Mcclenon · Jennifer Mccullough · Jennifer Mcfadden · Jennifer Ratcliffe · Jennifer Richardson · Jennifer Rowland · Jennifer Ruby Privateer · Jennifer Westerman · Jennifer White · Jennifer Wolfe · Jenny Cattier · Jenny Lee · Jenny Stein · Jenzo Duque · Jeremiah · Jeremiah Follett · Jeremy Cohen · Jeremy Ellsworth · Jeremy Fried · Jeremy Peppas · Jeremy Radcliffe · Jeremy Rishel · Jeremy Smith · Jeremy Smith · Jeremy Van Cleve · Jeremy Walker · Jeremy Wang-Iverson · Jeremy Welsh · Jeremy Wortsman · Jerry & Val Gibbons · Jerry Englehart, Jr · Jerry Krakoff · Jerry Pura · Jess Chace · Jess Fitz · Jess Higgins · Jess Kemp · Jess L. · Jess Mcmorrow · Jess Voigt · Jesse Brickel · Jesse Hemingway · Jessi Fierro · Jessica · Jessica · Jessica Allan Schmidt · Jessica Bacho · Jessica Bifulk · Jessica Eleri Jones · Jessica Fiske · Jessica Ghersi · Jessica Hampton · Jessica Martinez · Jessica Mcfadden · Jessica Mcmillen · Jessica Mcmorrow · Jessica Partch · Jessica Poulin · Jessica Shook · Jessica Spence · Jessica Stocks · Jessica Suarez · Jessica Vanginhoven · Jessica Yu · Jessie Gaynor · Jessie Johnson · Jessie Lynn Robertson · Jessie Stockwell · Jett Watson · Jezzka Chen · Jijin John · Jill · Jill Cooke · Jill Ho · Jill Katz · Jillian Mclaughlin · Jillian Mcmahon · Jim And Loretta · Jim Haven · Jim Kosmicki · Jim Lang · Jim Mccambridge · Jim Mcelroy · Jim Mckay · Jim Moore · Jim Redner · Jim Stallard · Jim Taone · Jimmy Orpheus · Jincy Kornhauser · Jjamms Hoffman · Jo Ellen Watson · Joachim Futtrup · Joan Basile · Joan Greco · Joann Holliday · Joann Schultz · Joao Leal Medeiros Hakme · Joddy Marchesoni · Joe Callahan · Joe

Dempsey · Joe Kukella · Joe Kurien · Joe Romano · Joe Stuever · Joe Williams · Joel Bentley · Joel Kreizman · Joel Lang · Joel Santiago · Joey & Berit Coleman · Joey Hayles · Johanna Pauciulo · Johanna, Finja, & Charlie Degl · John & Minda Zambenini · John Artrock77 · John Baker · John Bannister · John Bearce · John Borden · John Bowyer · John Cahill · John Cary · John Charin · John Debacher · John Ebey · John Gialanella · John Hawkins · John Hawkins · John Hill · John Justice · John Karabaic · John Keith · John Kornet · John Lang · John Mcmurtry · John Muller · John Onoda · John P Monks · John P Monks · John P Stephens · John Pancini · John Plunkett · John Poje · John Pole · John Prendergast · John Repko · John Ricketts · John Sarik · John Semley · John Terning · John Tollefsen · John Tompkins · John W Wilkins · John Walbank · John-Fletcher Halyburton · Johnston Murray · Jokastrength · Jon Englund · Jon Folkers · Jon Senge · Jon Stair · Jonas Edgeworth · Jonathan Brandel · Jonathan Deutsche · Jonathan Dykema · Jonathan Fretheim · Jonathan Jackson · Jonathan L York · Jonathan Meyers · Jonathan Van Schoick · Jonathan Wenger · Jordan Bass · Jordan Bell · Jordan Campo · Jordan Campo · Jordan Hauser · Jordan Katz · Jordan Kurland · Jordan Landsman · Jordana Beh · Jorge · Joseph · Joseph Buscarino · Joseph Edmundson · Joseph Fink · Joseph Marshall · Joseph Miebach · Joseph Pred · Josh "The J-Man" Kjenner · Josh Houchin · Josh Mason · Josh Rappoport · Josh Tilton · Joshua Arnett · Joshua D. Meehl · Joshua Farris · Joshua Harris · Joshua Lewis · Joslyn Krismer · Jowi Taylor · Joy · Joyce · Joyce Hennessee · Jozua Malherbe · J.P. Coghlan · Jeremy Radcliffe · Jt Chapel · Juan Mapu · Jude Buck · Judi L Mahaney · Judith · Judy B · Judy O'karma · Judy Schatz · Julena Campbell · Julia · Julia · Julia Bank · Julia Buck · Julia Fought · Julia Henderson · Julia Kardon · Julia Kardon · Julia Kinsman · Julia Kochi · Julia Meinwald · Julia Pohl-Miranda · Julia Slavin · Julia Smillie · Julia Streit · Julia Strohm · Julia Strukely · Julian Gibbs · Julian Orenstein · Juliana Capaldi · Julianne Rhodes · Julie · Julie Fajgenbaum · Julie Felix · Julie S · Julie Schmidt · Julie Stampfle · Julie Vick · Julie Wood · Jumpsaround · June Speakman · Justin Barisich · Justin Foley · Justin Guinn · Justin Katz · Justin Owen Smith Stockard · Justin R. Lawson · Justin Rochell · Justin Wilcox · Justin A. · Justo Robles · K. Edward Callaghan · Kaat · Kai Van Horn · Kaitlyn Trigger · Kali Sakai · Kane E. Giblin · Kara Richardson · Kara Soppelsa · Kara Ukolowicz · Kara White · Karan Rinaldo · Karen · Karen Enno · Karen Gansky · Karen Gray · Karen Hoffman · Karen Holden · Karen K. · Karen Stilber · Karen Unland · Karin Gargaro · Karin J. · Karin Ryding · Karl Gunderson · Karl Petersen · Karla H. · Karla Hilliard · Karolina Waclawiak Derosa · Karrie Kimbrell · Kaspar Hauser · Kat Lombard-Cook · Kat Marshello · Kate · Kate Aishton · Kate Berry · Kate Brittain · Kate Bush · Kate Fritz · Kate Kapych · Kate Ory · Kate Semmler · Kate W. · Kate Webster · Kath Bartman · Katharine Culpepper · Katherine · Katherine Buki · Katherine Harris · Katherine Love · Katherine Minarik · Katherine Sherron · Katherine Tweedel · Katherine Weybright · Katherine Williams · Kathleen · Kathleen Brownell · Kathleen Fargnoli · Kathleen O. · Kathleen O'gorman · Kathleen Ossip · Kathleen Seltzer · Kathleen Stetsko · Kathryn Anderson · Kathryn Bumbaugh · Kathryn Flowers · Kathryn Holmes · Kathryn Kelley · Kathryn King · Kathryn Lester · Kathryn Page Birmingham · Kathryn Price · Kathy Harding · Kati Simmons Knowland · Katie ·

Katie · Katie Chabolla · Katie Dodd · Katie Jewett · Katie Lewis · Katie Linden · Katie Love · Katie Mcguire · Katie Y · Katie Young · Katielicious · Katmcgo · Katrina · Katrina Dodson · Katrina Grigo-Mcmahon · Katrina Woznicki · Katryce Kay · Katy Carey · Katy Orr · Katy Shelor Harvey · Katya Kazbek · Kayla M. Anderson · Kaylie Simon · Keiko Ichiye · Keith Cotton · Keith Crofford · Keith Flaherty · Keith Morgan · Keith Van Norman · Kellie · Kellie Holmstrom · Kelly · Kelly Browne · Kelly Conaboy · Kelly Conroe · Kelly Cornacchia · Kelly Doran · Kelly Heckman · Kelly K · Kelly Marie · Kelly Miller-Schreiner · Kelly Wheat · Kelsay Neely · Kelsey Hunter · Kelsey Rexroat · Kelsey Thomson · Kelsie O'dea · Kemp Peterson · Ken Flott · Ken Krehbiel · Ken Racicot · Kendel Shore · Kendra · Kendra Stanton Lee · Kenneth Cameron · Kerri Schlottman · Kerry Evans · Kev · Kev Meister · Kevin And Kim Watt · Kevin Anderson · Kevin Arnold · Kevin Ashton · Kevin Camel · Kevin Cole · Kevin Cosgrove · Kevin Davis · Kevin Eichorst · Kevin Felix · Kevin Freidberg · Kevin Gleason · Kevin Hunt · Kevin Johnson · Kevin Keck · Kevin Lauderdale · Kevin Mccullough · Kevin Mcginn · Kevin Mcginn · Kevin Mcmorrow · Kevin O'donnell · Kevin Spicer · Kevin Vognar · Kevin Wynn · Kevin Zimmerman · Khalid Kurji · Kickstarter · Killer Lopez-Hall · Kim · Kim Baker · Kim Ku · Kim Sanders · Kim Wishart · Kimberley Mullins · Kimberley Rose · Kimberly Grey · Kimberly Hamm · Kimberly Harrington · Kimberly Nichols · Kimberly Occhipinti · Kimberly Rose · Kira Starzynski · Kirsten Zerger · Kitkat · Kitz Rickert · Kj Nichols · Knarles Bowles · Knut N. · Kom Siksamat · Kori K. · Kris Majury · Kris S. · Krista Knott · Kristan Hoffman · Kristan Mcmahon · Kristen Ann Tymeson · Kristen Brooks · Kristen Easley · Kristen Miller · Kristen Reed · Kristen Reed · Kristen T Easley · Kristen Westbrook · Kristi Vandenbosch · Kristin M. Morris · Kristin Mullen · Kristin Nielsen · Kristin Pazulski · Kristin R Shrode · Kristina Dahl · Kristina Harper · Kristina Rizga · Kristine Donly · Kristine Donly · Kristy Kulp · Kristyn Dunn · Krisztina Bunzl · Krystal Hart · Kuang-Yi Liu · Kunihiro Ishiguro · Kurt Brown · Kurtis Kolt · Kyle Dickinson · Kyle Garvey · Kyle Jacob Bruck · Kyle Lucia Wu · Kyle Prestenback · Kyle Raum · Kylee Panduro · Kyra Rogers · L.n. · Landy Manderson · Lang Thompson · Langston Antosek · Lani Yamamoto · Lara Kierlin · Lara Struttman · Larisa Shambaugh · Larry Doyle · Larry Farhner · Launa Rich · Laura · Laura · Laura Bauer · Laura Bennett · Laura Bostillo · Laura Buffington · Laura Celmins · Laura Dapito · Laura Farris · Laura Hadden · Laura Howard · Laura Nisi · Laura Owens · Laura Schmiedicke · Laura Scott · Laura Stevenson · Laura Thomas · Laura Vigander · Laura Weiderhaft · Laura Williams · Laurel · Laurel C · Laurel Chun · Laurel Fedder · Laurel Flynn · Laurel Hall · Lauren Andrews · Lauren Groff · Lauren Isaacson · Lauren O'neal · Lauren Peugh · Lauren Powers · Lauren Rose · Lauretta Hyde · Laurie Bollman-Little · Laurie Ember · Laurie L Young · Laurie Major · Laurie May · Laurie Young · Lawrence Bridges · Lawrence Porricelli · Layla Al-Bedawi · Leah · Leah Browning · Leah Dieterich · Leah Mallen · Leah Murray · Leah Swetnam · Leanne Stremcha · Lee · Lee Ann Albury · Lee Brumbaugh · Lee Harrison · Lee Roe · Lee Smith · Lee Syben · Lee Trentadue · Leigh Vorhies · Leila Khosrovi · Lene Sauvik · Lenore Jones · Lenore Rowntree · Leonard · Leone Lucky · Les Edwards · Lesley A. Martin · Leslie · Leslie Bhutani · Leslie Cannon · Leslie Kotzas · Leslie Maslow ·

Leslie McGorman · Leslie Mclinskey · Leslie Woodhouse · Lester Su · Lewis Ward · Lex Leifheit · Lian Fournier · Lila Fontes · Lila Lahood · Lillian Rachel Taft · Lily Mehl · Linda Cook · Linda Given · Linda Ocasio · Linda Ostrom · Linda Parker Gates · Linda Schroeder · Linda Skitka · Linda Troop · Linda Weston · Lindsay Hollett · Lindsay Mcconnon · Lindsay Morton · Lindsey · Lindsey Darrah · Lindsey Eubank · Lindsey Shepard · Lindsey Spaulding · Linn Elliott · Linne Ha · Lisa Berrones · Lisa Brown · Lisa Ellis · Lisa Janowski Goode · Lisa M. Geller · Lisa Pearson · Lisa Ryan · Lisa Thaler · Lisa Vlkovic · Lisa Winter · Living Life To The Fullest · Liz Benson · Liz Crain · Liz Flint-Somerville · Liz Nord · Liz Weber · Liza Behles · Liza Harrell-Edge · Lloyd Snowden · Logan Campbell · Logan Hasson · Logan Wright · Lois Denmark · Lora Kelley · Loredana Spadola · Loren Lieberthal · Lorenzo Cherubini · Lori · Lori Blackmon · Lori Cheatle · Lori Dunn · Lori Felton · Lori Fontanes · Lori Hymowitz · Lorie Kloda · Lorin Oberweger · Lorna Craig · Lorna Forbes · Lorraine Dong · Lotus Child · Lou Cove · Louis Loewenstein · Louis Mastorakos · Louis Silverman · Louisa · Louise Marston · Louise Mccune · Louise Williams · Luca Maurer · Lucas Foster · Lucas Hawthorne · Lukas Drake · Luke · Luke Benfey · Luke Burger · Luuly Tran · Lyn Walker · Lynn Farmer · M Robertson · M. Koss · Madeleine Watts · Madeline Jacobson · Mae Rice · Maggie Rotter · Maggie Stroup · Magnanimus · Maia Pank Mertz · Mainon Schwartz · Maitri Sojourner · Majelle · Major Solutions · Manca G. Renko · Mancinist · Mandy Alysse Goldberg · Mandy Brown · Mandy Kinne · Manion · Mara Novak · Mara Zepeda · Marc Atkinson · Marc Beck · Marc Lawrence-Apfelbaum · Marcella Forni · Marcello · Marcia Hofmann · Marco Buscaglia · Marco Kaye · Marcus Cade · Marcus Liddle · Margaret Bykowski · Margaret Cook · Margaret Grounds · Margaret Harvey · Margaret Kelly · Margaret Landis · Margaret Lusko · Margaret Newman · Margaret Peters · Margaret Prescott · Margaret Wachtler · Margo Taylor · Margot Atwell · Mari Moreshead · Maria · Maria · Maria Alicata · Maria Cunningham · Maria Faith Garcia · Maria Sotnikova · Maria Verloo · Mariah Adcox · Mariah Blackard · Mariah Blob Drakoulis · Marian Blythe · Marianne · Marianne Germond · Marie Dever · Marie Harvat · Marie Hohner · Marie Knight · Marie Marfia · Marie Meyer · Marielle Smith · Marina Meijer · Marinna Castilleja · Mario Lopez · Maris Antolin · Maris Kreizman · Mark · Mark · Mark · Mark Aronoff · Mark Beringer · Mark Bold · Mark Brody · Mark Dezalia · Mark Dober · Mark Dudlik · Mark Durso · Mark Fisher · Mark Fritzenschaft · Mark Gallucci · Mark Giordono · Mark Helfrich · Mark Himmelsbach · Mark Kates · Mark Levine · Mark Macleod · Mark Mandel · Mark Movic · Mark Novak · Mark Ramdular · Mark Reitblatt · Mark Riechers · Mark Ryan · Mark Southcott · Mark Van Name · Mark Weatherup, Jr. · Mark Wilkerson · Markus Wegscheider · Marlin Dohlman · Marlo Amelia Buzzell · Marna Blanchard · Marrion K · Marsha Nunley · Marsha Soffer · Marshall Farr · Marshall Hayes · Martha · Martha Benco · Martha Linn · Martha Pulleyn · Martin Berzell · Martin Cielens · Martin Gelin · Martina Radwan · Martina Schuerpf · Martina Testa · Marty Anderson · Mary · Mary Atikian · Mary Beth Hoerner · Mary Byram · Mary Christa Jaramillo-Bolin · Mary Dumont · Mary Durbin · Mary E I Jones · Mary Elizabeth Huber · Mary F Kaltreider · Mary Gioia · Mary Krywaruczenko · Mary Larson · Mary Lukanuski · Mary Mann · Mary Mannison · Mary Melville · Mary Nieves · Mary O'Keefe Bradley · Mary

Williams · Mary Z Fuka · Mary-Kim Arnold · Marya Figueroa · Marybeth Gallinger
· Maryelizabeth Van Etten · Mason Harper · Mateo Sewillo · Mathias Hansson · Matt
· Matt · Matt Adkins · Matt Alston · Matt Bouchard · Matt Conner · Matt Davis ·
Matt Digirolamo · Matt Fehrenbacher · Matt Gay · Matt Greiner · Matt Kelchner
· Matt O'brien · Matt Slaybaugh · Matt Slotkin · Matt Werner · Matthew · Matthew
Clark · Matthew Edwards · Matthew Grant · Matthew Honeybeard Henry · Matthew
Latkiewicz · Matthew Ludvino · Matthew Morgan · Matthew Morin · Matthew
Mullenweg · Matthew Rhoden · Matthew Robert Lang · Matthew Sachs · Matthew
Smazik · Matthew Storer · Matthew Swatton · Matthew Wild · Matthew Wood ·
Mattie Armstrong · Maureen · Maureen Mcbeth · Maureen Van Dyck · Maureen Van
Dyck · Max Elman · Maxime · Maximilian Virkus · Maxine Davies · May Ang ·
May-Ling Gonzales · Maya Baratz · Maya Munoz · Mayka Mei · Mayka Mei · Mayra
Urbano · Mbhsing · Mc Macaulay · Mckenzie Chinn · Meagan Choi · Mebaim · Meg
Ferguson · Meg Palmer · Meg Varley Keller · Megakestirsch · Megan · Megan ·
Megan Dowdle · Megan Marin · Megan Murphy · Megan Orsini · Megan Reigner-
Chapman · Megha Bangalore · Meghan Arnold · Meghan Smith · Meghan Walker
· Meghann Farnsworth · Megin Hicks · Meimaimaggio · Melanie Paulina · Melanie
Wang · Melia · Melia Jacquot · Melissa · Melissa Boilon · Melissa Locker · Melissa
Stefanini · Melissa Weinstein · Melissa Yes · Mellena Bridges · Melynda Nuss ·
Meredith Case · Meredith Davies · Meredith Payne · Meredith Resnick · Mette-
Marie Katz · M. Garvais · Mi Ann Bennett · Micaela Mcglone · Michael Angarone
· Michael Ashbridge · Michael Avella · Michael Barnstijn · Michael Bebout · Michael
Birk · Michael Boyce · Michael Denning · Michael Donahue · Michael Eidlin ·
Michael Gavino · Michael Gillis · Michael Gioia · Michael Glaser · Michael Greene
· Michael Hall · Michael Harner · Michael Ireton · Michael Kidwell · Michael
Laporta · Michael Legge · Michael Lent · Michael Marsicano · Michael Marx ·
Michael Mazur · Michael Moore · Michael Moorhouse · Michael Moszczynski ·
Michael O'connell · Michael Olson · Michael Patrick Cutillo · Michael Sciortino ·
Michael Sean Lesueur · Michael Thompson · Michaela Drapes · Michaelle · Micheál
Keane · Michel Ge · Michelangelo Cianciosi · Michele · Michele Bove · Michele
Fleischli · Michele Hansen · Michele Howard · Michelle · Michelle · Michelle ·
Michelle Akin · Michelle Badash · Michelle Castillo · Michelle Clement · Michelle
Cotugno · Michelle Curtis · Michelle Floyd · Michelle Matel · Michelle Nadeau ·
Mickey Bayard · Micquelle Corry · Miguel Duran · Mik · Mike · Mike Benner · Mike
Etheridge · Mike Golay · Mike Lee · Mike Levine · Mike Mcvicar · Mike Munsell ·
Mike Smith · Mike Thompson · Mike Zuckerman · Mikel Wilkins · Miles
Ranisavljevic · Milind Kaduskar · Mimi Evans · Misha Renclair · Missy Manning ·
Mitch Major · Mitchell Hart · Mo Lai · Moise Lacy · Moishe Lettvin · Mollie Brooks
· Molly · Molly · Molly Charnes · Molly Grpss · Molly Guinn Bradley · Molly
Mcardle · Molly Mcsweeney · Molly Murphy · Molly Ohainle · Molly Taylor · Mona
Awad · Monica Beals · Monica Fogg · Monica Tomaszewski · Mono.kultur ·
Morningstar Stevenson · Moshe Weitzman · Moss · Muckdart · Mudlarque · Mudville
· Murray Gm · Murray Steele · Mygreensweater.com · Myron Chadowitz · Myrsini
· Mythmakers · Nadia Ibrashi · Nadine Anderson · Nai-Wen Hu · Nakiesha ·
Nakiesha Koss · Nalden · Nancy C. Mae · Nancy Folsom · Nancy Friedman · Nancy

Goldberg · Nancy Hebben · Nancy Jamieson · Nancy Jeng · Nancy Keiter · Nancy Riess · Nancy Rosenberg · Nancy Rudolph · Nancy Smith · Naomi Alderman · Naomi Firestone-Teeter · Naomi Pinn · Nara Bopp! · Nat Missildine · Natalie · Natalie · Natalie · Natalie Gruppuso · Natalie Hamilton · Natalie Strawbridge · Natalie Ung · Natalie Villamil · Natasha Boas · Nate Arnold · Nate Corddry · Nate Merchant · Nathan Chadwick · Nathan Pyritz · Nathan Rostron · Nathaniel Weiss · Navjoyt Ladher · Neal Cornett · Neal Pollack · Ned Rote · Neda Afsarmanesh · Neil · Neil Blanck · Neil Rigler · Neil Shah · Nelly Ben Hayoun · Nesher G. Asner · Newtux · Nic Barajas · Nicholas Almanza · Nicholas Bergin · Nicholas Herbert · Nicholas Maggs · Nicholas O'neil · Nicholas Van Boddie Willis · Nicholas Walker · Nicholson Baker · Nick · Nick Brown · Nick C. · Nick Cooke · Nick Fraenkel · Nick Kibodeaux · Nick Miller · Nick Peacock · Nick Plante · Nicky Montalvo · Nicolas Llano Linares · Nicole Avril · Nicole Carlson · Nicole Elitch · Nicole Flattery · Nicole Howard Quiles · Nicole Mandel · Nicole Pasulka · Nicole Rafidi · Nicole Ryan · Nicole Yeo · Nicoletta · Nicoletta Beyer · Nicolette Blum · Nigel Dookhoo · Nigel Taylor · Nigel Warren · Nighthawk · Niina Pollari · Nikil · Nikki H · Nikki Thayer · Nil Hafizi · Nils Normann · Nina Drakalovic · Nion Mcevoy · Nirav · Nitsuh Abebe · No · Noah Miller · Noah Slo · Noelle Greene · None · Nora Caplan-Bricker · Nora L · O. Dwyer · Ofpc Llc · Ola Torstensson · Oleg · Oliver Emanuel · Oliver Grainger · Oliver Kroll · Oliver Meehan · Oliver Mooney · Omar Lee · Owl · P. E. Zalinski · P.M. · Pamela Marcus · Pamela Pugh · Pamela Rooney · Papermantis · Parashar Bhise · Paris Ward · Parker Coddington · Pascal Babare · Pascalle Burton · Pat Jenatsch · Pat Wheaton · Patience Haggin · Patricia Baas · Patricia Bindert · Patricia Iorg · Patricia Miller · Patricia Parker · Patrick · Patrick Cates · Patrick Cox · Patrick Dennis · Patrick Ducey · Patrick M. Freebern · Patrick Maier · Patrick O'driscoll · Patrick Rafferty · Patrick Schilling · Paul · Paul · Paul Bielec · Paul Bloom · Paul Boxer · Paul Braidford · Paul Cancellieri · Paul Curtin · Paul Debraski · Paul Degeorge · Paul Durant · Paul Dutnall · Paul Eckburg · Paul Ferraro · Paul Ghysbrecht · Paul Kohlbrenner · Paul Lasch · Paul Littleton · Paul Mikesell · Mike Sell · Paul Moore · Paul Nadeau · Paul Rosenberg · Paul Studebaker · Paul Upham · Paul Van Zwieten · Paula Palyga · Pauls Toutonghi · Pax · Payton Cuddy · Pedro Poitevin · Peggy Stenger · Penny Blubaugh · Penny Dedel · Peri Pugh · Perii & John Owen · Pete Mulvihill · Pete Smith · Petel · Peter · Peter Blake · Peter Bogert · Peter Bradley · Peter Brian Barry · Peter Fitzgerald · Peter Gadol · Peter Gerhardt · Peter Hoddie · Peter Hogan · Peter Maguire · Peter Mcnally · Peter Meehan · Peter Paul · Peter Platt · Peter Quinn Fuller · Peter Rednour · Peter Roper · Peter Woodyard · Phil Dokas · Phil Fresh · Philip Kor · Philip Kors · Philip Maguire · Philip Platt · Philip Scranton · Philip Wood · Philip Zimmermann · Philippa Moxon · Phillip Henderson · Phillip Johnston · Phyllis Tankel · Pia Widlund · Pierre L'allier · Pierre L'allier · Poilleux · Prisca Riggle · Priscilla Riggle · Priya Sampath · Prmes · Pro · Quim Gil · Quinn · Quinn Formel · R. Mansolino · Rachael Klein · Rachel All · Rachel Bartlett · Rachel Beal · Rachel Brody · Rachel Didomizio · Rachel Droessler · Rachel Fershleiser · Rachel Newcombe · Rachel Pass · Rachel R. Rdriguez · Rachel Sluder · Rachel Smith · Rachel Unger · Rachele Gilman · Radovan Grezo · Rami Levin · Rana · Randall Imai · Randolph Baker · Ravi And Kaela Chandrasekaran ·

Ray Adams · Raymond Desjarlais · Raymond Khalastchi · Raymond Zhou · Raysha Gallinetti · Rbeedee · Rea Bennett · Reality Connection · Rebecca · Rebecca · Rebecca Bame · Rebecca Calvo · Rebecca Ha · Rebecca Harlow · Rebecca M · Rebecca Martin · Rebecca Rubenstein · Rebecca Scalio · Rebecca Scalio · Rebecca Schneider · Rebecca Schneider · Rebecca Serbin · Rebecca Wilberforce · Reean · Reed Johnson · Reese · Reese Kwon · Reid Allison · Reina Castellanos · Renée Reizman · Renton Wright · Rich Hjulstrom · Rich Scott · Richard Busofsky · Richard Byrne · Richard Cripe · Richard Light · Richard Marks · Richard May · Richard Meadow · Richard Nisa · Richard Parks · Richard Rutter · Richard Sakai · Richard Sakai · Richard Stanislaw · Richard Stroud · Richard Tallmadge · Richard Winter · Rick Cox · Rick Lo · Rick Redick · Rick T. Morrison · Rick Webb · Riley · Riley · Rivkah K Sass · Rk Strout · Rkt88edmo · Rob Atwood · Rob Callender · Rob Colenso · Rob Knight · Rob Mishev · Rob Neill · Rob Wilock · Robby Sumner · Robert Amerman · Robert Archambault · Robert Biskin · Robert Brandin · Robert Brown Glad · Robert Denby · Robert Dickau · Robert Doherty · Robert Drew · Robert E Anderson · Robert Fenerty · Robert George · Robert Hilton · Robert Jacklosky · Robert Macke · Robert Okeefe · Robert Rees · Robert St. Claire · Robert Wilder · Robin Nicholas · Robin Olivier · Robin Ryan · Robin Smith Peck · Roboboxspeaks · Rob W · Rochelle Lanster · Ron Calixto · Ron Charles · Ron Sanders · Ron Wortz · Ronald Neef · Ronnie Scott · Rory Harper · Rosalie Ham · Rosanna Yau · Rose · Rosie Cima · Ross Goodwin · Rosy Capron · Rotem Shintel · Roy Mcmillan · Roy Mcmillan · Ruari Elkington · Russ Maloney · Ruth Franklin · Ruth Madievsky · Ruth Wyer · Ryan + Lucy · Ryan A. Millager · Ryan Abbott · Ryan Bailey · Ryan Barton · Ryan Curran · Ryan Hetherington · Ryan Molony · Ryan Pitts · Ryan Stenson · Rye Sour · S.P. Garrett · S. Tayengco · S. Grinell · Saelee Oh · Safwat Saleem · Sage Dahlen · Sairus Patel · Sal Macleod · Sally · Sally Brooke · Sally Jane Weed · Sally Macleod · Salpets · Sam · Sam Barrett · Sam Brightman · Sam Hockley-Smith · Sam Skrivan · Sam Sudar · Sam Sweeney · Sam Wright · Sam Zucchi · Sam Zuckert · Samantha · Samantha Armintrout · Samantha Bloom · Samantha Grillo · Samantha Hunt · Samantha Krug · Samantha Netzley · Samantha Schoech · Samia Haddad · Samir Shah · Samuel Cole · Samuel Douglas Miller · Samuel Preston · Sandra Delehanty · Sandra Edwards · Sandra Spicher · Sandy Cooley · Sandy Guthrie · Sandy Stewart · Sanford Nathan · Sara Arvidsson · Sara Corbett · Sara K. Runnels · Sara M · Sara Mouser · Sara Rowghani · Sara Satten · Sarah · Sarah · Sarah · Sarah · Sarah Aibel · Sarah Bacon · Sarah Bownds · Sarah Brewer · Sarah Burnes · Sarah Carter · Sarah E Klein · Sarah Elizabeth Ridley · Sarah Frazier · Sarah Getchell · Sarah Hotze · Sarah Hutchins · Sarah Johnson · Sarah Lavere · Sarah Lincoln · Sarah Litwin-Schmid · Sarah Lukachko · Sarah Maguire · Sarah Mundy · Sarah Rosenshine · Sarah Scire · Sarah Stanlick Kimball · Sarah Tiedeman Gallagher · Sarah Towle · Sarah Walker · Sarah Weissman · Sarita Rainey · Sasqwatch Watch Company · Savannah Adams · Savannah Cooper-Ramsey · Scooter Alpert · Scott A. Harris · Scott Bateman · Scott Callon · Scott Dagenfield · Scott Elingburg · Scott Farrar · Scott Ferron · Scott Malagold · Scott Mcgibbon · Scott Olling · Scott Paxton · Scott Rinicker · Scott Shoger · Scott Snibbe · Scott Stanfield · Scott Stelter · Scott Stelter · Scott Suthren · Scott Thurman · Scott Underwood ·

Scott Wahl · Scott Williams · Sean · Sean Baker · Sean Beatty Oaktown Ss · Sean Boyle · Sean Carr · Sean Harrahy · Sean Jensen-Grey · Sean Kelly · Sean Langmuir · Sean Mcindoe · Sebastian Campos · Sebastianfidler · Sebastien J Park · Segundo Nallatan Jr · Serjio · Seth Casana · Seth D. Michaels · Seth Fowler · Seth Reiss · Shane P. Mullen · Shane Pedersen · Shane Tilton · Shane Ward · Shannon Christine · Shannon David · Shannon Dunbar · Shannon Kelly · Shari D Rochen · Shari Rochen · Shari Simpson · Sharon Lunny · Shaun Bossio · Shaun Pryszlak · Shauna Sutherland · Shaunda Tichgelaar · Shawn Calvert · Shawn Calvert · Shawn Hall · Shawn Lee · Shawn Liu · Shawn Lucas · Sheenagh Geoghegan · Sheila Mennis · Shelby Black · Shelby Kling · Shelley Vinyard · Shelleyboodles Gornall · Shelleysd · Shelly Catterson · Sheri Kenly · Sheri Parsons · Sheri Sternberg · Sheridan Fox · Sherry Suisman · Shevaun Lewis · Shield Bonnichsen · Shih-Lene Jee · Shira Geller · Shira Milikowsky · Shoshana Paige · Simon · Simon Bird · Simon Groth · Simon Harper · Simon Hawkesworth · Simon Kuhn · Simon Nurse · Simon Petherick · Simon Pinkerton · Simon Smundak · Siobhan Dolan · Sisyphus · Smilner · Smivey · Solange Vandermoer · Solenoid · Somedaylee · Somrod Creative · Sona Avakian · Songeehn Choi · Sophie Malone · Sophine · Soraya Okuda · Spencer Coates · Spencer Nelson · Spencer Tweedy · Ssk · Stacey Pounsberry · Stacy Murison · Stacy Ryan · Stacy Saul · Stan Smith · Stanley Levine · Stef Craps · Stefanie Pareja Reyna · Steph Hammell · Steph Widmer · Stephan Heilmayr · Stephanie · Stephanie · Stephanie Anne Canlas · Stephanie Arman · Stephanie Goode · Stephanie Mankins · Stephanie Morgan · Stephanie Murg · Stephanie Wagner · Stephanie Wan · Stephanie Wu · Stephen Angelette · Stephen Beaupre · Stephen Benzel · Stephen Berger · Stephen Bronstein · Stephen Bryce Wood Jr · Stephen Fuller · Stephen Hahn · Stephen Hairsine · Stephen Kay · Stephen Littell · Stephen Mallory · Stephen Murray · Stephen Northup · Stephen Paul · Stephen Schifrin · Stephen Shih · Stephen Shocket · Stephen Smith · Stephen Tabler · Stephen Williams · Steve · Steve Beaven · Steve Berkovits · Steve Caires · Steve Clancy · Steve Conover · Steve Jackson · Steve Kern · Steve Kindrick · Steve Lewis · Steve Maher · Steve Marian · Steve Mockus · Steve Payonzeck · Steve Rivo · Steve Smith · Steve Sweet · Steve Thornbury · Steve Tsuchiyama · Steve W. Jones · Steven Canning · Steven Danielson · Steven Elias · Steven Friedman · Steven Friedman · Steven Hemingray · Steven Hudosh · Steven Jay Athanas · Steven Kindrick · Steven Lowry · Steven Marten · Steven Morley · Steven Powell · Stewart Davis · Stuart Macdonald · Stuart O'connor · Stuart Rosen · Sue Diehl · Sue Naegle · Sue S · Susan · Susan Auty · Susan Barrabee · Susan C. · Susan Clements · Susan Cooke · Susan Cormier · Susan D. · Susan Davis · Susan Eichrodt · Susan Fitzgerald · Susan Hobbs · Susan Hopkirk · Susan Ito · Susan King · Susan Loube · Susan Miller · Susan Morrissey · Susan Mosseri-Marlio · Susan Schorn · Susan Spradlin · Susan Strohm · Susan Yuk · Susanna · Susanne Durkin · Susanne Durkin-Schindler · Susheila Khera · Suzanna Zeitler · Suzanne Scott · Suzanne Scott · Suzanne Spencer · Suzanne Wilder · Suzi Albertson · Suzie Baunsgard · Syafii · Sydney Blackett · Sydney Morrow · Sydney Sattell · Sylvia Tran · Sylvie L. · Syncione Bresgal · Szienceman · T Cooper · T S Plutchak · T. L. Howl · T.m. Ryan · Tabitha Hayes · Tamar Shafrir · Tamara Zver · Tami Loeffler · Tami Wilson · Tangerine0516 · Tanya F · Taryn Albizzati · Taylor Baldwin · Taylor F. · Taylor Kearns · Taylor Pavlik ·

Taylor Smith · Taylor Stephens · Tdemarchi · Ted Jillson · Tedder · Teresa Hedin ·
Teresa Sweat · Terna · Terrence Hayes · Terri Arnold · Terri Coles · Terri Leker · Terry
Morris · Terry Wit · Tershia D'elgin · Tess Kornfield · Tess Marstaller · Tess
Swithinbank · Tessa Holkesvik · Thanh Tran · The Creature · The Duke Of Follen
Street · The Haikooligan · The Lance Arthur · The Nyc Cooper Clan · The Shebooks
Team · The Tomato Head, Inc · The Typewriter Revolution · Thedammtruth.com
· Thempauls · Theo Ploeg · Theresa · Theresa C Kratschmer · Thientam Nguyen ·
Thierry / On The Road To Honesty · Thomas Barron · Thomas Belote · Thomas
Demarchi · Thomas Green · Thomas Kiraly · Thomas La Farge · Thomas Moore ·
Thomas Moore · Thomas Pluck · Thomas W. Conway · Thomas Weverka · Thousand
· Tieg Zaharia · Tiff Chau · Tiffany · Tiffany Cardoza · Tiffany Holly Lyon · Tiffany
Peon · Tiffany Tseng · Tim Gaffney · Tim Keogh · Tim Larrison · Tim Lash · Tim
Perell · Tim Ruszel @ Ruszel Design Company · Timothy Blackett · Timothy Clark
· Timothy Johnstone · Timothy Mey · Timothy N. Towslee · Timothy Paulson · Tina
Burns · Tina F. · Tinderbox Editions · Tirza Ben-Porat · Tobias Carroll · Tobin Moss
· Tod Story · Todd · Todd · Todd Abbott · Todd Barnard · Todd Bever · Todd Fell ·
Tom Fitzgerald · Tom Garbarino · Tom Gonzales · Tom Head, Ph.d. · Tom Hood ·
Tom J Clarke · Tom Joiner · Tom Keekley · Tom Marks · Tom Skoda · Tom Steele ·
Tom W. Davis Iii · Tomasz Werner · Tony Puccinelli · Tony Solomun · Tori Bond ·
Tracey A Halliday · Traci Ikegami · Tracy Cambron · Tracy Middlebrook · Travis
Burton · Travis Gasser · Trevor Burnham · Trey Kuchinsky · Tricia Copeland · Tricia
Psarreas · Triscuit Vallejo · Trisha Bunce · Trisha Weir · Tristan Telson · Troy Goertz
· Troy Napier · Tttt · Tucker Christine · Turner Partain · Turtlepants · Tyler Cazes
· Tyler Cazes · Tyler Cushing · Tyler Munson · Tyler Robertson · Tyler Smith · Uccf
· Uncle Doug · Under Construction Dvd.com · Uttam Kumbhat Jain · V
Hollingsworth · V. · V. Stoltz · Vaia Vaena · Val Emmich · Valerie Gprman · Valerie
Seijas · Valerie Sonnenthal · Valerie Woolard · Vanasa Bowden · Vanessa Allen ·
Vanessa Kirker · Vaughn Shields · Veena · Vera Hough · Vernon · Veronica V-V ·
Victor Jih · Victor Kumar · Victoria Bartelt · Victoria Davies · Victoria Evert ·
Victoria Marinelli · VII · Vika · Viken · Viktor Balogh · Vinay · Vincent Hsieh ·
Vinson Cunningham · Virginia E Mead · Virginia Killfoile · Vitor Neves · Vivian
Wagner · W.C. Beck · Waipo5kathryn Blue · Wayfarer · Wayne Gwillim · Wendi
Aarons · Wendy Ju · Wendy Koster · Wendy Molyneux · Wendy O'neil · Wes Wes
· Whitney Isenhower · Whitney Pape · Wiebke Schuster · Will Brodie · Will
Cavendish · Will Johnson · Will Mellencamp Leubsdorf · Will Ramsey · Will
Skelton · Willa Köerner · Willh · William · William · William Amend · William
Donahoe · William Farley · William Hatt · William Kirchner · William Mascioli ·
William Noonan · William Ross · William Smith · William Van Zandt · William
Woolf · Willliam Merrill · Winnie Dreier · Winston Finlayson · Wire Science ·
Www.smltalk.com · Wythe Marschall · Xiangyun Lim · Yahaya Baruwa · Yang Dai
· Yani Robinson · Yeekai Lim · Yew-Leong Wong · Yodiez · Yosef · Yoshihiro
Kanematsu · Yotta Sigma · Yuen-Wei Chew · Yukiko Takeuchi · Yvette Dezalia ·
Yvonne Mains · Yvonne W · Zabeth Russell · Zach · Zach Blair · Zach Lascell · Zach
Lipton · Zachary Amundson · Zachary Beamer · Zachary Doss · Zack Daniels · Zack
Peercy · Zain Khalid · Zainab Juma · Zalfer · Zanne Cameron · Zoe Laird

Proud Supporter of McSweeney's

EXTRA-SPECIAL THANKS TO
THE FOLLOWING DONORS

Illustrations by Agata Nowicka

Arianna Reiche

Dan Pasternack

*Annette Toutonghi
and Bruce Oberg*

Damian John Bradfield

Candice Chiew

Debbie Millman

Green Apple Books

EXTRA-SPECIAL THANKS TO
THE FOLLOWING DONORS

Illustrations by Agata Nowicka

David Hodge   Rea Bennett   Marlys Morgan   Scott Patrick Thurman

Jordan Kurland   Nicole Avril   Duane Murray

The Lynch Family

ALSO AVAILABLE FROM McSWEENEY'S

store.mcsweeneys.net

ART & COMICS

BOOKS FOR CHILDREN

ALL THIS AND MORE AT

store.mcsweeneys.net

ALSO AVAILABLE FROM McSWEENEY'S

FLOWERS OF ANTI-MARTYRDOM
by Dorian Geisler

Dorian Geisler's beguiling debut collection solves the problems of audacity—with audacity. A darkly uncanny romp through everyday American life, Geisler's understated poetry and minimalist aesthetic conveys a burgeoning landscape featuring Main Street America in all its often-questionable Americanness.

    Flowers is Kafka mixed with Tarantino. It's *Invisible Cities*—except instead of beautiful, imaginary cities, the poet introduces us to disconcertingly realistic humans in all their casual perversity, exalted banality, and moral questionability. *Flowers* holds the mirror up to contemporary America—reader be warned.

"Flowers of Anti-Martyrdom... *is exactly the book you need to read right now... a mix of cautionary wit, a dash of profound sadness, and a heavy dose of quiet empathy.*"

— *Dorothea Lasky*

ALSO AVAILABLE FROM McSWEENEY'S

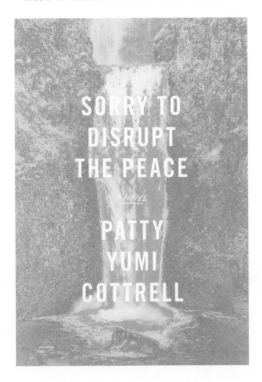

SORRY TO DISRUPT THE PEACE
by Patty Yumi Cottrell

According to the internet, there are six possible reasons why her brother might have killed himself. But Helen knows better: she knows that six reasons is only shorthand for "the abyss." Helen also knows that she alone is qualified to launch a serious investigation into his death, so she purchases a one-way ticket to Milwaukee. There, as she searches her childhood home and attempts to uncover why someone would choose to die, she will face her estranged family, her brother's few friends, and the overzealous grief counselor, Chad Lambo; she may also discover what it truly means to be alive.

"This book is not a diversion—it's a lifeline." —Jesse Ball

"Her voice is unflinching, unforgettable, and animated with a restless sense of humor."
—Catherine Lacey

ALSO AVAILABLE FROM McSWEENEY'S

The Abridged History of Rainfall   Jay Hopler

THE ABRIDGED HISTORY OF RAINFALL
by Jay Hopler

Jay Hopler's second collection, a mourning song for his father, is an elegy of
uproar, a careening hymn to disaster and its aftermath. In lyric poems by turns
droll and desolate, Hopler documents the struggle to live in the face of great loss,
a task that sends him ranging through Florida's torrid subtropics, the mountains
of the American West, the streets of Rome, and the Umbrian caountryside. Vivid,
dynamic, unrestrained: *The Abridged History of Rainfall* is a festival of glowing
saints and fighting cocks, of firebombs and birdsong.

*"By these poems, your faith will be shattered and restored, restored and
wondrously shattered again." —Craig Morgan Teicher*

ALSO AVAILABLE FROM McSWEENEY'S

ONE HUNDRED APOCALYPSES
AND OTHER APOCALYPSES
by Lucy Corin

Lucy Corin's dazzling collection is powered by one hundred apocalypses: a series of short stories, many only a few lines, that illuminate moments of vexation and crisis, revelations and revolutions. An apocalypse might come in the form of the end of a relationship or the end of the world, but what it exposes is the tricky landscape of our longing for a clean slate.

"Unforgettable voices resist description. Lucy Corin sounds like no one; prickly, shrewd, faintly paranoid or furtive, witty and also savage, she has something of Paley's gift for soliloquy combined with Dickinson's passionate need to hold the world at bay, that sense of a voice emanating from a Skinner box. Her achievement is already dazzling, her promise immense."

—Citation of the American Academy of Arts and Letters Rome Prize

ALL MY PUNY SORROWS
by Miriam Toews

Elf and Yoli are sisters. While on the surface Elfrieda's life is enviable (she's a world-renowned pianist, glamorous, wealthy, and happily married) and Yolandi's a mess (she's divorced and broke, with two teenagers growing up too quickly), they are fiercely close—raised in a Mennonite household and sharing the hardship of Elf's desire to end her life. After Elf's latest attempt, Yoli must quickly determine how to keep her family from falling apart, how to keep her own heart from breaking, and what it means to love someone who wants to die.

> *"Irresistible… its intelligence, its honesty and, above all, its compassion provide a kind of existential balm—a comfort not unlike the sort you might find by opening a bottle of wine and having a long conversation with (yes, really) a true friend."*

> —*Curtis Sittenfeld, the* New York Times Book Review

ALSO AVAILABLE FROM McSWEENEY'S

MY DOCUMENTS
by Alejandro Zambra

My Documents, from Alejandro Zambra, the award-winning Chilean writer whose first novel was heralded as the dawn of a new era in Chilean literature, is described by Junot Díaz as "a total knockout." In his first short story collection, Zambra gives us eleven stories of liars and ghosts, armed bandits and young lovers—brilliant portraits of life in Chile before and after Pinochet. The cumulative effect is that of a novel—or of eleven brief novels, intimate and uncanny, archived until now in a desktop folder innocuously called "My Documents."

*"In his new book, Zambra returns to the twin sources of his talent—
to his storytelling vitality, that living tree which blossoms often in these
pages, and to his unsparing examination of recent Chilean history."*

—James Wood, the New Yorker

ALSO AVAILABLE FROM McSWEENEY'S

THE BEST OF
MᶜSWEENEY'S
INTERNET TENDENCY

INCLUDING:

IT'S DECORATIVE GOURD SEASON,
MOTHERFUCKERS.

ON THE IMPLAUSIBILITY OF THE DEATH
STAR'S TRASH COMPACTOR.

I REGRET TO INFORM YOU THAT
MY WEDDING TO CAPTAIN VON TRAPP
HAS BEEN CANCELED.

HAMLET (FACEBOOK NEWSFEED EDITION)

I'M COMIC SANS, ASSHOLE.

IN WHICH I FIX MY GIRLFRIEND'S
GRANDPARENTS' WI-FI AND AM HAILED
AS A CONQUERING HERO

AND MORE OF THE BEST OF FIFTEEN YEARS
OF THE WEBSITE.

Edited by CHRIS MONKS and JOHN WARNER

THE BEST OF McSWEENEY'S
INTERNET TENDENCY
edited by Chris Monks and John Warner

Back in 1998, the internet was young and wild and free. Along with listservs, pornography, and listservs dedicated to pornography, there was a website that ran all its articles in the same font and within abnormally narrow margins. This site was called McSweeney's Internet Tendency, and many dozens of people read it. Every year or so, we collect some of the site's better material and attempt to trick readers into paying for a curated, glued-together version of what is available online for free. This collection is the best and most brazen of such attempts. Please enjoy it, after you have paid for it.

"{The Best of McSweeney's Internet Tendency} is just like those chocolates
that hotels put on pillows, if the chocolate were laced with acid."

—*Michael Agger, the* New Yorker

ALSO AVAILABLE FROM McSWEENEY'S

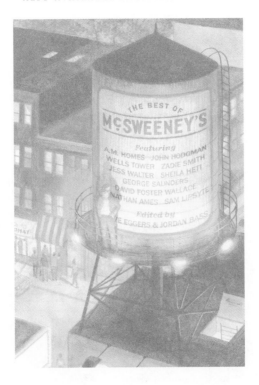

THE BEST OF McSWEENEY'S

edited by Dave Eggers and Jordan Bass

To commemorate the fifteenth anniversary of the journal called "a key barometer of the literary climate" by the *New York Times* and twice honored with a National Magazine Award for fiction, here is *The Best of McSweeney's*—a comprehensive collection of the most remarkable work from a remarkable magazine. Drawing on the full range of the journal thus far—from the very earliest volumes to our groundbreaking, Chris Ware–edited graphic novel issue to our most popular project yet, the full-on Sunday-newspaper issue known as *San Francisco Panorama*, *The Best of McSweeney's* is an essential retrospective of recent literary history.

"The first bona fide literary movement in decades."
—*Slate*

ADVERTISE IN

McSWEENEY'S QUARTERLY CONCERN

"A key barometer of the literary climate."
—*The New York Times*

By supporting McSweeney's you will gain access to our growing audience.

Monthly Newsletter Subscribers: 312,000
Unique website visitors: 1.5M per month
Twitter followers: 258,000
Facebook page likes: 131,000
Instagram followers: 20,000
Quarterly Concern subscribers: 8,000

Some of the most innovative brands in culture advertise in McSweeney's publications.

HarperCollins
Drawn & Quarterly
FSG
Third Man Records/Books
AWP
Temporary Residence
SPD
Bookforum

Granta
The Paris Review
Yale University Press
Harvard University Press
Doubleday
PEN
The Drawing Center
Sub Pop Records

To advertise in *McSweeney's Quarterly Concern*,
contact: *claire@mcsweeneys.net*

SUBSCRIBE TO

McSWEENEY'S QUARTERLY CONCERN

Four times a year, you'll receive a beautifully packaged
collection of the most groundbreaking stories we can find,
delivered right to your doorstep for $95

THE BASIC SUBSCRIPTION: $95

Four (4) issues of McSweeney's Quarterly Concern

THE DELUXE SUBSCRIPTION: $135

Four (4) issues of *McSweeney's Quarterly Concern*;
Two (2) classic back issues: Issues 42 and 34;
Two (2) classic hardcover McSweeney's books:
Michael Chabon's *Maps and Legends* and
Dave Eggers' *A Hologram for the King*

Subscribe at store.mcsweeneys.net

Founded in 1998, McSweeney's is an independent publisher based in San Francisco. McSweeney's exists to champion ambitious and inspired new writing, and to challenge conventional expectations about where it's found, how it looks, and who participates. We're here to discover things we love, help them find their most resplendent form, and place them into the hands of empathic, engaged readers.

THERE ARE SEVERAL WAYS TO SUPPORT MCSWEENEY'S:

Support us on Patreon
visit *www.patreon.com/ mcsweeneysinternettendency*

Volunteering & Internships
email *interns-sf@mcsweeneys.net*

Subscriptions & Store Site
visit *store.mcsweeneys.net*

Books & Quarterly Sponsorship
email *kristina@mcsweeneys.net*

To learn more, please visit *www.mcsweeneys.net/donate* or contact Director Kristina Kearns at kristina@mcsweeneys.net or call 415.642.5609.

All donations are tax-deductible through our fiscal sponsorship with SOMArts, a nonprofit organization that collaborates with diverse artists and organizations to engage the power of the arts to provoke just and fair inclusion, cultural respect, and civic participation.